The New Comedy Writing
Step by Step

Revised and Updated with Words of Instruction,
Encouragement, and Inspiration from Legends of the Comedy Profession

By Emmy Award-Winning Writer

Gene Perret

Foreword to the New Revised Edition by Joe Medeiros
Foreword to the First Edition by Carol Burnett

Quill
Driver
Books

Sanger, California

Printed in the United States of America.

Published by
Quill Driver Books/Word Dancer Press, Inc.,
1254 Commerce Ave, Sanger, CA 93657
559-876-2170 / 800-497-4909
QuillDriverBooks.com

Word Dancer Press books may be purchased for educational, fund-raising,
business or promotional use. Please contact Special Markets, Quill Driver Books/
Word Dancer Press, Inc. at the above address or phone numbers.

Quill Driver Books/Word Dancer Press Project Cadre:
P.J. Dempsey, Doris Hall, Stephen Blake Mettee, Carlos Olivas

First Printing

ISBN 1-884995-66-1 • 978-1885956-66-9

**To order a copy of this book, please call
1-800-497-4909.**

Library of Congress Cataloging-in-Publication Data
Perret, Gene.
The new comedy writing step by step : revised and updated with words of
instruction, encouragement, and inspiration from legends of the comedy
profession / by Gene Perret.

p. cm.

ISBN 1-884956-66-1

1. Wit and humor—Authorship. I. Title.

PN6149.A88P47 2007

808.7—dc22

2007009901

In memory of Bob Hope
My inspiration
My mentor
My friend

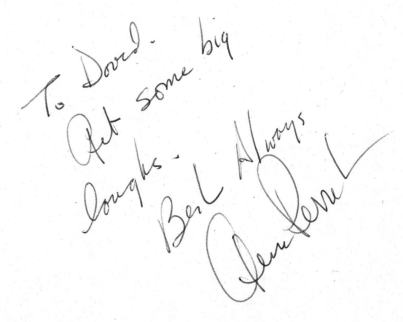

Contents

PART ONE
DECIDING TO WRITE

1. You Can Write Comedy 3

Working in a universally practiced art...the little matter of disciplining your wit, then refining your basic comedy skills...why beginning writers are afraid...the "I'm not a joke writer" syndrome...how would-be writers defeat themselves before they start...learn how to play the percentages.

2. Yes, It Can Be Learned 11

You aren't born a comedy writer...you have to learn everything somehow...inexperienced writing isn't bad writing...why only you can teach yourself...water knowledge and wine knowledge.

3. The Skills You'll Need... 15

Analyzing comedy: the dissected frog analogy...preparation and practice (and practice and practice)...defining a sense of humor...the mental process of joke writing...what most jokes are...going beyond the obvious ...why anyone can write a joke—and why a writer can't depend on coincidence.

4. Comedy as a Hobby 24

Humor and the quality of life...when the reward is in the doing ...challenge, entertainment, stimulation—and you can't top it for convenience... comedy as a group effort...the pleasures of personalizing humor...and tangible products to boot.

PART TWO
BUILDING YOUR SKILLS

geration and distortion: allowing your mind to play...exploiting clichés for fun and profit...getting 'em wholesale: formula jokes.

Foreword
to the New Revised Edition

When Gene Perret asked me to write a foreword to this new version of his book, he said in his quipping, good-natured way, "Make me look more intelligent and powerful than I am."

To me, Gene's credibility doesn't need to be artificially inflated. I can say unequivocally that if I hadn't benefited from Gene Perret's advice and comedy writing knowledge, today I wouldn't be the head writer of *The Tonight Show with Jay Leno*, TV's number one late night talk show.

I can trace the steps that took me here from January 1983. I was working as a copywriter in a suburban Philadelphia ad agency. During one lunch hour, I went to a bookstore in a local mall and stumbled upon Gene's book, *How to Write and Sell Your Sense of Humor*, an earlier edition of the book you have in your hands right now. (Literally I stumbled because I accidentally knocked it off the shelf.)

Reading the first few pages, I was astounded to see that Gene was an ordinary guy from Pennsylvania who started writing jokes in his kitchen and ended up working in television. That's what I wanted to do! And this guy did it. I'm from Pennsylvania like he was. I have a kitchen. How hard could it be? So I bought the book. *Step One.*

Well, it turned out to be harder than I thought because if I wanted to become a big time comedy writer like Gene, I'd have to work at my craft every day. Luckily, Gene's book wasn't filled with a lot of comedy theory and show business war stories like many of the books I'd bought before. It had practical exercises in it. They were difficult at first, but became easier the longer I kept at it. Since I had a fulltime job and a family, my joke-writing time was limited. I sacrificed sleep by getting up at 5:00 A.M. every morning and cracking Gene's book. *Step Two.*

Before long I had stockpile of jokes I'd written. But Perret teaches that you can't keep them in a drawer or on your hard drive forever. You've got to overcome your fear and get them out there. Following his advice, I started sending material to comics, DJs, publications that went to DJs, greeting card companies—anyone who needed jokes. (This was in that god-awful time before the Internet when you actually had to read classified ads in the back of writing magazines to see who was buying humor.) It worked. Over the next four years, I sold over a hundred jokes a month. *Step Three.*

Next came the biggest step of all. I had a friend who had a friend whose brother grew up in South Philly with Gene and still kept in touch with him. Jackpot! In the book, Gene tells about the value of networking, so I got up my courage and wrote him a letter asking his advice. *Step Four.*

Well, twelve weeks went by and he didn't write back. Of course, now I know why. Being on a busy TV show myself and getting dozens of letters like mine every week, I know how impossible it is to answer them. But back then, I didn't give up. I wrote another letter. I didn't give up. *Step Five.*

This time, I tried a different approach. I opened his book to the section where Gene talked about networking and quoted what he'd said about it. I sent the letter off. A week later, I got a reply from him. He said he'd never been shamed by his own words into writing a letter, but he graciously answered my question. The question: How do I make a living writing comedy? His answer: Write for better paying comedians. (Back then I was being paid $2 to $10 per joke and that meant having to sell tens of thousands a year to make a living wage. Gene's advice made sense.)

Gene also invited me to a conference he was having in Los Angeles for aspiring comedy writers. I flew out and attended. That's where I met the man. I was happy to see he wasn't some slick, insincere "Hollywood type," but a friendly, genuine, low-key, self-effacing family guy who was also devastatingly funny. I've never told Gene this, but because of his beard and his calm, almost stoic manner, he's always reminded me of a Greek philosopher—sort of a Comedy Socrates (minus the hemlock).

I came away from that weekend with the following: A) some new friends and contacts whom I still have today; B) the knowledge that Gene was the type of guy whose advice I could trust; C) some added self-confidence because I found that I could hold my own in a room full of joke writers; and D) the fact that Jay Leno was buying jokes at $50 a pop.

Meeting other writers for information, competition and support: *Step Six.*

Then came the day in August 1988 that Jay Leno was performing in my area. Back then, he was guest hosting *The Tonight Show* for Johnny Carson on Monday nights. So I watched when Jay was on, taped one of his monologues, typed it out to get the rhythm of his speech, wrote a bunch of jokes in what I thought was his style, and had my wife drop them off at the box office of the theatre where he was performing. I went off to my day job with my fingers crossed. *Step Seven.*

Then on November 30, 1988, came the *Ultimate Step.* I got a call at my office from Jay Leno. He said that NBC was letting him put together a writing staff for his weekly guest hosting spot. I was hired. He said, "You start tomorrow." The first person I told after my wife was Gene.

For the next four years, I worked out of my house in Glenside, Pennsylvania. When Jay took over *The Tonight Show* in 1992, my family and I moved to Los Angeles where we still live and where I am, gratefully, still working for *The Tonight Show* and Jay.

That was my step by step approach to getting here. And it all started because of this book and following every bit of the step by step approach that Gene Perret has so marvelously laid out in it.

I hope you'll have a similar story to tell. You won't know, though, unless you trust this book, trust Gene Perret, and trust yourself. Take the first step.

Joe Medeiros
Head writer, *The Tonight Show with Jay Leno*
December 2006

Foreword
to the First Edition

Every convenience that we enjoy around us—the automobile, the dishwasher, the toaster, the hot comb, and the flip-top-lock baggies—began as an idea. Someone had to think that these things were possible and then work to make them a reality. Ideas keep the world progressing.

When someone has a funny idea and can put it on paper, that someone is a comedy writer. It's astounding to think that the wildly warped philosophy and insightful humor of James Thurber and the charmingly funny characterizations of Neil Simon were once blank sheets of paper.

Each morning in Hollywood a battalion of brilliant writers enter their offices, gulp down their coffee, and insert glaringly white sheets of paper into their IBM Selectrics. Then wheels start turning in their heads. Their fingers begin tippy-tapping at varying rates of speed, and humor magically appears on the page. Seemingly from nowhere, words, sentences, and scenes take shape.

It all begins with the words. They beget scenery, costumes, props, and most of all, glorious laughter.

We all depend on the writers. The first thing the performer asks when she shows up for work on Monday morning is, "Where's the script?" Without those pages there would be no reason for showing up at work.

Bob and Ray once did a routine in which they were supposedly performing in a summer theatre with a local, nonprofessional cast. One, as the interviewer, said, "Things seemed a bit ragged on stage tonight." His partner replied, "Oh. You're probably referring to that hour-and-a-half stretch when nobody said anything." That's where most of us would be without writers…we wouldn't say anything.

Outside of a relatively few classics, there aren't many "golden oldies" in humor. For comedy to work, it has to be unique. There will always be room for talented, imaginative new comedy minds.

If this book is your first endeavor in humor, hurry up and learn your craft. We need you.

Carol Burnett
May 1982

Introduction
Why an Update?

Whenever a TV commercial would boast that a product—a brand of soap or toothpaste—was "new and improved," I would ask, "What was wrong with the old one?" I'd been loyal to this sponsor, using their product for years, and now they tell me it's inferior. "This will make your teeth brighter and whiter," they'd claim. So all these years it's been making my teeth dull and what—sort of like an oyster gray?

You may wonder the same thing about this book. Why an update? What was wrong with the original text? Responding as humbly as I can, nothing was wrong with the earlier version.

"Wait a minute," you argue. "It must have needed some revision. After all, it was first published in 1983. Surely comedy has changed since then, hasn't it?"

Well, yes and no. Let's step away from comedy for a moment and take a look at the music profession. The changes are more pronounced in that art form. Today's rap stars don't sound at all like Perry Como crooning "Catch a Falling Star and Put It in Your Pocket." Modern rock bands are quite unlike Les Brown and his Band of Renown. But even in light of these divergent examples, there are similarities. There are still eight notes in an octave. You begin with "do" and you progress through "re"-"mi"-"fa"-"so"-"la"-"ti"- and as Julie Andrews advises us, that will bring you back to "do."

There are still 88 keys on the piano—some of them black and more of them white. They were there when Bach played, when Liberace played, and they're there when Harry Connick, Jr., plays.

A C chord will always be produced when you play the notes C, E, and G. If Beethoven wanted a C chord, he wrote those three notes. If a rap star wants a C chord throbbing behind his lyrics, the band plays those same three notes.

So the stylings change, but the mathematical rules of harmony and music theory are unchanged.

This is true of comedy, too. The styles and the language may change, but the basic elements remain the same. This text—both in the original and the update—deals with basics. A joke is the building block of humor. A joke is anything that gets a laugh. Certain fundamentals produce laughs. Follow the fundamentals and you'll get laughs—you're writing comedy.

Certainly there are innovations in today's comedy. David Letterman's "Top Ten Lists," for example. They're clever, they're funny, and they're as current as this morning's headlines. Dennis Miller, with his "rants," has something to say and he drives his points home with passion and hip humor. Political humor is not new. Will Rogers, Bob Hope, Mort Sahl, and Mark Russell all commented on elected officials, but Jon Stewart's *Daily Show* has modernized political satire and commentary—given it a fresh format. Comics like Chris Rock, George Lopez, and Margaret Cho present ethnic humor from their own experience.

Monty Python's Flying Circus, Saturday Night Live, In Living Color, Blue Collar Comedy have all added up to date variations to television sketch comedy.

Jerry Seinfeld, Rita Rudner, Drew Carey, and many other well-known comics have improved the art of stand-up comedy. And there are countless unknown comics struggling through the comedy club circuit right now who are brilliant humorists and who will go on to be the legends of tomorrow.

You should learn from all of these funny folks. That's the nice part of studying the comedy craft—your teachers are easily accessible. If you want to learn stand-up, visit the clubs. If you want to write hilarious TV sketches, watch the hilarious shows. If you want to write great screen comedy, go to the movies that have audiences buying tickets and laughing out loud.

Sure comedy changes. You want to write for today's world so you should be well versed in today's comedy.

However, in studying the trend-setters, don't neglect the geniuses that went before. I once worked on a show called *Bob Hope and Other Young Comedians*. On that show we presented several stand-up comedians who were considered the up and comers. During one meeting with the comedians, one of them said, "My dad always tells me to be more like Jack Benny. I never saw Jack Benny. I don't know what to do to be like him."

One of the other comics on the show mildly rebuked her. He asked, "How can you be in this profession and not know what some of the old masters did?"

That belief is part of this new edition, too. I respect the "old-timers" because watching them taught me to write. I also worked with several of them and they helped me to hone my craft. I've included the techniques they taught me in this book.

It's very tempting for some readers to say, "Sure, the ideas you present worked for Red Skelton, Milton Berle, George Burns, and guys like that, but they were the *old school of comedy*. I want my stuff to be hip, sharp, pointed, on the cutting edge."

Well, that's what comedy should be to be effective. Sometimes, though, we become biased. We think because a gag is old, it's old-fashioned. That's not necessarily so. Following are a few gags about marriage. See if you can tell which are dated and which are current.

a) I chased a girl for two years only to discover that her tastes were exactly like mine. We were both crazy about girls.

b) Marriage is an adventure—like going to war.

c) Getting married is like sitting in tub of hot water. After you've been in it for a while, it's not so hot.

d) Marriage is forever—some days longer.

e) All women should marry—and no man.

f) Always get married in the morning. That way if it doesn't work out you haven't wasted the whole day.

g) I love being married. It's so great to find that one special person you want to annoy for the rest of your life.

Have you read them carefully? Have you made any decisions? Are some definitely old? Some definitely new? It's hard to tell the new from the old, isn't it?

Just for the record:

a) This gag is attributed to Groucho Marx—definitely *old school.*

b) This one's from G. K. Chesterton—even more *old school.*

c) This is a Minnie Pearl line, so it's not exactly current

d) This one is only four years old. I wrote it as the title for a joke book about marriage.

e) Benjamin Disraeli wrote this one. How *old school* can you get?

f) This one is from Mickey Rooney, who's not exactly knocking 'em dead in today's comedy clubs.

g) This one is from Rita Rudner—definitely today's comedy.

One of my main reasons for updating this book is to show, by including more examples from the current crop of successful and up-and-coming comics, that using the basic elements to create humor still works. Going back to the fundamentals that we deal with in this book still produces laughs. It produced laughs in the time of Hope, Berle, and Burns; it'll produce laughs in the heyday of whichever comic is enjoying his or her heyday right now.

Even though you want your comedy to be hip, current, cutting edge, there are two things you should remember about the comedy greats of previous eras. First, they were on the cutting edge *in their own day*. Their careers progressed because they appealed to their audiences. They were hot, hip, and popular. They were yesterday what you want to be today and tomorrow.

Second, they endured. Their popularity lasted for decades. They must have been doing something right to have made it to the top and to have stayed on the top. So, they had something that you can study and benefit from.

So, yes, analyze today's comedy and comics, but respect those who brought it to this level. Keep in mind that all comedy has one basic purpose—to be funny.

In this book I'll deal with that basic building block—the joke. Master that and you can restyle, reformat, retool, change the structure in any creative way you like. As I said, Letterman's "Top Ten List" is innovative, but it is a collection of ten jokes. Dennis Miller's "Rants" are incisive, but they are a series of jokes formed into a monologue.

Jeff Foxworthy gained popularity with his "You know you're a redneck if..." routines.

"You know you're a redneck if your dad walks you to school because you're in the same grade."

"You know you're a redneck if the 5th grade is referred to as 'your senior year.'"

Foxworthy's routines are current, hot, and funny. Yet they're not too much different from the late Red Buttons' "Never had a dinner" routines. Red would speak at roasts and would complain about all the famous people who, unlike the guest of honor, never had a dinner.

> *"Vincent Van Gogh, whose mother once said to him,*
> *'Vincent, everything I say to you seems to go in one ear*
> *and out the same one?—never had a dinner."*

> *"Jack the Ripper, whose mother once said to him,*
> *'Jack, how come I never see you with the same girl*
> *twice?—never had a dinner."*

It was true yesterday and it remains true today that jokes are the bulk of comedy. Often, it's the packaging that's different. This is not to trivialize that. Sometimes the package sells the product. Nevertheless you shouldn't confuse the packaging with the product.

Your goal as a comedy writer is to generate good, solid, laughs. And let's face it—laughs are what make the comedy world go 'round.

Have fun reading and writing.

PART ONE
DECIDING TO WRITE

"A writer is a person for whom writing is more difficult than it is for other people."

—Thomas Mann

- 1 -

You Can Write Comedy

I've had a *ball* writing comedy. I've written from my kitchen table back in Upper Darby, Pennsylvania, from a cocoon-sized office behind my house in California—even from a plane seat on the way to England to help write the command performance show celebrating the twenty-fifth anniversary of Queen Elizabeth's coronation.

I've been on vacations with my family where we crammed in a tiring day of sightseeing—and then while the rest of them slept, I shut myself in the bathroom, curled up in the empty tub with pencil and notepad, and turned out my next day's quota of jokes (...or gags. Throughout this book I'll use those terms interchangeably.)

I've written some good jokes in some bad places and some bad jokes in some good places, but I've been delighted with every minute of it. The one overriding message of this volume is that comedy writing is fun. It's a capitalized FUN...an underlined FUN. It's *fun* in italics, and fun in foreign languages: C'est tres amusant, es muy divertido, es macht mir Freude.

Now my wife is gong to object when she buys a copy of this book and reads those opening paragraphs. She has had to listen to my complaints over the years about recalcitrant associates, egomaniacal performers, moronic producers, asinine executives, and people in audiences who wouldn't know a good joke if it jumped off the stage and extracted a belly laugh from them surgically. What she doesn't realize is that my complaining about the business is fun to me—*she's* the only one not having a good time.

My Comedy Ego and How It Developed

I've exulted in all the stages of my career—good and bad. When my career first showed signs of progress, I was so delirious that it wore a bit on my friends and family. I was proud of hobnobbing with celebrities and rarely stopped talking about my accomplishments. Every conversation was sprinkled with my latest witticisms.

In short, I was a bore. You'll notice as you read through the book that I've not been totally cured of this.

While I was in the most critical stage of the disease, I eagerly anticipated taking my checks from Phyllis Diller to the bank each Friday. I'd try to look my humblest—all the while waiting for the teller to notice the celebrity name on the check.

One lady saw the signature, chuckled a bit, and said, "Phyllis Diller, huh?" I modestly lowered my eyes and replied, "Yeah." Then she called another teller over and showed her the check. Pride swelled so much in me that it seriously threatened the buttons on my shirt.

"Is she anything like the *real* Phyllis Diller?" the teller asked.

"That *is* the real Phyllis Diller. She's a personal friend of mine." (I had talked to her on the phone.)

The lady calmly studied the check and signature with that air of expertise instinctive to bank tellers, began stamping the documents with whatever they stamp documents with and said firmly, "No, it's not."

I never did convince her it really was the *real* Phyllis Diller. In fact, she almost had me believing I was working for a fraud. This incident was not among the highlights of my career, or even of that particular day, but since then it has been good for laughs.

Another time my wife and I had a few laughs over an experience that is almost the flip side of the Phyllis Diller story. We had been vacationing (please don't think that all comedy writers do is vacation) at a California resort and were checking out when the cashier informed me that I had received a call from Bob Hope. I was on Hope's writing staff at the time, and he frequently called in the middle of vacations. In fact, he frequently called in the middle of anything I was doing. The clerk asked, "Is this the real Bob Hope?" I assured him that it was and he offered me a telephone a few feet down the counter.

While I was on the phone, another couple came to check in. The first thing the clerk said to them was, "Have you ever heard of Bob Hope?" They were a little confused as to what this had to do with check-

4

ing into a hotel but said they had. The counter man motioned toward me with his thumb and said with feigned matter-of-factness, "He's talking to him."

I've even had some recognition that I didn't merit. Our writing staff was nominated for an Emmy one year, so the producer invited me to share his rented limousine for the evening—we wanted to arrive in style.

The festivities were being held very near my home, so my four youngsters rode there on their bikes and got right up front behind the police barricades. Our limousine pulled up to the front of the building, we stepped out, and my kids and their friends immediately went wild with screams of delight. Being an incurable ham, I turned and waved to the adoring throng. Now everyone in the crowd started screaming. The fact that they didn't recognize me as a big star didn't deter them. They figured scream now and ask questions later.

One lady, though, turned to my most vocal daughter and said, "Who is that?" My daughter told her, "My daddy."

There's a flip side to that tale, too. (Are you beginning to notice that all my stories have their own rejoinders?) Once we were at a rehearsal for a Bob Hope show originating from Palm Springs. Former President Gerald Ford was to attend the gala that evening, and some Secret Service men were combing the ballroom with dogs trained to locate bombs. Hope was on stage with a handful of script pages, saw me, and shouted, "Hey, Perret. They keep sniffing out your jokes."

You may be fearful now that you spent your hard-earned money on a book of Gene Perret anecdotes (I warned you that I'm not completely over my self-aggrandizement phase yet), but I'm just trying to illustrate and emphasize the laughs I've had with my comedy-writing career.

That's really the main reason for this book. I've had so much fun writing humor that I wanted to help other people share some of that. And you can.

A Universal Form

You may not believe it, but there is a fear of comedy writing. People feel that it's almost a sacred profession; the Deity must reach down and anoint their heads before witticisms will germinate.

Nonsense. Comedy is a universally practiced art form. Anyone who has ever performed stand-up comedy knows that the guy at the table in the front who's had one too many cocktails and is trying to impress his date thinks he can shout out funnier things than you've been writing and rehearsing.

Wisecracks are universal. Every time your family gets together I'm sure friendly insult jokes pepper the room. Any time old friends gather, good humor is an invited guest, too. Everybody does jokes.

In my rookie year as a television staff writer, the producers asked our team to come up with a new line for a guest performer. We were doing a tribute to Las Vegas and needed a joke between verses of a song. Ten of us, newcomers and veterans, gathered in a room to write one joke. We threw ideas from 10 A.M. until 1 P.M. without one gag satisfying our collective judgment. When we broke for lunch, most of us stopped in the CBS restroom.

There was a nicely dressed youngster of about 10 in there washing his hands. His hair was neatly combed, but one cowlick stood up in the back. I touched the recalcitrant locks and spoke to his image in the mirror.

"What's this?"

"Oh, that," he replied. "That's my personality."

And he walked out with the swagger of a performer who had just delivered a gem.

We professionals had just spent thirty man-hours with no results, and this kid came up with a great ad lib in a split second. There's a touch of comedian in everyone.

I was once the guest of honor at a dinner in my hometown. In attendance was a remarkable former teacher of mine. Remarkable because she was a strong-willed woman of 93 who had never been married. She taught me in the fifth grade and I must admit she looked 93 back then, too. (To her credit, she was the kind of person you could say that to.) A rumor was floating around the banquet hall that this lady had specified in her will she was to have no male pallbearers.

As the guest of honor, I dared to ask her if it were true. She admitted it was. I asked why. "The bastards never took me out while I was alive," she declared, "I'll be damned if they'll do it when I'm dead."

You don't get many lines funnier than that.

Of course, comedy isn't restricted to the cuteness of the very young or the very old. I once spoke to a group about comedy writing and during question and answers someone asked how many writers were typically on the Bob Hope staff. I started to count on my fingers and replied, "Let me see. He has the one good one."

I thought that was a pretty clever response until someone in the audience hollered out, "And then there was you."

Everybody tries to be funnier than the performer—and this guy succeeded. (But I got even. I stole that joke from him and use it in my banquet speeches to this day.)

A Matter of Discipline

Being witty upon occasion, though, or even every day, isn't the same as turning out enough humor to submit to a magazine or to a comic. The difference is not so much in the skill as in the discipline. The discipline can be learned and acquired. As a result of that training, your basic comedy skills can be refined.

When I first began writing for Phyllis Diller, I'd send her two routines a week, which amounted to about sixty jokes. The first time I met Phyllis after working with her over the phone and through correspondence, she said, "You don't write enough." I immediately set a quota of ninety jokes per week. It was difficult, and quite a strain for many weeks. Today, in contrast, I can come home from a full day of TV writing and production and, after a relaxed dinner, turn out 120 gags to be delivered to a freelance client the next morning.

Beginner's Fear

In dealing with beginning writers, the phrase I hear most often is, "Would you just read over my stuff and tell me whether it's any good or not?" Now when these same people watch TV or go to a nightclub or read a book, no one has to tell them when to laugh. They know a good joke as well as anyone else. They know which material they're proud of and which they're not sure about. The statement—"Tell me if it's any good or not"—expresses fear of mixing with the professionals.

People sometimes label themselves as amateurs and the selling writers as professionals. That's technically correct, but amateurs don't have to remain amateurs. Good amateurs become good pros. Many of today's boxing champions are former Olympic medalists—good amateurs. Now they're knocking the blocks off of the professionals. We in the humor business know that there are amateur writers out there who will one day will knock our comedy blocks off.

One of the beginner's fears is caused by comparing his or her writing to the best. But nightclub routines and television shows are the products of many minds. They've been rewritten and polished many times over. There's no way that you can sit at your kitchen table and duplicate that kind of communal expertise, but the important thing is that you don't have to.

Young comics have come to me and other writers many times and asked for just one piece of material that will get them a spot on Letterman or Leno, catapult them to national prominence, and allow them to set up residence on Easy Street for the rest of their professional lives. They promise to send the writer a few bucks after they've made it.

If I could write the piece of comedy that would accomplish that, I'd deliver it myself and build my own abode on Easy Street. But I can't do that. My friends can't do that. Neil Simon can't do that. Nobody can sit in front of the keyboard and create that piece of material. Why should a beginner expect to?

> ✔️ Ed Simmons was a writer who broke into television when television was just breaking on the scene. He wrote for Martha Raye's show, Martin and Lewis, Red Skelton, and others. He won five Emmys as the producer and head writer of The Carol Burnett Show. He said this about television writing opportunities:
>
> On the down side, TV is not accessible to new writers, the door is closed and new writers are neither needed nor wanted. That's what some say. Yet, on the up side, every year dozens of new writers break through. There is no set formula. One of the best ways is to get an agent who cares about new writers. There aren't too many. Another way is to get your material to an established writer who cares about new writers. Surprisingly, there are more of them than you would imagine.
>
> The important thing to remember is that as a would-be, could-be, or should-be writer, you have the edge. A writer doesn't have to sell himself. His pages speak for themselves. All you need is the right person to read them.

Playing the Percentages

To be a good writer, *everything* you write doesn't have to be good— just a fair percentage of it. A baseball player doesn't hand in his spikes and burn his bat if he doesn't hit a home run each time he steps to the plate. If he gets a hit just a third of the time, he can ask for a hefty raise next season. Pretty much the same percentages apply to comedy writers.

One comic I worked for had me and eight or nine other writers doing twenty to thirty jokes on a given topic. That meant he'd have available anywhere from 200 to 300 jokes on one topic. And only fifteen of those jokes at the most would be included in his finished monologue.

Occasionally I deliver some of my own material at after-dinner speeches. (The checks aren't as large as for writing, but it's nice once in a while to experience the laughter myself.) For each topic I speak on, I write twenty-five to thirty-five gags. Rewriting, I cut this down to twelve or fifteen of the best. Composing the final speech, I slice even more of the funnies. After I deliver the talk once or twice, it will be obvious that certain lines aren't working. From the original thirty, six to eight solid jokes might result. And that's my own brilliant stuff I'm cutting.

TV shows are rewritten endlessly. If some producers and writers had their way, they'd make changes even as the show was being broadcast.

Years ago, my writing partner and I wrote a script for *All in the Family*. The producer of the show worked in offices right near ours. Each time we passed in the corridor, he'd ask us to come back and submit new ideas so we could write a second script for him. When our episode finally aired, only one line in the entire half-hour script was one we had written. Our script had been completely redone, yet they wanted us to come back and do more.

Another writer friend of mine went to watch a show he had written being taped. His script was rewritten so completely that when the producer came to him after the taping and asked him to do another one, he replied, "I don't have to. Just use the one I gave you in the first place."

Don't defeat yourself before you get started. If you can write funny and are willing to learn and apply some of the skills, you can be a humorist. Every line you write doesn't have to be a gem. There just have to be enough gems there to be worth mining.

Folks who don't write professionally are sure they never will. I was in this class. I wrote a few funny fillers for magazines, but I convinced myself that I was really just collecting rejection notices as a hobby. Then something happened—I got a check for one of my jokes. My life changed. But before that I was among those who have what I call the "I'm not a joke writer" syndrome. Such people envision themselves as homemakers, or electricians, or salespeople. Someone *else* is always the humorist.

That's baloney. People are selling their first gags to magazines or comics all over the nation every day.

As I mentioned, I began early in my career writing material regularly for Phyllis Diller's nightclub act. I was gleefully wallowing in my own image of myself as a writer. I went to see Phyllis appear on *The Mike Douglas Show*. While I was waiting outside the studio with everyone else in the audience, a gentleman came up to me and said, "Are you Gene Perret?" I told him I was and he said, "Phyllis wants to see you in her dressing room before the show goes on."

After a brief meeting with Phyllis, I talked with the man. I was curious. We had never met before, yet in the mass of people he came right up to me and asked if I were Perret. I wanted to know how he managed that. A bit reluctantly he told me that Phyllis asked him to bring me backstage. He asked, "How will I know who he is?" Phyllis said, "Just walk along the line, find the guy who looks least like a comedy writer, and bring him up here." He did.

If you have a sense of humor, if things appear funny to you, if you think you can write—you can.

- *2* -

Yes, It Can Be Learned

Some of my comedy-writing colleagues will chastise me for authoring this book. They'll argue that you can't teach anyone to write comedy.

That reminds me of an assignment I had before turning to humor for a livelihood. Working in the electrical engineering department of a large corporation, I was slated to computerize the engineering logic we used. My job was to assemble all our engineering reasoning, organize it, and reduce it to a form that could be fed into a computer.

The first phase of this investigation was to interview the engineers. The engineers objected. "You can't do that," they insisted. "Too many variables exist to ever compile what we know for a nonthinking machine."

"But don't you go through a series of steps to compile your information?" I asked.

"Certainly," they conceded, "but the logic is too complex to be fed into a computer."

"But if you could," I persisted, "how would you go about it?"

"The first thing I'd do," each replied, "would be to..." and then each in turn furnished me all sorts of information. Each engineer defined for me in detail what he said would be impossible.

We have the same phenomenon here. Professional comedy writers insist that no one can write professional comedy except professional comedy writers. Yet their existence contradicts their precept. They weren't born comedy writers, so they must have learned it somehow.

Why do they maintain that no one else can learn it? Well, they know that because they've been writing comedy now for twenty or twenty-five years. Yet when they boast of their longevity, they're implying that during those years they've learned about comedy. If comedy can't be learned, how did they accomplish it?

This "can't teach" bromide is particularly insidious because it prevents many talents from developing: "What's the point in trying to become a writer," some fledglings say, "if it simply can't be done?"

Young writers occasionally have asked me to review and critique their work. Often my first inclination is to say, "This is terrible." Then I'll review my own writings from twenty-five years ago and find it was just as bad as the sample I'm reviewing. The moral is that there is potential there. The writing isn't bad; it's just inexperienced. That writer can improve as he or she learns or is taught.

An Ongoing Process

The truth is, all of us—beginners and veterans—can improve. We improve by eliminating errors. We learn not to make those mistakes any more. In this sense, the beginner can learn much more than the old pro simply because the beginner has more mistakes to remove.

Over the years, I've learned a few things about humor writing. Perhaps I've read about it, or learned from listening to more experienced writers, or discovered through trial and error some of those things I should or shouldn't do. Why can't I tell a less experienced writer what I've learned? Isn't that teaching? If she listens, isn't she learning?

You may argue that you can't "teach" the basic something that makes a person funny. And while that argument may technically be true, in practice it just doesn't wash. You can't teach that innate something that makes an athlete a baseball player, a football player, or a tennis star, yet every professional team has high-paid coaches who teach players how to field ground balls, or how to block, or how to hit an overhead smash. Once you concede that a person has a certain amount of coordination, you can teach that person to use that talent more efficiently and more intelligently. You can't teach a person to be fast or agile, but a wily old pro can instruct a novice in how to use the speed and agility to his advantage. The veteran has taught; the youngster has learned. We may play with semantics all we want, but certain aspects of humor can be taught, they can be learned, and each of us can improve.

Another harmful response to this "can't be taught" cliché is that if you can't teach everyone to become another Woody Allen, why bother with instructions at all? The reason is because hobbyists, part-timers, and those with a professional career in mind are all entitled to learn as much about the business as they want.

Here's another example. I've always been a frustrated musician and annoyed many a comedy-writing partner with my constant humming or whistling because there's always a melody rolling around in my head. Over the years I've attempted to learn the harmonica, the ukulele, the banjo, and the guitar. My family has been extremely patient throughout this ordeal. (They're thankful I never tried to master the drums.) I did manage to acquire some self-taught proficiency with the guitar, but it was limited. Finally, I decided that if I were going to play the instrument, I should learn about it. I enrolled in a class on music theory and another in playing skills. Music began to lose its mystery as I learned the logic and the mathematics behind it, and my fingers took on dexterity as I was faithful to my practice assignments.

The storybook end to this anecdote would be that I now play with a jazz group on weekends for some inordinate amount of money. I don't. In fact, I still have trouble getting the family to listen. The important point is this: I can play reasonably well and I get hours of relaxation and enjoyment from my guitar strumming. No one can tell me I shouldn't have invested time and money into lessons simply because I would never become another Segovia or Eric Clapton.

If the only people who took piano lessons were those who were assured of becoming virtuosos, the world would be deprived of a lot of music.

Teaching Yourself

There are two types of knowledge—intellectual and practical. To illustrate the difference, let's suppose there was a very intelligent college professor who wanted to learn all he could about swimming. He studied textbook after textbook on the different strokes. He even studied anatomy to learn which muscles should be developed for swimming proficiency. However, in the course of this extensive research, our professor never went near water. He never swam.

Now, let's suppose another young man took a job as a lifeguard. He went through the Red Cross lifeguard certification course, and each day had to swim two miles for training. During the course of his job, he was involved in many lifesaving ventures under varying conditions.

Now assume that you were drowning. Which of our two characters would you choose to save you?

Certainly, the professor had all the intellectual knowledge he needed about swimming, but he never learned firsthand how to swim. The second man knew little about the anatomical mechanics of swimming, but he knew how to swim.

✔ The late comedy genius Steve Allen said this about practice and experience:

> You could have a gift for, let's say, playing the trumpet. But if you don't buy a trumpet and don't practice it every day, you're going to end up either not playing the trumpet or you'll be a lousy, third-rate trumpet player. Nobody should think they can just coast through life on the basis of gifts—gifts that they have nothing to do with in the first place. You have to, to use the tiresome phrase, pay your dues and do your homework. You have to get the experience.

The ideal, of course, is to combine both forms of knowledge. Learn what to do and how to do it. With comedy, you can learn what to do by studying, observing, and analyzing. Watch good comedians work in the clubs, watch well-written TV shows and films, read funny scripts and plays. Then begin applying what you learn.

In the practical sense only you can teach yourself to write with your own writing, writing, and more writing.

- 3 -

The Skills You'll Need

When I was teaching a course in comedy writing, a student told me analyzing comedy was like dissecting a frog: "You may learn a little bit about it, but the poor creature dies in the process." That may be the way some readers are feeling at this point… "Enough *about* comedy. When are we going to *write* some?"

I honestly sympathize with you because I know the feeling well. The tendency when given a comedy-writing assignment is to just sit down and crank out the funnies—that's what we're paid for, that's what's fun.

Prepare! Prepare!

Having been faced with many difficult assignments with distressingly pressing deadlines, I've learned one thing—get them done quickly so that I can get back to relaxing. Naturally, I want to do them well so that I still have a job next week to pay for my relaxing.

I've also learned through experience that the quickest and easiest way to complete an assignment well is not to rush headlong into it but to spend some time preparing. It makes the job easier and the end results better.

That's why I'm taking this chapter to discuss the skills necessary for comedy writing, so you'll be aware of them and can practice and develop them.

For example, you now know how I took courses to learn about music in general and the guitar in specific. Undeniably, it was tedious learning scales, then chord formation. At first, none of it seemed to have any application toward helping me to play the guitar. But with patience, study, and diligent practice, it all came together. I found I could play more and varied pieces. I could ad-lib or improvise with my instrument. I was playing music. Somehow the frog had lived.

You will feel the same as you study and practice your comedy skills. No one thought or idea will hit you and change your work in a single instant, but gradually, almost unwittingly, you will absorb what you learn and it will become part of your writing arsenal.

Let's discuss some of the skills that you will need for your writing. When we get to Part Two in this book, we'll actually write—I promise.

A Sense of Humor

Perhaps it's silly to list this as one of the skills. It's like all of us sitting in a guitar class that we paid $120 to take, each with a $600 guitar on his knee, and the teacher starting out by asking, "How many of you like to play the guitar?"

Obviously, you have a sense of humor or you wouldn't have been attracted to this book. However, we might learn a bit about comedy, and about ourselves, by briefly studying the sense of humor.

I define a sense of humor as the ability to:

- *see* things as they are
- *recognize* things as they are
- *accept* things as they are

To illustrate, let me recount a minor setback that recently happened in my household. I had a leaky roof.

Certainly, it had to be repaired, but the sequence of events leading up to that decision should illustrate what I mean by *seeing*, *recognizing*, and *accepting* things as they are.

See Things as They Are

One can't fix a leaky roof until one sees that one has a leaky roof. My wife and I noticed one day that there were water stains on the plaster ceiling in one room of our house. My wife asked, "I wonder what's causing those water stains?" I answered, "Water." That's why on tax returns I'm listed as "head of the household."

The point, though, is that if we had never seen those stains, we never would have known that there was a problem in that area of the roof. That's *seeing* the facts as they are.

Recognize Things as They Are

Just seeing it, though, didn't resolve the mess. The question now was why there was a problem. Since the stains were in an area where there were no pipes or plumbing of any sort above that ceiling, it had to be a leak in the roof above the ceiling. We had to get up there and find where the leak was. That's *recognizing* the facts as they are.

Accepting Things as They Are

Now we knew there was a leak in the roof and we knew exactly where it was, but that still didn't resolve the problem. When we actually called a qualified roofer and paid out hard-earned, joke-writing money to have him fix the leak, that was *accepting* the facts as they are.

That finally resolved the problem. (Except I then had to repaint the ceiling, which is a whole different domestic difficulty.)

You're probably wondering what seeing, recognizing, and accepting have to do with a sense of humor. Just as the leaky roof would never have been repaired if we hadn't fulfilled all three steps, so you'll fail to see humor in any topic if you don't satisfy all three. Here's another illustration:

I once gave a seminar with probably the most-quoted joke writer of all time, Robert Orben. Bob has written for Red Skelton, was a speechwriter for President Gerald Ford, and has published numerous joke books and newsletters. During a question and answer session someone asked, "To be a good comedy writer, do you have to be bald?" Bob and I both sport the same skin-prominent hairdos.

It could have been an awkward and embarrassing moment—for either the questioner or for us, the bald-headed seminar leaders. Bob, though, immediately seized the humor in the question.

He replied, "When we're born, each of us is given only so many male hormones. If you want to use yours to grow hair, go ahead."

17

Seeing the problem was easy. Our heads glowed in the overhead lighting. Recognizing the problem was a tad more subtle. Some people might hope that the audience won't notice. Both of us knew the audience could see our empty pates. Now by accepting those facts, Bob could kid about it.

Orben got a big, appreciative laugh from the audience. (Although later I got even when someone asked, "What do you do when the jokes don't work?" I immediately turned to Orben and said, "I think this question's aimed at you, Bob.")

It's especially important to be aware of these three abilities in speaking to audiences because not all audiences have a sense of humor about all topics. You must know what they see, recognize, and accept before kidding them. (I knew that Robert Orben had a big enough sense of humor to accept the friendly barb I had just aimed at him.)

Humor and Well-being

Completely aside from comedy writing, developing a sense of humor will help your well-being. Many times you will be in situations that test your patience; if you can learn to see, recognize, and accept reality, and then be able to laugh about it, it will be much easier on your nervous system. Reality is usually easier to handle than the fantasies that we can create in our own minds.

I was a speaker on a cruise line for several years. During the course of a two- or three-week cruise I would give several lectures on the value of a sense of humor. This philosophy of seeing, recognizing, and accepting things as they are was the theme of my talks.

At the end of one cruise, the cruise line had a logistics problem. The result was that many of us who were booked overnight in the top-rated hotel in the area had to be relocated to a different, less exclusive resort. Many of the passengers rebelled. As we sat on the bus that was to transport us to the *inferior* inn, they demanded an audience with the captain. They insisted that their original reservations be honored. However, whatever the problem was, there simply was no room at the hotel they wanted. Still furious, they were forced to board the bus and accept the lesser booking.

As one angry gentleman walked down the aisle of the bus, he noticed me. He said, "Well, how's your sense of humor holding up now?"

The irony was that my sense of humor and my wife's sense of humor were serving us well. We were content. We were resigned. We saw there was a problem; we recognized why the change was necessary; we accepted the new accommodations (which, by the way, were very elegant).

This gentleman didn't and it bothered him. I'm sure his brief stay at the *inferior* hotel was not nearly as pleasant as ours.

✓ Arnie Kogen is a wildly inventive comedy writer who has written for variety shows, sitcoms, and individual performers. When he and I shared an office, we would boast that I wrote for Bob Hope and Phyllis Diller; Arnie Kogen wrote for everyone else. Here he tells us what he looks for in aspiring writers:

If these writers are gifted, if they're wildly funny, if they can put it on paper and be funny in a room, then they will be working in television and will be hugely successful.

By "funny in a room" I mean contributing to a script rewrite after you've been hired on staff. Many new people don't realize it, but this is a major part of the TV writing process.

It also helps if you're "fast." Can you rewrite a scene in a few hours? Can you do a complete script in a week or ten days? These are not imperatives—"good" is still better than "fast"—but it's a big plus if you can write quickly.

We once hired someone for staff based on an incredible spec script he wrote. We discovered later that it took him five months to write it. I think in five months my dry cleaner could come up with a decent script. The thing is, under pressure, can you produce?

The Ability to Analyze and Prepare

There are two general thought processes involved in writing a joke. The first is rapid, and almost unnoticeable. It consists of rolling different ideas through your brain and instantaneously analyzing them for any relevant connection with another thought.

In general, a joke comprises two distinct ideas that come together to form one. Think of a few of your favorite one-liners and you'll discover that there are two thoughts there. Sometimes the thoughts are strikingly similar; other times they are intriguingly opposite. Sometimes they are totally nonsensical and other times simply ironic. But a majority of jokes are two ideas tied together in a funny way.

For example, Carol Leifer has a line that reads, "Sex when you're married is like going to a 7-Eleven. There's not much variety, but at three in the morning, it's always there." The two ideas tied together are marital sex and a twenty-four-hour convenience store.

In forming the joke, your mind begins with one idea and then with computer-like speed generates and appraises other ideas for a humorous connection with the original. When it strikes that deliciously witty combination, the joke pops out of your head.

Since our minds are so active, that combination can happen by accident. That's why anyone can write a joke.

However, writers can't depend on accidents or coincidences. That's why the second thought process is so important. It is slow and methodical. It is simply a method of preparing the mind to go through the first process.

All jokes are generated by the first process, the rapid assessment of ideas rolling through your brain. However, it stands to reason that the more thoughts you can get rolling, the better selection you will have. Consequently, the more jokes you'll generate and the better they will be.

These two thought processes are similar to the way your mind functions in playing a game of Scrabble. You have seven letters arranged in no particular order in front of you. You struggle to get the word with the highest point value. You mentally rearrange the letters and pass judgment on the arrangements. You mind rejects W-E-L-B as a nonword, but BLEW pops into your mind as acceptable. The more ways you can rearrange those letters, the better selection of possible words you have. When that high-scoring word finally pops into your mind, it feels as though it literally came from nowhere.

As a humorist, you will want to be able to thoroughly dissect a topic and prepare a list of relationships before getting around to the actual joke creation.

The Ability to Correlate Ideas

As part of analyzing and preparing, you need to find words, phrases, events, people, facts, things, and symbolisms that are either similar or opposite to the main topic.

It's not unlike the faculty you use in doing crossword puzzles. When given one word, you mentally search for all other words that have a relationship to the clue until your mind presents you with the right one.

The Ability to See Nonstandard Meanings

A good humorist must learn to go beyond the obvious. When you see a picture, a word, or a phrase, you are aware that it has a standard meaning. With a little bit of effort, however, you can create another meaning for it. Often, that other meaning will lead to the joke you are looking for.

For instance, a man in a tuxedo is a man in a tuxedo, but he can also be a penguin. A man in a white dinner jacket can also be a Good Humor man, or a doctor.

Roseanne Barr has a joke that presents a funny image of a husband of a few years:

> *"You may marry the man of your dreams, ladies, but*
> *fourteen years later, you're married to a couch that burps."*

This device works equally as well for words as for visualization. Here's an Emo Philips gag that illustrates that:

> *"I went into Gus's artificial organ and taco stand. I*
> *said, 'Give me a bladder.' The guy said, 'Is that to go?' I*
> *said, 'Well, what else would I want it for?' "*

And here's an old joke that demonstrates the same principle: "Can you tell me how long cows should be milked?" You expect an answer relating to time: five or ten minutes. The comic reply is, "The same as short ones." A different meaning was found for the question.

The Ability to Scan Ideas

You probably have noticed that most of these skills run together. The comedy writer must utilize all of them at the same time when he sits to compose his jokes.

The ability to scan ideas is one of the most important, though. It basically is the gag-writing process. The writer analyzes and lists all her correlations to a given topic, but to write she has to roll all these

21

ideas through her head one by one until she hits a joke. Generally, she starts with what she wants to say, then scans her brain searching for that perfect second idea to form a funny line.

Eventually, a writer learns to do this mentally, but I recommend that the newcomer actually write out these lists to help stimulate the funny bone.

The Ability to Visualize

This is a mental skill that will produce many jokes. If you analyze some of your favorite gags, you'll notice that many are funny because they conjure up a ridiculous image. Here's a very bizarre image that another Emo Philips line creates:

> *"My cousin just died. He was only 19. He got stung by a bee—the natural enemy of a tightrope walker."*

You can almost see this poor fellow high up in the air and reacting to the sting of a bumblebee.

As a comedy composer you take the realistic image in your mind and distort or exaggerate it out of all proportion to see what funny images you can visualize. Then you find the right words for the new image.

A Facility with Words

Most of our comedy is expressed in words, so naturally it behooves the writer to be proficient with them. Some of our gags even depend *entirely* on the words. Here's a line from British comic Harry Hill that has some fun with words:

> *"I was doing some decorating so I got out my stepladder. I don't get on with my birth ladder."*

The writer has to develop an ear for words and phrases, even compiling a list of some of the trendier ones so that they can be used in joke writing. In this gag, Garry Shandling has some fun with a current phrase:

> *"I practice safe sex. I use an airbag."*

The Ability to Pick up Comedy Rhythm

This skill is largely inbred. You hear rules like the comedy rule of three, and putting the punch line close to the end of the joke, and that words with *K* in them are funny. All these rules apply, but the rhythm and timing of a joke are mostly individual, and we're not going to make any attempts to teach it in this book.

I have seen a team of comedy writers argue for hours over the precise wording of a particular joke. No one was right and no one was wrong—it's an individual judgment.

Don't be frightened away by all these seemingly complicated skills that are required for comedy writing. Most of them are inherent in anyone with a sense of humor. Chapter 8 contains exercises that work on different aspects of gag writing, and we'll go through each aspect in detail. You'll find that all these techniques come easily. (At least more easily than I've explained them.)

They are listed here mostly for you information. We're dissecting that poor frog again.

- 4 -

Comedy as a Hobby

I once attended a writers' workshop where the main speaker was Charles Schulz, creator of the comic strip *Peanuts*. During his talk, Mr. Schulz mentioned that Snoopy, the precocious beagle in the strip, was a frustrated author. Though he worked at his craft seriously and with foolhardy optimism, Snoopy, Mr. Schulz conceded, had not and would never sell any of his writings.

A questioner from the audience then stated that many of us attending were like the pen-and-ink beagle. We might never make a literary sale either. Did Mr. Schulz, she asked, have any words of encouragement for these people?

I recall feeling some sympathy for Schulz when the question was asked because he and the audience had been referring to Snoopy and frustrated authors in a spirit of fun. Now this query turned it all into a heavy and rather depressing topic.

But Charles Schulz never faltered. "I certainly do," he said, "The reward is in the doing."

The Rewards of an Avocation

I've always believed that we need an escape from the stressful, results-oriented world where we make our living. Now there's nothing wrong with results, and there's certainly nothing harmful about earning our daily bread. The problem is that the two of them are so dependent on each other. It's refreshing to struggle with some challenge and never really be worried about the results, since it's not a matter of economic survival.

When I wrote the first edition of this book I was an avid tennis player and many of my illustrations and anecdotes had to do with tennis. Since then I've abandoned tennis for the less strenuous hobby, golf. I'm equally as bad at golf as I used to be at tennis. The same principle applies, though—I play the game for relaxation. I like to win, but if I lose, it's not catastrophic. Being defeated in golf takes no food from my table, nor does it hurt my career. Naturally, I dislike losing, but the after effects are mild. I've lost nothing but a golf match.

The other side of the coin is that it's nice once in a while to earn a little bread that you didn't expect. A hobby can do that for you, too.

I don't play golf for much money— if I did, I wouldn't earn much— but I did make money with my hobby of writing comedy. In fact, when people ask how I got started in the business, I tell them that it was a hobby that got out of hand. People embark upon a career in comedy writing the same way a person enters into a life of sin. First you try it for the fun of it. Then you begin entertaining a few close friends. Then you say, "What the hell, I might as well make a buck at it."

That may be an irreverent way of stating it, but it serves as notice that your hobby could very well lead to a part-time business and perhaps a full-time career. We'll discuss those in the following chapters.

I found, though, that when my hobby became a profession, I still needed a diversion. The guitar, tennis, and now golf, came to my rescue.

We all need some activity where the reward is in the doing. We need some pleasurable pastime where we can charge full speed ahead and "damn the results."

Humor writing can fill that need. It's certainly convenient. You don't have to buy a kit. You need no expensive equipment. In fact, all you need is a pen and a blank sheet of paper. It fits into anyone's schedule because there's no time-consuming preparation necessary, nor any cleanup afterward. You can write on a bus, during your lunch break, while shaving—almost any time you have a free moment or two.

My children once cajoled me into taking them across town to see a Marx Brothers movie that had just been rereleased. They had been enthused about it for some time, but just as we were leaving, I got a call from one of my clients to do some monologue material. Unfortunately, the material had to be ready within the hour. When the youngsters heard the news, they were disappointed and annoyed at me for reneging on a promise. I did feel guilty—but some ingenuity saved the day and my parental reputation.

The theatre was about a forty-five-minute drive from our house, so I issued each of my four children a notepad and pencil. The oldest one was to copy the first joke I recited. The next in age was to jot down my second witticism, and so on. As I drove I dictated my gags as they popped into my head, and the children dutifully recorded them. We arrived at the movie house, bought our popcorn, settled into our seats—then they watched the film while I collected the notebooks, put the gags in logical order, and called in the routine to my unsuspecting client. A fair percentage of the gags worked, the Marx Brothers were hilarious, the children were delighted, and I was a good daddy.

I classify this incident in the hobby area because by the time I paid for the theater tickets, the gas, and then treated everyone to dinner afterward, I made no profit on the deal. It does show, though, that comedy can be created under any conditions. You can't top that for convenience. Imagine the confusion if I had tried to complete a crossword puzzle or knit a sweater while navigating the Los Angeles freeways.

Humor writing is a provocative, entertaining, and exciting hobby because it employs many different skills. As we saw in Chapter 2, it requires a facility with words, visualization, memory recall, and a touch of psychology. It's demanding and challenging.

Humor is also a fun hobby. You know how entertaining it is to listen to a smart comic. It's that much more invigorating to create the humor yourself.

It can be fun on a shared basis, too. When I worked in an engineering office, a group of us used to devise humor projects. One that I recall was a variation of "The Great Carsoni." That was a routine that the late Johnny Carson would include occasionally on *The Tonight Show*. As a mentalist, Carson would give the answer to a question that was sealed inside an envelope. When that question was read, it was really the punch line to the joke.

Our gang would submit a few standard phrases, quotations, or sayings that had been in the news. These were something like, "a hole in one," or "have a Coke and a smile."

Then each of us would spend some time during the week, working during lunch hour or during our free time at home—or perhaps when we should have been doing engineering—creating funny questions that might have generated those replies, such as:

"When Robert Ford met the James Brothers, what did he leave?" (...a hole in one.)

"What will two dollars get you today at the local bordello?" (a Coke and a smile.)

You can see that a bit of competitive enjoyment is thus added to the hobby. You not only have the fun of making humor but delighting in what other people have created too. In Chapter 8 we'll discuss writing exercises, some of which can be converted to enjoyable group projects.

Humor writing can also be of practical use. When I first began in comedy, I discovered firsthand how much people love to be kidded. My writing got me a bit of a reputation and I was asked to be master of ceremonies at banquets. I always wrote comedy material specifically about the guest of honor. It would be gentle insult humor, the kind we hear of at celebrity roasts nowadays. After the ceremonies, the guest of honor usually asked for a copy of my monologue as a memento. Eventually, I began putting a nicely typed copy into a binder as my gift to the honoree.

Your humorous writing can create many treasured gifts. Your own ingenuity will provide an endless supply of innovative ideas, but here are a few that I've enjoyed.

I've written monologues for and about family and friends and put together bound collections of humor, cartoons, and original one-liners for special occasions like showers, birthday, or anniversaries, composing personalized captions for family photo albums or collections of old movie photos or monster pictures to be made into a friend's life story. I've made funny, personalized greeting cards and individualized cartoons that are drawn large enough for framing.

There's no end to the ideas that can be conceived for using comedy. As we said in the beginning of this chapter, though—or as Charles Schulz said—the reward is in the doing. And that reward is multiplied when you share it with others.

- 5 -

Comedy as a Second Income

With all due respect to the "reward is in the doing" quote, Charles Schulz during his lifetime and throughout his enormously successful career proved that there's nothing wrong with getting a bit of remuneration for your efforts. Creating humor is fun—but so is going shopping with the checks you receive in return.

The value of money doesn't have to be touted by this author, but I can tell you that there's a fringe benefit in being compensated for your writing—a check is one of the greatest inspirations to team up with your keyboard again. It's a driving force that keeps you writing. Friends and acquaintances may say you're funny and laugh hysterically at your creations, but when you get something you can take to the supermarket, you *know* you're a writer.

Comedy writing can be an excellent second income. You can work at home, at your own convenience, and you can pretty much be your own boss.

I began writing in 1959 and it took me almost ten years to break into television and the "big time." During that decade of apprenticeship, I made enough money to justify the time and effort I put into my writing. My income from writing ranged from $1,500 to $10,000 per year. Today, those figures could probably be doubled or tripled.

The important thing is that I maintained a steady job during all this time and didn't overtax my leisure. My moonlight income was almost all profit, too, because comedy-writing overhead is minimal. A typewriter (this was in the precomputer age), some blank pages (not blank for long, we hope), a bit for postage (nowadays you can use e-mail), maybe an extra phone call now and then, and that's pretty much the expense budget.

The marketing possibilities for comedy skills on a part-time basis are practically limitless. It's largely dependent on your own ingenuity and enterprise.

During my apprenticeship, I wrote several humor columns for newspapers. These consisted of twelve jokes on a local topic. I wrote them in the morning—notepad at the ready on the countertop—as I shaved before going to work. Each morning I made ten bucks while I shaved. (Today I have a full beard, so you know I either can't land another newspaper column or I'm independently wealthy.)

In time, though, I became frustrated that my career wasn't proceeding as quickly as I would have liked. I wanted to take a correspondence course in comedy writing, but the cost for me at the time was prohibitive. So I contacted a local comic. I told him my plans and sold him the rights to all my homework from the writing course. He got material rather cheaply—and I got to learn a little bit more about comedy writing.

Humor is in demand in every community. You'll be able to find the need and fill it where you live right now. Following are just a few suggestions that might stimulate your thinking.

Magazines

Many magazines solicit fillers and short humor pieces of varying descriptions. *Reader's Digest* is probably the periodical most known for its short humor pieces. They're one of the most generous markets, too. As of this writing, they pay $300 for any anecdote that they publish. They also accept contributions over the Internet. Go to rd.com and then click on "Laugh Lines." They'll give you full instructions on how to submit your funny stories or one-liners over the Internet.

A good writer's market will list those periodicals that accept fillers and short humorous pieces. *Writer's Market* (Writer's Digest Books) and *The American Directory of Writer's Guidelines* (Quill Driver Books) are two of the best. *Writer's Market Online*, www.writersmarket.com allows you to search out certain magazines, keep track of your submissions, and a whole lot of other bells and whistles.

Various writers' magazines, like *Writer's Digest* and *The Writer,* also publish books on writing. Here you can find how-to books on writing short humor pieces and fillers for magazines. They'll go into more detail than we can in this book and they may even list markets that you can approach.

Humorous Articles

Many magazines also publish humorous essays or features, either in every issue or whenever a funny piece comes in that thrills the editors. Editors love genuinely funny articles, but rarely get enough of them.

I've sold humorous pieces to *McCall's*, *Good Housekeeping*, *Parenting*, and several other national magazines. I've also written a humorous column called "WitStop" that's been featured in *Arizona Highways* since 1995. It's a fun style of writing, and one that calls on all of your joke-writing skills.

Again, a good writer's market will tell you which periodicals buy humorous articles.

To learn more about this genre, I suggest reading my book *Damn! That's Funny* (Quill Driver Books/Word Dancer Press, 2005).

Humor Services

These are services that offer jokes, one-liners, and quips to people who need a steady supply of humor. Most of these are probably published online nowadays. You can probably search out a few on the Internet to see which ones are buying from freelancers.

Enterprising writers who aren't afraid of writing a lot of material might even begin their own comedy newsletter. If you know your way around the Internet and can generate enough material, you might even begin finding subscribers for you own comedy service.

Greeting Cards

No doubt you've noticed over the years the trend has been away from sentimental and toward impertinent greeting cards. Consequently, there is a demand for inventive witticisms from all such card manufacturers.

Here again, I suggest a good book to learn the basics of this sort of writing and marketing. Check the backlists of publishers who specialize in books about writing. Also, search whatever market lists you can find for up-to-date marketing information.

Cartoonists

Being blessed with artistic skills doesn't always mean someone is also blessed with comedic talent. Most cartoonists are looking for a supply of comedy to illustrate.

The same two principles apply—a good book on fundamentals found through writers' magazines or by searching book sellers on the Internet and a comprehensive market list.

Newspaper Columns

You have an advantage over nationally syndicated columnists like Dave Barry in that you can *localize* your humor. Some local newspapers are willing to pay for comedy dealing with the specifics of their community.

Here you may do a little speculative work writing a few columns that deal with local headlines and presenting them to editors.

I've done several columns of this type during my writing career and have always found them to be popular, for two reasons. First of all, people love comedy, especially in the midst of all the negative news on the front page. Second, readers enjoy a few clever comments about their hometown—things no national columnist could be aware of.

Try the suburban weeklies and other small papers, which are much easier to crack than the metropolitan dailies. You can always work up.

Radio and TV Personalities

Disc jockeys and local television personalities have a lot of air space to fill. They're desperately in need of comedy material. Most of them subscribe to one or more of the comedy services, but again, you have an advantage—you can write on national topics, but you can also do material that only locals will know and appreciate. That's valuable to a local personality.

Here the best approach is a letter of introduction with a sample of the sort of material you can write. If the personalities are impressed with your skill, they'll get in touch, and both of you can take it from there.

Many of these local celebrities do as much work off the air as they do on. Their marquee value gets them many local speaking engagements. They'll need material for most of these appearances, too. (See how easy it is!)

Professional Speakers

A whole subculture exists that many of us know nothing about—the professional and corporate speaking circuit. These are people who deliver lectures on technical subjects, motivation, and salesmanship or are simply humorists who entertain at banquets. Almost all of them are searching for a good supply of wit because even the technical and the motivational speakers find that some humor is required to keep an audience awake and listening.

Many of these people belong to the National Speakers Association located at 1500 South Priest Drive, Tempe, Arizona. You can check this association out on the Internet at nsaspeaker.org.

Executives

Management is discovering that a dash of wit in a presentation helps listeners not only to listen but also to retain what they've been listening to. Consequently, business executives are searching for humor consultants to add a bit of flair to their speeches.

It may be difficult to find buyers in this market because you won't find them listed in most market lists. However, with some advertising and marketing innovations on your part, you may be able to reach those executives who will buy. Often, too, your local reputation will precede you, and they may find you.

I once had a very well-known and successful business executive call me for comedy material. He found me by asking Bob Hope for a recommendation. I called Bob and asked him what I should charge. Bob said, "Charge him a lot. He's very rich." I made a mental note to remember that advice the next time I negotiated my contract with Bob Hope, who was fairly well off himself.

Your Own Speaking

People hunger for the lighter touch—especially people who are constantly subjected to heavy, technical dissertations. The program chairman of every organization forages each year for one or two speakers who can introduce fun into the proceedings.

This is actually how my career as a writer began—as a speaker. People who had heard about my custom-tailored comedy hired me as an after-dinner speaker for business meetings. That led to other people hearing about my comedy and offering to buy it. Eventually, writing became more lucrative than speaking, and I devoted full time to the typewriter.

Now I've begun doing some speaking again and have discovered an interesting phenomenon—people who won't pay for speakers will pay for humorists. The reason many organizations don't normally pay for speakers is because they can get their fill. Local service clubs usually don't have to reimburse lecturers for their weekly or monthly meetings because businesses will gladly provide spokesmen as a community service or for the promotional return. However, if the organization can find a good humorist who'll lighten up their meetings occasionally, they'll offer a fee.

There are other avenues for a writer who can also function as a humorist or an emcee. Every bowling, softball, and bridge league has an awards banquet sometime during the year. Leagues avoid hiring professional comics for these things because they generally don't have the funds, but you can step in there for a smaller fee—one they can afford.

Speaking is excellent training for a comedy writer. Writing for others, you're tempted to just do adequate material and let the comic suffer through it. When you're up there on your own, though, you learn what good and bad material can do for or against you. You appreciate the need for quality material. You learn what the performer has to endure when the material is "only good enough."

Local Comics

Almost every area has its own "Mr. (or Ms.) Comedy." Larger cities may have several comics vying for the title. These local celebrities need material as much as Jerry Seinfeld or Rita Rudner do—maybe more.

Selling to them is beneficial for two reasons. First of all, you get a check. Second, you get a chance to learn by studying audience reaction. That's almost as good as being up there delivering the lines yourself.

With local comics, you can travel to their appearances with them and study the audience as they perform. With national comics, you can't always afford that luxury. You get your feedback secondhand.

Some of my writing in the early years was for local comics and people who worked at their trade on weekends only. With one gentleman, I drew up a contract to receive a weekly stipend in exchange for a set amount of gags. With another comedian, I wrote a set amount of material, but received a percentage of his fee for each appearance. There are countless ways to negotiate these partnerships, but we'll talk more about that a little further on.

National Comics

It is quite possible to sell to many big-name performers without ever leaving your hometown. I wrote for Phyllis Diller for many months before I ever met her. Most of our dealings were by mail and phone (again, this predated fax machines and e-mail).

Comics who buy are usually not listed in a writer's market—you have to discover them on your own. The weekly *Variety* lists the appearances of many well-known comedians. If you keep track of them through the pages of *Variety*, you may be able to contact them by mail or phone at the club where they're appearing. You may be surprised to find that most comedians will at least look at material. They need it so badly, they're not likely to pass up a potential source of comedy.

Some writers feel that they're not competent or experienced enough to write for the "biggies." This story may change your mind. An aspiring writer came to one of our comedy-writing seminars. He was selling well to local comics, but was eager for more. He spoke to many of our faculty members and they all told him the same thing—offer your material to big-name comics. He took their advice and within months was writing for three of the biggest names in comedy.

The moral—don't turn down your own sales pitch. Bring your work to the "names" and let them decide.

Television

I list this category as a caution only. It's very difficult for a part-time writer who doesn't live in New York or Hollywood to sell material to network television.

Television material changes almost hourly. You may sell a story idea in the morning and be called to a meeting in the afternoon to get notes on the "new" storyline. Then you'll write it and present it to the producers, and it will be changed as you sit there. After the final draft is written, it will be changed again, and will constantly undergo modifications even until—and while—they're taping it.

It's difficult to do this sort of work by mail. It's almost impossible to do it with five or six writers in the room—but through the postal services, forget it.

Even story ideas or series ideas are not easily sold from a distance. Television executives buy names rather than stories or ideas. Ninety-nine percent of these ideas are purchased from established writers. The reputation is being bought in the hope that a workable idea will follow.

It's not impossible to sell a sitcom script from your home, but it's rare. Until your reputation is more firmly established, I suggest that you would serve your writing career better by forgetting network television and concentrating on more accessible markets.

Local Television and Cable

Not all television today originates with the networks. Everything that's a drawback for a local writer who wants to work for network television becomes an asset in writing for locally produced shows. You're accessible. You're available for meetings. You can localize your writing.

You can generate your own market list for local TV shows. Watch them, note those you feel you can write for, and contact the producers or the stars through the station.

Your Hobby Expertise

In the last chapter we discussed gift ideas based on humor writing. Other people may enjoy these items and want them for friends. You might pick up a few second income dollars doing photo albums or writing personalized monologues about people you don't even know.

These are only some of the ways you can enjoy your comedy-writing habit and generate a supplemental income at the same time. Probably you've already got several variations on these or entirely new schemes running through you head. Explore them.

How Much Is It Worth?

We may be getting a little ahead of ourselves here, but you could be wondering how much to charge for all these services. In many cases—such as for magazine fillers, humor services, greeting cards, and cartoonists—the fee is predetermined. In other instances, the fee structure is personal. Charge enough to make it worth your while to do it.

A danger here is that beginning writers may read about how much money an established writer makes, then try to set their fees comparably. You must realize that we all lie about the money we make and the rates we charge. (I would be a happy and comfortable man today if I made as much as I told my friends I did.) Besides, those writers have built their way to that fee.

It's better to charge less than you think is fair, to gain experience and collect another credit. Each time you sell comedy you establish more credibility—which means your services will be worth more in the future. Should you begin too high, you may not *have* a comedy-writing future.

Be fair to yourself, but not unreasonable. Eventually you will get so much work that you can be selective, and then you can accept only those assignments that pay the highest return.

For an Emmy-cast tribute to writers, I was asked to write a pithy phrase that explained what a good joke was. I submitted this:

> ✔ Martha Bolton has run the gamut of writing, from hobbyist to part-timer to staff writer for Bob Hope for over seven-teen years. She's been nominated for both an Emmy and a Writers' Guild Award. She's now a magazine columnist and has published over fifty humorous books. Martha offers this advice for both hobbyists and part-timers:
>
> Get started. That's the main thing. I did a lot of volunteer writing and that's how I got started. Anybody that would ask anything from me, I would do it for free. You have to let people know that you can write and are willing to write. Then it's from word of mouth. I got to where I was writing roasts for businesses and then the jokes would be quoted in the paper. It just kept going on.
>
> People now call me to do those and I charge. So that turns itself into money. Basically now, the same things I was doing for free, I now charge a fee. But I had to start doing it for free because no one is going to come to your door and say, "Will you write this for me and I'll pay you $1,000." You have to prove yourself first.

"A good joke is a series of words that ends in a paycheck."

- 6 -

Comedy as a Career

Before Ed Simmons began a long and successful career as a Hollywood producer and writer, he was a baby photographer. In his own words, "I spent my days eliciting laughter from toddlers. After a few years, I became power-crazed. Getting one baby to laugh wasn't enough. I started to concentrate on twins, then graduated to triplets, and by the time I was exclusively into quadruplets, the short supply sent me into bankruptcy. Then television came into being and I luckily rode in on the first wave."

That's a whimsical bit of underplay. Mr. Simmons was indeed a baby photographer, but—along with a partner—he worked evenings writing song parodies. Successes in this endeavor led to writing for some well-known nightclub comics. When the young TV industry was looking for writers who weren't jaded by years of radio writing, one producer turned to Ed and his partner. This led to a string of credits that included Dean Martin and Jerry Lewis, Danny Thomas, Eddie Cantor, Martha Raye, George Gobel, Red Skelton, and the show where Ed was my boss for five years as the producer-head writer: *The Carol Burnett Show*.

The progression from baby photographer to head writer and producer of major television shows sounds bizarre, but it really isn't. Each writer in Hollywood has his or her own strange tale of transition to comedy writing. I was an electrical engineer before being invited into television. One of the chief writers on Jay Leno's late night show was in advertising before moving full-time to TV writing. Some sitcom writers graduated from mid-level careers as stand-up comedians. But I've also met and worked with doctors and lawyers who abandoned their practices to make it in show business. There is no one road that leads to professional comedy writing, but there is also no place from which you can't get there.

Regardless of what your present occupation is, a comedy-writing career is always possible. Whether it is easy or not requires a qualified answer. It cannot be accomplished without a great deal of effort, perseverance, and diligent study. In that sense, it isn't easy. But if you're willing to put in the necessary apprenticeship and keep at it, it's almost impossible to fail. In that sense, it's easy.

I equate it to learning a musical instrument. When I see a person playing a piano, my mind tells me that it's impossible to see musical notes scribbled on paper, make sense of them, translate them into physical movements, and then have ten digits make those varied moves simultaneously— all of this, oftentimes, while singing. It's so complicated that it would seem to be an unattainable skill. Yet anyone with professional lessons and devoted practice can learn to play a piano. It's not a gift given to a select few—anyone can play a piano. How well you play it depends on how much time you're willing to put into your education and your practice.

Working on variety shows, I have met many of the top musicians in the country. I've asked them how much time they devote to practicing. Even after they are accomplished professional musicians, they sometimes practice six to eight hours a day to become better musicians.

I don't tell you this to scare any fledgling writers away from a career, because musicianship is much more difficult than writing. It's a much more exact skill. You have to hit the right notes at the right time…if you can't, you can't play with a group. Writing doesn't require that sort of precision. Also, writing doesn't demand physical dexterity as musicianship does. But writing does illustrate the different meanings of "easy." If you are willing to work, learn, and stick with it, a writing career can be easy. If you are not, a writing career may be almost impossible.

The Luck Factor

Many talented people—not only writers—are tempted to use "luck" as an excuse for not embarking on a new career.

"Oh, I couldn't make it as a comedy writer. You have to be lucky to do that."

"Oh sure, she made it, but that's because she got lucky."

Let's look at two professional comedy writers who are both temporarily out of work. Writer A keeps calling his agent to find him some kind of work because he has to pay the bills. Writer B pesters her agent, too, but while she's on a forced hiatus, she creates and outlines twenty-six ideas for situation comedies.

Finally A does get a job and commands a nice salary. B sells one of her pilot ideas. It's a hit, and she becomes a millionaire. Now Writer A sits in his office and moans, "Oh sure, Writer B is on Easy Street now because she got lucky."

Luck is something that happens after the fact. It didn't cause Writer B's success. If none of these shows had sold, chances are B would have created more shows, then more, until one of them sold—and then that moment would have been termed "lucky."

The phenomenally successful screen actor Sylvester Stallone began his meteoric rise to fame and wealth with the screenplay that he wrote himself, *Rocky*. How lucky can you get? One screenplay generated all that income and all that fame. But Stallone wrote nine or ten other screenplays on speculation before he sold *Rocky*. That's not luck. That's dedication.

We create our own good fortune. Don't use luck as an excuse to avoid the challenge, and don't depend on it for your success. Substitute confidence and diligence instead—and then let Writer A complain about how "lucky" you got.

Why New Writers Break In

The popular misconception is that comedy writing is a "closed" profession—no newcomers are needed or welcome. That just isn't true. The door to a writing career is not standing wide open, but it is ajar.

Even if those of us already in the field wanted to make writing an exclusive fraternity, we couldn't do it for the following reasons.

Comedy Is Popular

Humor is a commodity in constant demand because it is tremendously popular. If you study most fields of entertainment, you'll discover that comedy is the big moneymaker. Good comedy is what's wanted most in the movie industry, in television, in books, and in nightclubs (even singers are doing comedy lines). The public's appetite for comedy is so voracious that no fixed group of writers could ever satisfy it. We will always need more and more suppliers to meet the demand.

Comedy Changes Constantly

At one time, most comedians were the stand-up variety. Lenny Bruce introduced a new and unique style. Bill Cosby came up with yet a different kind of comedy routine. Steve Martin brought some innovations to that. Today we have people like Steven Wright, Emo Philips, and Paula Poundstone adding even more subtleties.

As I mentioned in my introduction, the basics remain, but the stylings may vary. Not all of us can write in all of the different styles. I remember once when I was a beginning TV writer I was penning lines for Bob Hope and just finished a season with the very successful, and at that time innovative, show *Laugh-In*. When I began working on a new variety show staff, I wrote and turned in what I thought was a creative and funny script. When the star of the show read it, he tossed all the copies *out the window* onto Beverly Boulevard and said, "I'm not Bob Hope and I'm not *Laugh-In*." I quickly had to learn to write a new style of comedy.

Many innovations in comedy styles open the door for the new breed of comedy writer.

Comedy Is Not Recyclable

Start telling a joke and people will hold up their hands and say, "I heard it." No one enjoys a comic story they've already heard. But no one does that to a singer. If Michael Bublé starts crooning "Save the Last Dance for Me," no one in the audience says, "Don't sing that song. We've already heard it."

Comedy material is used up at an alarming rate. And it has to be fresh. Once it's on the airwaves, it's gone. Many comics who appeared as guests on variety shows I've written for wanted the staff to write new material for them. They didn't want to do their own tried and true material. Why? Because once it was exposed on television, they couldn't use it in their nightclub and concert appearances. People had already heard it.

With the enormous demand that all entertainment forms create, and since humor can't be reused too soon or even copied too closely, fertile new comedy minds are always wanted to fill the bill.

A Constant Supply of Comedy Is Needed

Because you usually can't recycle comedy, people who buy it always need a fresh source. Comics, television hosts, and other comedy consumers work constantly yet can't use the same material. So they need someone who can always bring them fresh ideas. This creates a tremendous need for comedy minds. Here's a story that shows how much comedians crave new material:

Bob Hope had just wrapped up the last television special of the season and all of the writers were gathered in his dressing room for our good-byes. Hope was leaving the following day for a tour of several universities beginning with Notre Dame. He said to the staff, "Hey guys, get me some good football jokes for tomorrow, will you?" One writer objected. (It wasn't me. I was a dutiful writer.) The writer said, "We've been writing football jokes all season. You haven't used all of them. Why do you need new football jokes?"

Hope crossed over to this writer and said, "I pay you with new money, don't I?"

We did new football jokes.

Humor is the lifeblood that keeps careers alive. Entertainers can never be satisfied with what they have because in a short time it will be gone. They can only relax when they know there is an inexhaustible supply of neatly typed gags sliding under the office door. That's why we always need a steady influx of new comedy thinkers in the profession.

Good Writers Move On

One of the most difficult problems of staffing a television show is finding good writers. Good writers quickly become unavailable because they advance to script consultants and story editors. Eventually they become producers and executive producers. This movement upward creates a vacuum that has to be filled with new talent.

New Writers Are Desirable

For comedy to be anything at all, it has to be fresh, enthusiastic, and exciting. Those are the qualities that new writers are infused with. Veteran writers are eminently competent but (much as I hate to admit it) sometimes competence isn't enough. It has to be combined with flair—something unique, something different, something daring.

In all fairness, you sometimes pay a price for the individuality of eager young writers. Sometimes their friskiness has to be tempered with the wisdom of the veterans. The National Football League would be a shambles if we allowed the players to run things. The coaches' know-how and discipline are necessary—yet what a sad team you would field if it comprised only 40- and 50-year-old coaches.

There's room in comedy for both dependable pros and zealous newcomers.

> ✓ Budd Friedman, who founded the Improv comedy club in New York in 1973, has helped many stand-up comedians begin and further their careers. Just a few of the well-known comics who got their start from the Improv are Richard Pryor, Lily Tomlin, Rodney Dangerfield, and Jay Leno . . . the list goes on and on. Budd offers this advice to comedy performers, but it applies to aspiring writers, too:
>
> To be a star you have to be creative, original, and resourceful. You must have a lot of stick-to-itiveness. It's a tough business and there are very few overnight sensations.
>
> Don't give up. I'll never tell you you're no good. I'll say you're not right for us, but I'm not going to be the one to say "get out of the business."
>
> I think you just have to stick to it, be original, do your own thing.

Begin Where You Are

We mentioned earlier that each successful writer has tried his or her own peculiar road to professionalism. Your story will be as distinctive and remarkable as each one of these. They all have one common feature, though—each began small.

Having heroes like Dave Barry or Ray Romano is commendable, but the beginner must be careful not to try to parallel their success from the start. Today's name writers and comics began with unlimited potential and no successes. Gradually, they converted their potential to fulfillment.

You must begin your career right where you are. I've often heard people say that they were going to try to come to Hollywood to "make it." That's fine, because that's probably where most television writers do make it. But they begin "making it" in their own hometowns.

Hollywood or New York is the ultimate goal for most writers, but you should establish a solid foundation in your craft before attacking either town. Arriving there too soon can be hazardous. It is much safer to have an extensive background and then extend it further to Hollywood or New York rather than come to the big city as a raw beginner and risk being rejected completely. Many would-be-successes never recover from that first rejection.

I had written for Phyllis Diller for several months, via telephone and mail, before I met her when she was appearing at the Latin Casino in Cherry Hill, New Jersey. I visited with her backstage between shows and the first thing she said to me was, "You're my best writer." I was thrilled and flattered and tried to capitalize on it. I said, "Then how come I'm not in Hollywood?" She answered, "Because you're not ready yet."

I never appreciated Phyllis's wisdom until I arrived in Hollywood. Naturally, my rookie year coincided with the first year of many other writers, and I could see the difference. Those of us who had served an apprenticeship adapted more readily to the rigors of the weekly television deadline. We may not have been great writers, but we could alter our styles as we learned what TV needed. Many of those first-year writers with less background than I had haven't survived in television.

In an interview in the pages of comedy writers' newsletter *Round Table,* Phyllis Diller was asked what the biggest piece of advice she could offer to young writers would be. She said, "Start right where you are. You offer to do it for nothing at first. You get paid a little if you can. But you have to prove yourself right where you are. Work banquets, send lines or monologues to local TV hosts, try to send out material regularly. Some say you have to go to Hollywood or New York to get into the business. I say, a trip around the world starts with the first step, and the first step can only be taken in one spot—where you're standing right now."

In constructing your comedy-writing career, you must build on small successes and transform them into larger ones. As Phyllis Diller advised, do free assignments for a while. If you do well at these, you'll eventually be able to charge for them. That's taking one success and building it into a bigger one. I've already told you how I began doing master of ceremony chores where I worked. This was great training, though I received no salary for it. But it provided excellent exposure because people in the audience organized different functions outside the company. They had seen my work, and hired me—at a small fee— to entertain outside, too.

Almost any assignment, performed well, can multiply into other assignments. You'll also discover that the marquee value increases as you go along. That is to say, you might write for a local comic, then a not-too-well-known national comedian, then a well-known comic, then perhaps television or the movies. The name value of the people you work for will increase the assignments you get—and the price you can command.

In beginning a professional comedy career, all the markets we mentioned in the previous chapter on part-time writing apply. The difference between a second-income career and a full-fledged pro career is simply a matter of degree. Some people decide that they are putting enough time and effort into their writing and are satisfied with the returns. But a would-be professional must continue to grow.

In Part Three of this book I'll discuss how to market your skills to build a professional career. The first step, though, is to know that it can be accomplished. Your efforts would be fruitless—and practically impossible to undertake—if you didn't think you could make it. The second step is to get to work and do it.

Again, I offer a word of caution. Developing your skills may take much energy and certainly some time. A successful career requires, along with determination and toil, a bit of patience and understanding. Patience because you must allow time for your apprenticeship, and understanding because you must realize that even after you perfect your craft and become supremely accomplished, it will take time for buyers to realize that. You must not only become proficient, but you must prove to others that you are. Both take time.

The Way I Did It

It took me nine years from the time I committed to a writing career until I became a full-time professional. Simply to serve as an example, I'll list my progress here. My path is longer or shorter or otherwise different from that of other writers. Besides, there is no guarantee that the routes I chose were most correct or most efficient. My narrative isn't included as your unalterable road map to success, but simply so you can see what someone else experienced—and perhaps know what you might encounter on your own journey.

I thought I had the skills necessary for comedy and wanted to try it. I had no contacts or education in the field but determined to give it a try anyway. My thinking was that it would be better to try and fail than to spend my later years saying, "I wish I had tried that when I was younger."

I began by taping all of Bob Hope's television monologues, then typing them out, studying them, and trying to duplicate the joke forms and styles with different topics. (Years later, when I got a call from Bob Hope to do some material for his Academy Awards performance, I wrote about 300 jokes. He used ten of them on the telecast. When we talked later he said, "Your material looked like you'd been writing for me all your life." I said, "Mr. Hope, I have, only you didn't know about it.")

Magazines seemed an easy way to make a bit of money, so I began sending short filler jokes to several of them. With a lot of bookkeeping effort and some postage I could sell about twenty dollars worth of comedy a month. (At today's fees, that might amount to about a hundred dollars a month.) It wasn't much, but it was at least some remuneration for my time and effort.

Simply as a comedy-writing exercise, I captioned a book of baby pictures about the office where I worked. This led to my being invited to emcee several twenty-fifth anniversary and retirement parties. This was both speaking and writing training, but it had another fringe benefit—it was great exposure.

In my hometown of Philadelphia, someone who knew a local comedian mentioned to him that I was funny. He called and asked me to write some material for him. The material never sold, but he recommended me to a local television host who wanted a writer for his daytime show and a ghost writer for a humorous newspaper column. I did both, but again, never sold them. However, a visiting comic saw my material and my letterhead on the TV host's desk and called me to write for him. That led to a fairly lucrative contract that ran for six years.

During this time I was also visiting every nightclub in the Philadelphia area, calling on comics with copies of my most recent and brilliant gags. I made a few sales but mostly learned to cope with rejection. (The list of comedians who've turned me down is much longer than the ones who've hired me, but ones who hired me paid more.)

Finally, I connected with and impressed Phyllis Diller. She prompted me to write more and better material. Eventually, she starred in a network TV show and hired me to do the monologues. This introduced me into television—and then one job led to the next.

It started small. It started in my hometown. It progressed gradually. It was fun all along the way, and it was an education that served me well when I reached Hollywood.

Your journey is ahead of you, but the groundwork must be laid now. I envy you because it should be exciting and it should be fun.

Part One of this book was to help you overcome that first great obstacle—that little something inside you that whispers, "I can't write." Yes you can. You know you have a sense of humor and perseverance if you have managed to listen to me for this long.

Move on with me to Part Two where we'll convert your potential to product. As we say in the profession, "We'll put it on paper."

PART TWO
BUILDING YOUR SKILLS

"It's not necessarily what career you pick. It's about how you do what you do."

—Cory Doctorow

- 7 -

Write, Read, and Listen

Before going any further, we should both understand our roles in this volume. This is definitely a "how-to" book, but it's not the complete, definitive, solitary bible on comedy. It has suggestions for beginning your comedy writing and some hints for sharpening your comedy skills, but the genius must come from you.

Comedy is such a subjective art that no one can or should have all the answers. If anyone ever did, comedy would no longer exist. To be anything at all, humor must be fresh and ever changing, innovative and inventive. It must be *surprising*. If anyone had all the answers, there would be no surprise. For your comedy to be bright, it has to have a touch of *you* in there—certainly not all me.

One head writer I've worked with many times kept a sign prominently displayed in his office that read, "There are few good judges of comedy. And they don't agree." One day the writing staff had a serious discussion about that sign. Some of the writers wanted to change it to read, "And *we* don't agree." That's how subjective comedy is.

We couldn't agree on whether it should say ". . . *they* don't agree" or ". . . *we* don't agree."

I hope the material in this book will help you. However, don't permit anything in here to stifle your creativity or your particular brand of zaniness. This volume doesn't have all the answers—simply a few of the things I've learned from doing comedy and from listening to others do comedy. But the tips are available to help you get started and learn on your own.

This book is like the faint outline on needlework patterns—it's there as a guide to get you started. The real artistry appears when you provide the stitchery.

Or better yet…the book is like a blasting cap. It will provide a spark; the explosion will come when you start generating your own comedy.

The lessons and the exercises in these pages are very fundamental. I wanted the book to be a step-by-step progression so that any reader, whether acquainted with comedy writing or not, could pick it up, follow it through, and be turning out humor with professional potential by the back cover.

At the same time, if you are already an experienced humorist, it can serve as a refresher course and reminder of the fundamentals of good comedy technique. Professional golfers sometimes have to remind themselves to keep their heads down or their wrists firm. Writers may also get a bit lax on good basic technique occasionally.

A good percentage of these pages are devoted to joke or gag writing and monologues. That's because I feel that comedy is based on jokes, the basic building blocks of humor. If you were to compile a list of very successful humor writers, you'd find many of them served an apprenticeship as gag writers. Norman Lear, who was the force behind the very successful *All in the Family* on TV, wrote nightclub material for many comics, including the team of Lewis and Martin. Larry Gelbart, who has done TV, movies, and Broadway plays did one-liners for Bob Hope. Woody Allen's delightfully bizarre movies evolved from his experiences as a gag writer for newspaper columnists. Neil Simon, one of the most successful playwrights of our time, began as a gagster on Sid Caesar's legendary show.

I don't mean to imply that stand-up, one-line routines are the only or even the best form of comedy. However, they do serve as a superb apprenticeship for all other varieties of humor writing.

Picture yourself buying a tennis racket, a can of balls, a cute little dress, and walking out to a tennis pro and saying, "I want to be an attacking player. I'd like to hit the ball crosscourt most of the time, then close in to the net for the put-away shot." He'd say, "Fine, we'll work a few weeks on the backhand stroke, then a couple weeks on the forehand. We'll practice your volleys, your overhead, and get fundamentals down." That way you'll discover your strengths and your faults—and your preferences. From that you'll be able to design your strategic game plan.

The same logic applies in music, dancing—almost any learning process. That's why we'll be devoting most of our time to the simpler humor forms, although we will discuss other writing after learning the "strokes."

This book can only be your third best teacher of comedy. The first two will always be your own writing and reading and listening to other humorists.

Learn by Writing

Some readers may be shy about sitting before a blank sheet of paper and turning out humor. They ask, "Should I write if I don't feel I'm ready?" Certainly. That's *how* you get ready.

How many people would be playing golf today if they refused to pick up a club until they knew they could shoot in the low 80s? If no one were willing to be a clumsy beginner, tennis courts would be deserted. No one would ever learn to play a musical instrument. You learn by doing—in fact, it's the only way to learn.

In working with newcomers, the best advice I can give (and the advice that is least followed) is to set an unyielding quota and then stick to it. There's no need to make the quota unreasonably demanding. That sort of bravado only makes it easier to abandon. Make it simple on yourself. Start with three jokes a day or ten jokes a week, but be faithful to it. Adjust it as you progress to keep making it a challenge, but one that is attainable.

✔ Comedian Drew Carey says this about a regular writing routine:

You have to treat comedy—writing and performing—like a job. One of the ways I did that was to set minimums for myself—like writing 10 jokes a day. I told other comics about this and they did it and it helped them. I got really good feedback from the 10-jokes-a-day method.

If you write 10 jokes a day and you get one good joke—that's all you want out of the whole day—and you do that five days a week, that's five good jokes a week. If you do that all year, 50 weeks a year with two weeks off, that's an hour's worth of material. If you're a stand-up comic and you can come up with an hour a year, that's amazing. It really, really is. You'll be the most prolific comic on the road.

I'm telling you, set a minimum for each day and stick to it and you really can't go wrong.

Doing your own writing consistently and religiously will help in the following ways.

Improvement by Repetition

I disagree with the popular saying that "practice makes perfect." Practice leads to perfection *only* if you're practicing the correct technique. If a novice tennis player practices faithfully, at the end of the year he won't be a Roger Federer or an Andy Roddick. He might not be a tournament player or even a real good club player, but he will be hitting the ball well—certainly better than he did a year ago. Even if he hits the ball incorrectly, he will be hitting it incorrectly *consistently*. I've played against unorthodox tennis players who do everything wrong, but they win. Repetition does beget improvement.

Obviously, the optimum course is the combination of study with practice. *Learn* how to do it correctly, and then practice doing it correctly. With this mixture you improve correctly. However, study or training with no practical application is virtually worthless.

Gaining Confidence

"Having written" is the greatest proof that you can write again. Each time you do an exercise or assignment, you'll do one or two little things that delight you. You may not be entirely happy with the results, but there usually will be a few gems in there to thrill you.

Again I'll use tennis to illustrate this point. I've played with folks who were having particularly bad days, but when they hit a rare good shot they'd say, "Ah, that shot made it worth getting up early." It's those brilliant moments that convince you you can do it.

As you work on your writing, you'll be faced with exercises or assignments that initially seem impossible. Yet you'll persevere and complete them, and the next time you face an "impossible" assignment, it won't seem nearly as threatening because you know you've completed similar ones before.

Many times I've been assigned to write jokes on topics that simply aren't funny, or I've been faced with deadlines that are unmeetable. But because I've faced those seemingly insurmountable odds before—and conquered them—I set my schedule, turn on my computer, and complete the chore.

Discovering Your Strengths and Weaknesses

Hanging in my office is a cartoon from the Sunday papers that I cut out and had framed. It tells a beautiful story about writers. (I know because I've mentioned this story to other writers and they say, "I have that same cartoon hanging in my office.") The cartoon strip is from many years ago. It's from a cartoon strip called *Shoe* drawn by McNelly. The first four blocks of the strip picture an owl (the Professor) seated at a typewriter, struggling to come up with an idea. The balloon above his head, though, is blank each time. Then, in the fifth frame, he strikes a great thought. In the balloon over his head is a glorious, ornate letter "A." Inspired with this stroke of genius, he taps his typewriter, looks at what he has just written—and it's just a simple, typewritten letter "A." In the final frame he crumples up the paper and goes back to his empty thinking.

I keep this in my office to remind me that sometimes there's a tremendous gap between what we *conceive* and what we *execute*. It's easy to say, "I want to write the greatest love song of all time." It's difficult to deliver.

All writers discover their inadequacies sooner or later. William Saroyan said, "You write a hit play the same way your write a flop." Perhaps Robert Benchley, a humorist from the early 1900s, best expressed this realization when he said, "It took me fifteen years to discover that I had no talent for writing, but I couldn't give it up because by that time I was too famous."

There will be certain types of writing you do very well and some you have to struggle to complete. Some of your work will be excellent, some adequate. Only by writing and trying different types of composition can you learn which is for you and which isn't.

You'll also learn which you prefer and which you'd rather not be bothered with. You'll learn which skills you'll have to practice more to improve.

Developing New Skills

As you write faithfully, you will discover and experiment with new talents. Ralph Waldo Emerson said, "Good writing is a kind of skating which carries off the performer where he would not go."

For all these reasons, as a form of training and discipline I once determined to write a full screenplay. Good, bad, or indifferent, I vowed to complete a full story and 120 pages of dialogue. I was prepared for extremely tedious work.

But I discovered a fascinating phenomenon—I got into my work and was enthralled by the characters. I couldn't wait to get to the computer each morning to find out what they'd do and say. I found out that I loved dialogue writing.

Other writers detest doing dialogue. But only by trying it do you discover whether you like it or not.

Listening and Reading

Listening and reading is the second best practice for a comedy writer because it is almost effortless learning. I've already mentioned how I taped and typed out Bob Hope's monologues, studying them for form and style. But I listened to many other comics, too, and I read as much comedy and about comedy as I could. You absorb something from all this contact.

We absorb more than we're aware of from contact with the greats. You can test this out yourself. Watch some of the newcomers in the comedy clubs or on comedy spots on television. If you're tuned in, you'll be able to recognize traces of some of the more established comedy performers. Some of the young comedians may not even be aware that they've adopted and adapted the styling of the other performers, but you'll be able to spot it.

Listening to other humorists and reading comedy will help you learn in the following ways.

Observe What Does and Doesn't Work

There is only one good judge of comedy and that is the audience. The rest of us are merely guessing. Remember that sign that producer had in his office: "There are few good judges of comedy. And they (or we) don't agree." I have written jokes that I've absolutely loved. I'd sit in the audience hardly able to contain my anticipation until the comic got to my treasured joke. Then he'd deliver it; it would get nothing. I'd convince him to try it again—again nothing. I'd work with the comic on the delivery. He'd incorporate my suggestions—again, stony silence. We might give it one more shot for good measure, and then I'd have to admit that it was a great joke, but nobody loved it but me.

Other times the audience responds to a simple joke with big laughs. Neither the comic nor I can explain it, but we enjoy it.

Watching other performers work and noting what sort of response they get will clue you in to the pitfalls of certain types of humor. The audience will always be the master of the comedy, but you'll learn to become one of the good guessers.

Joke Forms

Each comedian you listen to has his or her own particular speech patterns and joke forms. The peculiarities are almost as varied as the comics who use them. Wendy Leibman, for example, has a way of completing a sentence, but then not really completing it.

"Having an affair with a married man—I would never do that...again."

You learn the various devices that comedians use by listening to them and noting their gimmicks. Once you learn these tricks, they become convenient joke writing tools because they're largely "fill in the blank" type of writing.

"It was so cold out today that (fill in the blank)."

"Alimony is paying money to a person you're no longer married to. That's like (fill in the blank)."

"The way the new television season is going, NBC stands for (fill in the blank)."

You'll absorb many of these simply by hearing other comedians, and they will serve you well in the future.

New Topics and Slants

A writer on *The Tonight Show* staff told me once that the most difficult part of his job isn't the actual writing. The hard part is finding new topics to joke about each day. The work is relentless because it's five days a week, fifty-two weeks a year. Writing isn't always tough—but finding out what to write about can be.

Listening and reading will give you a whole new catalog of topics. You'll discover what humorists are talking about and what audiences are responding to.

You will also learn from other comics how to give a standard topic a fresh slant. By a slant, I mean the way you approach the humor in a given topic.

Recently, Vice President Dick Cheney made the headlines when he accidentally shot a friend during a hunting outing. The topic didn't immediately lend itself to humor because Cheney's companion was seriously wounded in the mishap. Comics nevertheless jumped on this topic by focusing on the vice president's shooting prowess and avoiding any mention of the wounded man.

Jay Leno mentioned during his monologue that at the opening of the baseball season in Washington DC, "President Bush threw out the first ball...and Dick Cheney shot the first fan out of the upper deck."

David Letterman said, "It was so cold in Washington DC, that Dick Cheney shot the weatherman."

Even President Bush got into the comedy on this topic. He entertained the collegiate champion rifle squad team—fittingly a team from West Point—at a reception in the Rose Garden. He told them, "If you fellows happen to bump into Dick Cheney while you're here, maybe you could give him a few pointers."

There is any number of slants or approaches you can take to a given topic, so it pays to learn as many as you can. It will not only help you on the particular topic but can also help you find an approach for topics that you may have to work on later.

Different Styles

The one thing that sets good comics apart from bad or mediocre ones is that the good comics have a definite style—a definable character. Jerry Seinfeld has some wonderful lines in his act. Robin Williams can't use them. Conversely, Seinfeld wouldn't use any of Williams's great lines either. Rita Rudner has hilarious one-liners; Ellen DeGeneres can't use them. I just selected these names randomly, but the principle applies to almost any top-notch comics. Their material isn't transferable because their styles and characters are unique.

Style and characterization are a larger part of comedy than most people realize. It's the stage persona that determines what type of jokes comics can do and how they do them.

It will serve you to watch and listen and become acquainted with as many different styles as you can.

How to Blend Styles

By exposing yourself to varied styles, you will begin subconsciously—or consciously—to adopt some of them. You'll start with a touch of Dennis Miller, sprinkle in a bit of Lewis Black, maybe add a dash of Chris Rock, and top it all off with a flavoring of Kathleen Madigan. Whatever combination you choose, you'll begin to fashion a brand new style—your own.

There's nothing wrong with borrowing from the greats. I once attended a banquet honoring George Carlin for his comedy career. During his acceptance speech, Carlin thanked many of the greats from radio, film, and television comedy. He was grateful to all of them because he learned from them and adopted some of their techniques to form his own individual brand of humor.

My wife, my mother-in-law, and my wife's grandmother all make spaghetti sauce from the same recipe. All of them are delicious and all of them are different. Why? Because each one puts a bit of her own personality into the cooking.

By being aware of different styles, you'll learn all the ingredients you can use in your own unique comedic recipe.

Inspiration

Listening to other humorists can be a stimulus to get you to the keyboard. When I was a youngster, I'd watch my brother play high school football on Sunday afternoons. The first thing I wanted to do when I got home was get a bunch of guys and play two-hand touch. Watching that much football made me want to go out and play some. So, when you see or read some excellent comedy, it might inspire you to try the same.

The big-time comics can add something intangible to your work, too. They instill something in you that makes you work better and harder. Often, when I must turn out fresh material for a client, I'll slip a tape into the video player and watch a bit of that comedian's past performances. This gets me inspired, into the flow, and I can attack the assignment with renewed vigor.

Now, as I promised at the beginning of this chapter, we're going to get you writing. Find some blank paper, a pencil, and turn the page.

- 8 -

Comedy-Writing Exercises

In Chapter 3 we discussed several comedy-writing skills. Many of these, though, involved preparatory work. When it comes to the actual writing of comedy, three skills become paramount. They are:

- Recognizing relationships and ironies
- Visualization and imagery
- Facility with words

It's easy to categorize these skills and list them separately, but in practice they are intertwined; in the creative process you employ them all as one.

We're back to dissecting our beleaguered frog again. You can study his cardiovascular system to see how it operates and what functions it performs. You can investigate the workings of his nervous system for its particular purpose. But if they're to work properly, they cannot be detached. The heart cannot beat without the signals from the nervous system. The nerves cannot operate without blood supplied through the circulatory system.

We will consider these skills separately, but be careful—you might find it cumbersome and fruitless to try to create comedy by using them apart from one another. Be inventive, using all of them, and let your meanderings lead you where they may.

Relationships and Ironies

Most comedy, as I've stated before, is a combination of two or more ideas. It's the relationship of these ideas that generates the humor. Some ideas are very similar; some are quite different. Some appear to be different, but are really the same and vice versa. The skillful humorist will discover these relationships.

> "The elderly don't drive that badly. They're just the only ones with time to do the speed limit."

That's a simple little statement created by Jason Love, but what an entertaining observation. Obviously, the joke stands on its own. Any joke that needs an explanation has something lacking. But for our discussion, we might look deeper into it.

The comedy basically comes from the fact that the statement, for the most part, is true. Or at least it has a recognizable element of truth in it. We've all berated the elderly driver of the car in front for driving so slowly, but then again, what does he or she have to rush for. We always seem to be in a hurry, but our older neighbors aren't. Probably anywhere they're going, they've already been. It's a nice little joke because the observation is recognizable, but is expressed unusually tightly. It took a creative humorist to do that.

> "If carrots are so good for the eyes, how come I see so many dead rabbits on the highways?"

Again, here is an observation that no one quite ever made before. Comedian Richard Jeni did, though. It's a concise little gag, but it says so much because the relationship and the irony not only are recognized but are also beautifully expressed.

Visualization and Imagery

Many jokes are pictures. That is to say, with words we create an image in the listener's mind. Notice this Rita Rudner line:

> "When my husband and I are in the car, I usually let him drive. Because when I drive, he has a tendency to bite the dashboard."

As soon as you hear this joke, you immediately get a picture in your mind of this poor fellow chewing on the car's interior.

When we create an image, the distortion or the ridiculousness of that image generates the humor. That's why puns have the reputation as the lowest form of humor. I have worked with clients who refuse to buy any gag that depends on pure wordplay. Words are powerful tools of the humorist—as we'll see in the following section—but comedy that depends on wordplay alone often does not create a graphic image in the mind of the listener; therefore, it's usually not as funny—clever, maybe, but not funny.

This is also one reason why humor is so subjective. Some people love a particular joke or story; others won't appreciate it at all because the image is different in each person's mind. The joke is not the collection of words; it's the scene that appears in the listener's mind as a result of those words. Skillful use of words will create a stronger image, but it is usually the image that produces the humor.

The mind can be extremely elastic, too, which is an aid to humorists. Our minds easily accept distortions and impossibilities. Think back to some of the dreams you've had. In them you wander from place to place with no trouble. People change before your very eyes. The situations become so bizarre that you can't even relate them coherently, yet during the dream your intellect accepts every outlandish occurrence without questioning it.

Humorists can often use the mind's flexibility to advantage. For example, consider these lines that I once wrote about Phyllis Diller's fictitious mother-in-law. In her act, Phyllis called her Moby Dick.

"Talk about fat people, you ought to see my mother-in-law. She's so big, she has two ZIP codes.

"The first time I met her, Fang (Phyllis called her husband 'Fang.') said, 'Who does Mom remind you of?' I said, 'North Dakota.'

"I don't know what her measurements are. We haven't had her surveyed yet.

"She's a nice woman, though. Nicest three acres of flesh I've ever met.

"She gave me one of her old dresses. I plan to have it starched and made into a summer home.

"Once she was coming to visit us, but I didn't want her staying with us. I made reservations for her at a motel. She stayed in Cabins 13, 14, and 15.

"When you get on an elevator with her, you'd better be going down.

"Once she got on a bus and six men got up and offered her their seat. If two more had done it, she could have accepted."

Notice the liberties I took with the imagery. First the lady is the size of two ZIP codes; then she becomes as large as a state. I define her as three acres and the mind accepts that. In another line she is no longer the size of North Dakota, only the size of a small house. She requires three motel rooms, but she can get on an elevator and a bus.

My descriptions of Moby Dick would hardly be acceptable evidence in court, but the adaptability of our minds allows me to have some fun—create some comedy—with exaggerated and distorted images of this lady.

Yet another mental phenomenon can be used advantageously by comedy writers—audiences tend to fill in any gaps. Our minds continue an image on to its natural conclusion and supply anything that might be missing. It's this peculiarity that makes stage magic work. Magicians show an audience only so much—the audience assumes the rest. The key to the trick is generally where that assumption is made. People say, "I know he put the coin in his right hand. I saw it there." They really didn't; they just assumed it should be there and so their minds told them they "saw" it there.

Humorists utilize this tendency by leading an audience's thinking in one direction and then suddenly changing that direction. The classic example of this is Henny Youngman's oft-cited line, "Take my wife . . . please." When he says, "Take my wife," the audience assumes he's just saying "Let's use my wife as an example." But the next word changes the meaning entirely. The comic is literally asking someone to *take his wife.*" We didn't expect that, so we laugh.

Comedy depends on the unexpected. (Remember no one enjoys

hearing a joke they've already heard.) A joke might even be diagrammed like this:

That indicates a thought continuing along in a certain direction and abruptly changing direction. That's what evokes the laughter at a man who slips on a banana peel. He's walking contentedly on his way. All of us assume he will continue to walk merrily along that same way. Suddenly, he is abruptly upended. That's the unexpected; that's what we laugh at.

✔ **Comic Tom Dreesen talks about the surprise element of comedy:**

Let me give you something to tell your writers: Comedy is nine-tenths surprise. The audience laughs because they didn't think you were going to say that. So remember when writing a joke, the setup line must totally hide the punch line. Take them down the path of believability and then drop the bottom out.

The silent screen comedian, W. C. Fields once said that real comedy was when you expected something to break and it only bent. Again...the unexpected.

As humorists, we can take advantage of people's thinking patterns. The following gag illustrates that:

> *"Dear Abby,*
> *I am 16 years old. I think I'm old enough to wear lipstick, rouge, and eye shadow. Yet every time my mother finds it, she throws it out and punishes me. Please answer and tell me who is right.*
> *Signed,*
> *Ralph"*

Notice how your thoughts were led in one direction and the last word of the gag abruptly changed that. The rug was pulled out from under your mind.

The principle applies in short one-liners, too. Jay Leno once commented on a news item:

*"A man who worked in a mortuary stole 157 pounds of
body parts. Bail cost him an arm and a leg."*

Our minds assume the comic is going to mention a monetary price.
No, he surprises us with the body parts.

Facility with Words

For the most part, words are the medium we use to convey our
witty creations. There are funny pantomimists, of course, and some jokes
are enhanced by facial expression or inventive stage business. None-
theless, most humor is conveyed by words.

Words have a playfulness all their own. Malapropisms are a good
example of this. Malapropisms are those words that are almost the right
word, but not quite. "Their marriage was never constipated." Sometimes the wrong version creates a new meaning that is almost as mean-
ingful, or even more so, than the right word. "We should study history.
It's part of the whole American heresy." "Why do I have to contribute
so much of my money to the Infernal Revenue?"

Some folks can misuse phrases so that their meaning is conveyed—
just about. The movie mogul, Sam Goldwyn, had so many that they
became known as "Goldwynisms." I think we all know what he meant
when he said, "Oral contracts aren't worth the paper they're written
on." And what could be more definitive than to say about someone, "I
never liked him and I probably always will."

One of my favorite misusages was uttered by my tennis partner
while we were being badly beaten in a match. "Okay," he said to me,
"we've got them right where they want us."

Word jokes have fallen into disrepute with the axiom about puns
being the lowest form of humor. But it simply isn't true: puns can be
really inspired at times. Samuel Johnson once boasted to his drinking
companions that he could instantaneously compose a pun on any subject. "The King," someone volunteered. Johnson replied, "The King, sir,
is not a subject."

I know I said earlier that puns weren't funny—you don't have to
start paging backwards now. That was when we talked about visualization and imagery. The point I was making then and still maintain is
that puns that depend *totally* on wordplay generally aren't funny. How-

ever, some puns can create a funny image and produce a good joke. For example, consider this line from Taylor Negron:

> "My father used to ground me—and then run electricity through me."

That's a play on the word "ground"—a pun. However, it also generates (no pun intended) a picture of a kid being jolted by live current circulating through his body. It's a great graphic.

Woody Allen is clever punster; here's one that's a classic—it not only got many laughs, it also got him sued. A news story had broken about his ex-wife having been molested. Allen said, "She claims she was violated. Knowing my ex-wife, it wasn't a moving violation."

There is hardly any word you can think of that doesn't have at least one other meaning—most have several. Once I was trying to disprove this statement, and a word I came up with that could have no possible other meaning was "butterfly." It could only mean an insect. But as soon as I said that, the obvious other meaning popped into my head. Literally, it can denote a dairy product that flies.

Try it yourself. Think of a word or two and almost immediately you'll discover another meaning for each word. Take an ordinary word like "house." As you read it, you instantly visualize what I mean by that word—but do you? Which of the following meanings of "house" was I trying to convey:

A dwelling?
A brothel?
A legislature?
An audience?
The management of a gambling casino?
A business?

A good humor writer, with effort and practice, can learn to use the idiosyncrasies of the language to good advantage.

Following are eight comedy-writing exercises that will help you develop your writing skills. Some favor language skills, others visualization, but, for the reasons we discussed earlier, no attempt is made to differentiate them. You do yourself no favor by separating the skills. If an exercise features language, the best jokes will be those that not only use words cleverly but that also conjure up a humorous image and present an ironic observation.

Have fun with these exercises. They're not homework assignments or chores. They're fun, provocative excursions into the creation of comedy.

(If you choose, you can attack these assignments with a purpose. As we discussed in Chapter 4, comedy writing can be practical. With a bit of ingenuity on your part, many of these exercises can become keepsakes.)

Work at them. The tendency among comedy writers is to quit too soon. You can just treat these exercises lightly and skim the surface, or you can put in a little more effort and surprise yourself with the results. If you apply yourself to these, it will be good training for the discipline you'll need to write good comedy material later on.

Exercise One

Step 1. Collect fifty jokes from any source. They can all come from a single joke book, they can be fillers from a magazine, or just some favorite jokes that you remember other comedians delivering on comedy albums or television. The only criterion is that these should be gags you particularly like. Don't just go to a joke book and jot down numbers 1 to 50.

Step 2. Type or print these jokes on a piece of paper and analyze them. List next to them what you think makes them funny and what form they take. Are they word jokes, or do you laugh because they create a funny image in your mind? Or both? You don't have to be too technical, just jot down the reason you like each gag.

This exercise serves several purposes. You'll familiarize yourself with the style and the form of some great jokes, and you'll begin to understand your own likes and dislikes and generate your own style of writing.

You'll see the different forms that gags can take. You'll learn what your own tastes are in comedy and, consequently, the type of comedy that you probably can write best.

Another important aspect of collecting a series of jokes you particularly like is that they will be an inspiration to you. Seeing expert craftsmanship can motivate you to simulate it.

This collection will also serve as a nice reference. As we discuss different types and forms of jokes later in the book, you can refer to your own compilation for examples and comparison.

Exercise Two

Step 1. Make a list of ten adjectives that you might use in comedy writing. These should be very simple, ordinary words.

Step 2. For each word on your list, compile a grouping of other words or symbols that can represent the original word.

As an example, suppose we select the adjective "white." Some symbols or other words that convey the same meaning might be

Movie screen
Good Humor man
Wedding dress
Purity
Snowman
Nurse
Blank pages
Paleness
Ghost
Bed sheets

This exercise is practice in discovering the relationship between words or facts. It will help you become skilled at finding a word or phrase that might substitute for the most obvious word in your joke.

Many gags are too obvious or too direct. These can be improved by substituting a word or phrase that *implies* the meaning rather than stating it directly.

It might be a good idea right now to refer to your joke collection from Exercise One to see how many of your jokes might employ this device.

In the previous chapter we reviewed several jokes that Phyllis Diller used about her immense mother-in-law, Moby Dick. Here's another—

"That woman is so huge that when she wears a white dress, we show movies on her."

This is a case where the related idea created a joke, but the wording implied the meaning rather than stating it. The same idea expressed in a much weaker gag would have been, "When she wears a white dress, she looks like a movie screen."

Many times you can use the symbolism to completely replace the meaning. In the last joke, we used the word "white" and a symbolic meaning along with it. Suppose, though, you meet a gentleman who is dressed in a white suit. You might say, "If I stick a carrot on your nose and a broomstick under your arm, will you stand on the front lawn for my kids?"

In this case, you're implying that he is wearing so much white that he looks like a snowman, but you never actually say it.

Exercise Three

Step 1. Collect a series of at least thirty unusual photos. They can be interesting baby photos, old movie stills, strange photos like those featured sometimes in photography magazines, or any other source you might discover.

The photos should be unusual in some way, so I wouldn't recommend family snapshots. (Unless you come from a stranger family than mine.)

Step 2. Write humorous captions for the photographs.

In writing the captions, try to create new meanings for your photos rather than just commenting on the action depicted in them.

We sometimes write jokes that are too direct or obvious; the same fault creeps into captioning. We tend to comment on the obvious—the photograph itself. It will be worth the effort to find a different meaning in your captioning.

For example, suppose your baby photo shows an infant with baby food all around his mouth. One caption might read, "Boy, do I hate spinach," or "That's the last time I ever let *that* lady feed me." Both of these still depict a child with food all over his mouth.

However, a caption like, "That's the last time I let my wife buy me spinach-flavored shaving cream," changes the action in the photo. It's no longer a baby, but a man whose wife bought him some exotic shaving paraphernalia.

If the photo lends itself to this, it might even be captioned, "Tell me the truth, Myrtle. Do I look like Brad Pitt in a moustache?"

Undeniably, some hilarious captions can be written directly about the activity in the photograph, but since avoiding the obvious is so important in comedy writing, I urge you to try to generate a new meaning for each picture you caption.

And remember, you can put this exercise to practical use by captioning the pictures for the gang at the office, the family, a friend, or whomever.

Exercise Four

Step 1. Collect at least twenty-five cartoons that you especially like. You can find these in newspapers or magazines.

Step 2. Recaption the cartoons with lines of your own. You don't have to limit yourself to one caption for each cartoon. Do a few.

This exercise is similar to Exercise Three, except in this case, you can't deny the activity in the drawing. It exists as the straight line, and you'll learn to use it as a springboard to other jokes. No matter how great the cartoon is, there's no guarantee that the caption already on it is the only one that can be written, or even the best one.

You might paraphrase the original caption, improving the wording, or you might go for a whole new angle on the joke. The caption you write may even have nothing to do with the original. Don't limit yourself.

A valuable lesson of this exercise is that you'll learn not to quit on a joke too soon. The cartoon has been well executed, purchased, and printed by a newspaper or magazine. The tendency is to feel that it cannot be improved. However, keep trying. You might surprise yourself. The important thing is to resist the temptation to surrender on it.

Many times you will be faced with a topic that seems to have nothing inherently funny in it. By perseverance, you'll find it.

Exercise Five

Step 1. Create at least twenty-five cartoons of your own, using common items as your "characters." These items can be simple geometric shapes, household items, objects that exist where you work, fruits and nuts, or whatever. (I know this sounds bizarre now, but I'll explain it more in the example.)

Step 2. Caption your creations.

The scenes that you create should be set up in your mind in such a way that they could actually be photographed or drawn. You needn't go to the trouble or expense, but the perspective should be real enough to translate to an actual photograph.

The following examples—using food as "characters"—should make this exercise clearer.

Picture: Two soft pretzels. One without mustard, and one covered with it. *Caption:* You're a nice girl, Mabel. It's just that you use too much makeup.

Picture: A peach next to a plum. *Caption:* I don't care how late we are. You're not leaving this house until you've shaved.

In another exercise that we labeled "Nicotine Nifties," we used only tobacco and smoking accessories.

Picture: Seven cigarettes standing in a line. One of them is a burned-out and crushed cigarette butt. *Caption:* All right, which of you men was off limits last night?

Doing a series of gags using geometric figures prompted the following:

Picture:

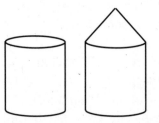

Caption: All right, Orville, the guests have gone. You can take off that silly lampshade now.

This is similar to Exercise Three, except here you have the thrill of beginning from scratch. You literally have the entire universe to choose from.

The following is an exercise that at first glance seems like a real toughie, but if you get into it and work at it—and allow others to work with you on it—you'll find that pretty soon you'll be bombarded with terrific jokes from people who never thought they could write a funny line before.

I guarantee you'll have fun with it.

Exercise Six

Step 1. Write 101 "Tom Swifties." A "Tom Swiftie" is a joke that uses a slightly different double meaning for an adverb. The Tom Swift series of children's books used this grammatical structure liberally, and now we're going to turn this same structure into gags.

Example: "I dove into the pool and knocked all my teeth out," he explained shallowly.

Obviously here we have the double meaning of the word "shallow."

You can get even more bizarre and give whole new meanings to the words you feature.

Example: "What this team needs is a good home run hitter," the manager said ruthlessly.

In that one, "ruthlessly" means without Babe Ruth. But you can become even more exotic and creative in playing with words.

Example: "I'm positive it was your dog that tore the back out of my trousers," the mailman said deceitfully.

Here "deceitfully" means "de-seat-fully." Other than that, just be creative, crazy, and have some fun.

Obviously, this exercise will develop your skill with words.

Should you think that 101 is too many and a totally impossible quota, I've listed my 101 and I will note that they're a totally different set of "Tom Swifties" from the ones that appeared in the previous edition of this book. I wrote new ones because I wanted to show that it is possible to write an endless number of these gags. Also, as an example and inspiration for you that it can be done. I strongly suggest that you begin writing your own and keep going until you're convinced that you can't create any more. And when you are convinced that you can't do any more, keep going anyway until you hit the magic number 101.

Stick with this exercise and I'm sure you'll have fun with it.

101 Tom Swifties

1. "No one seems to invite me to go hunting anymore," Vice President Dick Cheney said aimlessly.

2. "I'll get your golf ball back from that rottweiler," the man said off-handedly.

3. "My insurance wouldn't cover the entire operation, so the surgeon just did what he could," the patient said half-heartedly.

4. "Not tonight, dear. I have a headache," the wife said dispassionately.

5. "They should have just buried me," Ted Williams said coldly.

6. "Whoever said that the seat cushion could be used for a floatation device was a flat-out liar," the plane crash survivor said swimmingly.

7. "It's going to be difficult finding a hat to fit you because of the shape of your head," the sales clerk said pointedly.

8. "That's *Mister* Toulouse Lautrec to you," the artist said shortly.

9. "Forward march," the dyslexic drill sergeant said haltingly.

10. "If you say something is white, I'll say it's black," the photographer said negatively.

11. "Do I still have what it takes to be the host of *Jeopardy?*" Alex Trebec said quizzically.

12. "If we go down to the piers today, we might make a lot of money," the hooker said fleetingly.

13. "I've lived near this nuclear reactor all my life and it never affected me," the man said glowingly.

14. "I might have gotten carried away when I applied that hammerlock," the wrestler said disarmingly.

15. "I don't have a care in the world," the man exclaimed needlessly.

16. "The date on the bottle says the Viagra you sold me has expired," the customer said softly.

17. "Mine seems to have worked all right," another customer said longingly.

18. "I wonder what the abbreviation for apartment is," the man said aptly.

19. "Legally they can't do anything to us if we don't pay our electric bill," the man told his wife delightedly.

20. "They've closed down all my favorite saloons," the wino said disjointedly.

21. "We didn't put enough restrooms in the building," the architect said light-headedly.

22. "Baaa-aaa-aaa-aaah humbug," Ebenezer Scrooge said sheepishly.

23. "I have parsley, sage, and rosemary, but nothing else," the grocer said timelessly.

24. "This is the best bra I've ever owned," the woman said upliftingly.

25. "Mine is even better," her friend said pointedly.

26. "I've never owned a bra," the other said flatly.

27. "We have ways of punishing criminals here in Singapore," the judge said cannily.

28. "This ancient skull is cro-something or other," the scientist said magnanimously.

29. "I wonder what I'll get if I mix sugar and water," the chef said surreptitiously.

30. "Do you give up now?" the swordfighter said piercingly.

31. "You're standing on one of my tubes," the hospital patient told the visitor breathlessly.

32. "I've picked some pickled peppers but I have nothing to put them in," Peter Piper said impeccably.

33. "Someone stole everything I wrote during class," the student said denotedly.

34. "We only have home plate, first, and second," the umpire said debasedly.

35. "I like to sunbathe topless," the girl said barely.

36. "But I do wear a thong," she added cheekily.

37. "I'll never do another nude scene," said Sharon Stonily.

38. "I'm proud to be up here with Washington, Jefferson, and Lincoln," Theodore Roosevelt said stone-facedly.

39. "I may be the best racing driver of all time," said Richard Pettily.

40. "Vote for me and I'll deliver everything I've promised and more," the politician said unbelievably.

41. "You know, if we row, row, row, our boat in a very specific way, someone may write a song about it," the man said merrily, merrily, merrily.

42. "Let's tear down this barbed wire so our critters can graze freely," the sheepherder said defensively.

43. "I know I've lost my vim, but I've still got lots of that other stuff," the old man said vigorously.

44. "I'm waiting until someone has a good sale on light bulbs," the man said dimly.

45. "Who says I can't stand up in a canoe…whoops," the man said swimmingly.

46. "Here are all the things you'll have to do before we can admit you to our hospital," the administrator said precariously.

47. "My name is Pluto," the cartoon character pronounced doggedly.

48. "I can perform this vasectomy with my eyes closed," the doctor said snippily.

49. "Not on that part of me you won't," the man said privately.

50. "It's almost impossible to make the 7-10 split," the bowler said unsparingly.

51. "I feel like nipping on somebody's nose," said Jack Frostily.

52. "I'd like to come up with a good nickname for women," the chauvinist said broadly.

53. "Someone stole my thesaurus and my dictionary," the writer said wordlessly.

54. "This suit has been made completely without stitches," the tailor said seamlessly.

55. "This knit cap really works," he said hot-headedly.

56. "My pencil is not working," the student said pointlessly.

57. "Hey, if I press real hard on my pencil, the letters come out darker," another said boldly.

58. "It's just that I don't feel like making love right now and that's all there is to it," he said simply limply.

59. "If you wanted your drink *neat*, you should have ordered it *neat*," the bartender said icily.

60. "I just found out I'm the only one that Snow White hasn't slept with," the dwarf said grumpily.

61. "That's because I need at least one day of rest," Snow White said weakly.

62. "I come from a long line of morticians," the man said stiffly.

63. "I come from a long line of grave diggers," another said callously.

64. "I come from a long line of surgeons," another said cuttingly.

65. "I come from a long line of umpires," another said blindly.

66. "I come from a long line of opera singers," another sang out loudly.

67. "I come from a long line of lion tamers," another said cagily.

68. "I come from a long line of lawyers," another said briefly.

69. "I come from a long line of ministers," another said religiously.

70. "I come from a long line of hookers," another said horizontally.

71. "I come from a long line of people who have had enough of this particular joke form," another said boringly.

72. "I gained so much weight I didn't think I'd find a dress," she said fitfully.

73. "I don't like my soup to be too hot or too cold," said Luke warmly.

74. "My name is Hap and I just hit my golf ball into the water," said Hap hazardly.

75. "I've got all the raw cotton I need," said the manufacturer to the salesman balefully.

76. "You know, I think we've only got room for about five or six more residents," St. Peter said soulfully.

77. "I can handle plenty more," said Lucifer heatedly.

78. "I have conquered the entire world, but what I most appreciate is the glorious nickname you've given me," said Alexander Greatfully.

79. "But, Godfather, I spent time in prison for you. Why did you throw me into the river with my feet in cement," said the ex-con descendingly.

80. "Bring me four and twenty blackbirds baked in a pie," the King said tartly.

81. "If I have twin boys, I'm going to name both of them after the first Pope," the man said repeatedly.

82. "If I have twin boys; I'm going to name one of them Elijah and one Ezekiel," the man said prophetically.

83. "If I have twin boys, I'm going to divorce my wife," the man said impotently.

84. "We will never do *Hamlet* on this stage again," the theater manager said disdainfully.

85. "I'm going to stop this fan with my nose," the man said self-defacingly.

86. "I'm a mystic who sleeps on a bed of nails," the man said holily.

87. "I just fell through that window," the man said panefully.

88. "Welcome to the annual teetotalers awards banquet," the emcee said drily.

89. "What's a three-letter word meaning 'street' in French?" the man said ruefully.

90. "Being the royal executioner doesn't bother me at all," the black-hooded man said detachedly.

91. "I'm going to send this audition tape to the producer of *Saturday Night Live*," the comic said forlornly.

92. "I'm going to go on a fact-finding trip to the Bahamas at the government's expense," the politician said jauntily.

93. "I would like to build a canal that connects our lake to the Hudson River," the engineer said eerily.

94. "I have much more *fluous* than you," the man said superfluously.

95. "I've had just about enough of taking orders from Siegfried and Roy," the tiger said bitingly.

96. "I do all the tricks with my own two hands," the magician said sleightly.

97. "I forgot to phrase my answer in the form of a what?" the contestant asked Alex Trebec questioningly.

98. "Once I perform this sex change operation on you, Howard, there's no turning back," the doctor said demandingly

99. "I don't have that much to lose, doctor," the man replied shortly.

100. "I don't know if I want to have that many children," Peter Cottontail said to his wife hare-raisingly.

101. "I'm glad this exercise is finally over; now let's move on," said Tom Swiftly.

Exercise Seven

Step 1. Select a topic that you would like to write jokes about. It can be either a general subject or a topical subject chosen from the day's headlines.

Step 2. Research your selected topic and write a series of 20 factual statements about it. The sentences should not be comic in any way, nor should you attempt to make them humorous—simply list truthful statements about your subject. If you choose a statement from the newspapers, read through the article and list several of the sentences. "The price of stamps rose to 39 cents today." "The Postmaster General announced the additional cost was necessary to improve the efficiency of the mails." Should your topic be of a general nature, you can still find factual sentences, "I lost a lot of money in the stock market this year." "My stock broker promised me a modest return of eight percent on my money."

Step 3. Treat each of your factual statements as the setup for your punch line or as the "picture" that you are going to caption the same way you captioned the photographs earlier. When you're finished, you'll have 20 or more jokes. (You don't have to limit yourself to one caption per setup.)

Examples: "The price of stamps rose to 39 cents today. That settles it. I'm sending my Christmas cards out in the form of a chain letter this year."

"The Postmaster General announced the additional cost was necessary to improve the efficiency of the mails. Baloney. The best way to speed up the mails is to mail the postal workers their paychecks."

"I lost so much money in the market this year I can afford to tell the truth on my tax return."

"My stock broker promised me a modest return of eight percent, and he was right. I've now got eight percent of the money I used to have a year ago."

This exercise helps you learn how to analyze a topic in order to generate ideas for jokes. It also helps you to see how jokes are formed. In many cases a good gag is simply a caption for a factual statement.

Exercise Eight

Step 1. Make a list of fifty objects. You can get a little bizarre here because these words are going to be used for graphic jokes. You may want to pick the funniest ones you can think of.

Step 2. Divide the list into two groups. The first should contain twenty objects and the second thirty.

Step 3. Go down the first list and make each word the subject of your joke—combining it, however, with one of the words from the second list to make the punch line of your joke.

Example:

1. Fruitcake	**21.** Goat
2. Garbage truck	**22.** Peanut butter
3. Water buffalo	**23.** Floor wax
4. Shortstop	**24.** Jockey shorts
5. Odor eaters	**25.** Cross-Your-Heart bra
etc.	etc.

Example: "My grandmother made a fruitcake out of floor wax. When my grandfather ate it, it killed him, but he did have a fine finish."

This is a tough exercise that will teach you that writing jokes is not always easy. More important, though, it will show you that a joke is made up of two separate ideas. It's the combination of these ideas that often leads to bizarre comedy.

This exercise is good practice in looking for the attributes of each topic and rolling them through your head until you find that comic combination. In combining these two unconnected items, you're forced to search for several characteristics of each item. You must ask yourself questions like these: What does floor wax do? What is it good for? What are its bad qualities? When do people use it? And similar questions. Eventually you will find a characteristic of each object that will blend together in some way to form the joke.

Later we'll find that this skill will be especially useful in finding blend lines for a comedy monologue. When you want to switch from subtopic A to subtopic B, it's nice to find a joke that combines one element of each.

- 9 -

The Value of Monologues

In Chapter 7 we discussed the joke as the basic building block of humor, just as the brick is the basic building block in construction. However utilitarian it is, though, no one can live in a brick. It has to be bonded together with other bricks in some sort of predesigned form to create a useful structure. The same is true of comedy.

Jokes have to be coupled together with continuity and structure to fashion a practical humorous piece. This is a monologue.

Don't think that this minimizes the joke. Bricks or stones do not a cathedral make—but just try to build one without them. Even well-manufactured bricks are not particularly attractive piled helter-skelter on an empty lot, but those same bricks rearranged into an elegantly designed structure take on a new beauty.

In the same way, well-written gags, blended masterfully into a well-conceived routine, take on more mirth.

Certainly single jokes have their place. Magazines looking for fillers, cartoonists, and greeting card companies all buy single gags. And beginning with the next chapter, you're going to write some jokes. However, I recommend that you write a full routine rather than isolated jokes. Let's investigate some of the more important reasons why it's advantageous for you to write in the monologue form.

Good Showcase

The beginning writer should be building up a showcase portfolio of his material. Opportunity can knock at any time and when you open the door, you'd darn well better have some material to display.

I have worked with many novice writers. As I've mentioned before, my first advice is to set a quota each week and meet it. Since the advice is rarely followed, when I receive calls from producers looking for new one-liner writers for various television shows, there is no way that I can recommend these novices—I haven't seen enough to prove their talent, and they have nothing to show producers anyway.

That's why a portfolio is so important—you have to have something tangible to show a potential client. When you compile that portfolio, though, completed monologues are much more valuable than a collection of isolated jokes, regardless of how good the jokes are.

Disconnected gags are difficult to read. All the jokes in Dave Barry's best-selling books, for instance, are organized into delightfully readable essays. How many people do you think would read a book of collected jokes from cover to cover? I bet that hardly anyone ever has. It's almost impossible because reading single gags is tiring. Reading a collection of Dave Barry's or Lewis Grizzard's essays, or even my own book of travel humor, *Someday I Want To Go To All the Places My Luggage Has Been*, Arizona Highways Books, 2000 (take note, comedy writers—one has to promote one's work wherever and whenever one can) is exhilarating. Struggling through an assortment of disjointed one-liners is exhausting. If you're presenting your work to a prospective buyer, which would you prefer he have?

Jokes also suffer in comparison to each other when they are simply listed in catalog form. There is no way all your gags can be of equal value; consequently, the good ones stand out and make the others look weaker than they really are. They're just standing there for inspection like people in a police lineup. All their flaws are exposed to the reader's critical eye, which gets more critical as she gets more and more tired of reading them.

Let's go back to our building block analogy. No one looks at a completed structure and criticizes individual bricks or stones. The eye takes on the finished form and judges the separate components in relationship to the whole.

Jokes Are Enhanced

A well-organized routine not only hides the weakness of some jokes, but it can also actually make jokes funnier. In one of Paul Reiser's stand-up routines, he was discussing greeting cards:

"Suppose you're going to pick up a card for somebody you don't really care about. They should make a card that says, 'You're a friend of my wife's cousin—the hell with you.'" That's a funny concept that usually gets a nice laugh. But then as the laughter was continuing, Reiser would add, "We hardly know you. What did you expect—cash?"

More laughter—and usually stronger.

But that tag isn't a classic comedy line. You couldn't sell it to *Reader's Digest*. No cartoonist would purchase it. It would look silly all by itself in a greeting card. In that particular place, though, in that specific routine, it works. It gets a big response from the audience and that's what jokes are supposed to do.

It works in that spot because it's supported by the gags that surround it.

A good monologue works on a "peaks and valleys" principle. Not all gags have the same relative humor content. Even if they could, it wouldn't be any good anyway because that would become monotonous. Comedy has to be modulated. The laughs should build to a crescendo and then taper off, build up again, and gradually descend.

When you see a comedian that you don't particularly like, it's usually not because he isn't funny—it's because the material doesn't build properly. All comics, even the great ones, have moments that are not hilarious. They can't all be. During those moments, they are leading you somewhere—they are building. When they get you where they want you, they hit you with the payoff, the big laugh. Then, as a listener, you feel justified in having invested the time listening to the softer material. A poor comic often doesn't deliver that payoff. Consequently, you feel disappointed. Your time was wasted. You were used. The poor comic didn't need a whole lot of new material, simply a few strong jokes strategically placed.

Let me give you an example of what I mean by the "peaks and valleys" principle. Here's a routine kidding a guest of honor who was a not so accomplished golfer. I've numbered the different parts of the routine so we can discuss them later.

1. Charlie and I have played a lot of golf together. What can I say about Charlie's golf? Well, let me put it this

way, Charlie is to golf what Oprah Winfrey is to pole vaulting.

2.   He hits the ball all over the place, but he loves the game. Charlie has played golf in Mexico, Africa, Scotland. I know a lot of people have done that, But Charlie did it all in the same round.

3.   In his bag he carries thirteen clubs and a passport.

4.   He never rents a cart when he plays…because where he hits the ball, you can take public transportation.

5.   Let me give you an idea how erratic a golfer he is. There are about thirty-two golf courses in and around our neighborhood. Charlie never knows which one he's going to play until his second shot.

6.   He's not a long golfer; he's a wide golfer.

Now let's take a look at this brief routine and see how it follows the "peaks and valleys" principle.

Item 1 is not a real strong joke. It gets a laugh because it's making fun of the guest of honor, but it also serves the purpose of setting up the routine. The audience knows that we're going to talk about Charlie's golf. They realize this is not the big joke, so they listen more attentively in anticipation.

Item 2 is another soft joke that starts building to the big payoff. We establish that Charlie is not very accurate with his golf shots. He not only misses the fairways; he misses the entire country.

Item 3 just reestablishes that premise.

Item 4 is a much stronger gag. It paints a graphic picture of Charlie hitting the ball and then taking a bus to get to it. The audience is now getting eager to hear more about this man's bizarre golf.

Item 5 should be the "biggie." This gag is strong enough to justify the attention that the listeners have paid to the routine thus far. It is a satisfying joke.

Item 6 is a much weaker line that simply capitalizes on the laugh that was generated by the gag that went before. It piggybacks on that joke and pulls a little bit more laughter from the audience. It's also easing out of that routine and preparing the audience for whatever topic the comic is going to attack next.

That's another advantage of clever routining—it allows you to sustain the laughter from good material. It's a delicious moment when a surefire story or joke gets that explosive audience response. It's a pity to just allow it to dissolve. Some very soft jokes placed at the right spot can intensify the laughter and keep it rolling for much longer than the gag actually deserves.

In the above example, item 5 could have stood on its own, but it works much better when you build audience anticipation. Let them know something special is coming—and then deliver it.

✔ Legendary comedian Bob Hope built a career based on monologue comedy that spanned seven decades. Here's what he had to say about how valuable those routines—and the folks who wrote them—were to his career:

When I was in vaudeville I used to pick up jokes from books like College Humor, or I'd ask acts that came through town if they had any gags I could use. I picked them up anywhere I could get them, you know.

Then I hired a couple of guys to supply me with gags. But when I went on radio, I knew that we'd be using different jokes every week. We'd have to have the freshest, funniest monologues we could get, and we'd need a lot of it—and fast. So I hired the best writers I could find. And it worked.

Since then, I've always had the finest writers. I still do.

I know comedy. I've done it awhile and I could handle an audience. I could have made it in the business without writers. But I'll tell you this—I never would have made it big time without them.

Some Good Jokes Need Setups

Sometimes, even powerful jokes need a bit of explanation or setup to make them understandable, perhaps because the gag is based on a premise that's not easily recognizable. In other words, you've written a joke you're proud of, but it can't stand on its own. A monologue enables you to use that gag without any clumsy preamble. The jokes that go before it set it up or explain it.

For example, suppose you've created a fantastic gag about people who always cough at piano recitals. You might have to do a few simple gags that state the premise very directly, then deliver the line its pure form.

Comedian Billy Connolly has done this line about air travel:

> *"In airplanes, why is there no window in the toilet? Who on earth is going to see in?"*

That gag stands on its own. It needs no explanation, no setup. As soon as the comic tells it, the audience understands it.

Compare that with this line that Garry Shandling has done:

> *"When I get on a plane that smells like my grandmother's house, that's where I draw the line."*

It doesn't make much sense, does it? It means nothing. It requires an explanation. Shandling had been doing a routine about how commercial aircraft is aging, and we passengers have no idea how ancient a particular plane may be when we board it. In that context, this was a strong, effective payoff line for the entire routine.

So we don't eliminate a gag simply because it needs an explanation. No. We explain it in the monologue by doing some simpler jokes that set the required premise.

Years ago I did a banquet for a doctor who was being honored by his hospital. In gathering information about this "roastee," I learned that he and his wife had seven children and that he was constantly fidgeting with his pipe—either smoking it, or lighting it, or cleaning it. I wrote a line that that has always been one of my favorites, but I'm listing it here as an example of a flawed line.

Since I couldn't be sure that everyone attending the banquet knew these facts, I had to incorporate them into the joke as follows:

> *"Most of you know that Doc Wilson and his wife have seven lovely children. And all of Doc's friends know that he is constantly fiddling with his pipe. I spoke to his wife of twenty-eight years before the banquet and asked her if that annoyed her—that her husband was constantly playing with that pipe of his. She said to me, 'No, Gene, not at all. After seven children, I'm for anything that keeps his hands busy.'"*

The line worked well and, as I say, it has always been among my favorites. But isn't it awkward? The facts that he had seven children and that he was always toying with his pipe should have been explained earlier in the monologue. I could have accomplished that with a few lines about his large family followed by a few gags about his nervous pipe habits. Then the line would have been much simpler, more compact, and probably cleaner and more effective.

Monologues Require Preparatory Work

I consider a monologue to be a routine of twenty-five to thirty-five jokes. That's not a strict rule of comedy, it's simply a convenient measure that I use. In Chapter 10, we'll discuss the reasons for this number. For now, though, it's enough to say that it's a formidable task to begin with a blank sheet of paper, knowing you're going to have to create two to three dozen comedic gems. Consequently, you have to do some homework. You can't "wing it" for that much material. You have to get organized and do some research and planning—you'll find that your material will be more creative as a result.

Later chapters will discuss this preparatory work.

Monologues Force You to Write More

A tendency among comedy writers is to quit too soon, both on each joke and on each topic. I used to note that my strongest lines in a routine were the first one and about the eighth one. The reason was that the first gag I wrote was the inspired one—the one that popped into my head and motivated me to write the routine. Then I would do gags based on the standard, obvious concepts—the ones that everyone would think of. When those were exhausted (about the seventh line) I would be forced into being more creative.

Naturally, it's not as mathematically exact as that, but we all tend to hit that point when we say, "There is nothing funny left in this topic." It's when we struggle beyond that stopping point that the work becomes more inventive.

Monologue Writing Diversifies Your Style

A monologue is designed to be read or listened to as a complete piece. It has to be interesting enough to keep an audience captivated. Therefore, you have to incorporate a fair amount of variety into each piece. Even though the one-line joke form is essentially the same, you must invent ways of varying the presentation.

For example, take the standard joke form, "My brother-in-law is so lazy that…" You might be able to write fifteen variations on this joke, but you can't do a routine in which every gag begins with "My brother-in-law is so lazy that…"

You might come up with openings like the following:

> "My brother-in-law is so lazy that…(joke)"
> "I mean he really is lazy…(joke)"
> "I won't say he hates work, but…(joke)"
> "Let me give you an idea how bad he is…(joke)"

The very same joke form can be used by varying it with those opening handles.

You'll also learn to look for other variations to relieve the monotony.

By forcing yourself to write complete, structured monologues, you'll improve your writing style.

Monologues Do the Work for the Buyer

You'll have a better chance of selling anything if you make the sale easier on the buyer. Structured monologues do that.

If you present a comic with a collection of one-liners in no particular order, he'll find it hard to read—as we discussed before. Even if he likes some of the jokes, he still has to incorporate them into a routine. If they're already in a workable routine, his work is done for him.

Plus, the sheer volume of a routine makes a sale more likely. In a monologue of twenty-five to thirty-five jokes, the comic can edit out those gags she's not sure of and still have enough left for a respectable piece of material. Even if your monologue is edited down to eight gags from the original thirty-five, that's still enough to include in an act. However, if you turn in only five to six jokes and the comic edits the same percentage, she's left with only one or two jokes. That's probably not enough to include as a chunk of material in the act.

The joke remains the basic building block. We'll get started on that now.

- *10* -

Getting Ready to Write

I've read that nightmares of frustration are fairly common. Pilots have told me that they frequently dream of taking off and immediately confronting obstacles like overhead wires or bridges. When I committed to comedy as a profession, I had a recurring dream. I'd be attending some gala festivity and would be called up from the audience to dazzle the crowd with a few insightful witticisms. I would march up to the microphone to much applause, feeling a warm glow of excitement within. Then I'd get to center stage and have absolutely nothing to say. I couldn't think of a joke, a rhyme, a riddle...not even a simple song to sing. All I could do was stand there silently and wish that I could disappear.

Comedy requires preparation. Some comics are masters of the ad lib, and spontaneous humor brightens any presentation, but professionals never depend on spontaneity totally. They always have their standard surefire material to fall back on.

Once I worked with two comedy legends—Bob Hope and Lucille Ball—on a military show overseas. We needed to add time to the show, so I told Lucille Ball that Bob Hope wanted to do a short talk spot with her. She said, "Where's the script?" I told her that Bob just wanted to ad-lib. She said, "Oh no, I did that once before with him. I went out there with nothing and he had all kind of jokes. I want a script."

She wanted to be prepared.

You the writer must be prepared, too. After all, you're beginning with blank pages.

I'd like to travel through the joke-writing process with you from beginning to end. Obviously, a description of a thought takes longer than the thought itself, so this may seem a bit sluggish and unwieldy. Be patient. It's like reading the instructions to a new game—they sound complicated and take forever to get through, but once you begin playing the game, they are logical and become second nature to you. The same will happen with your writing. Journey through this deliberately with me a few times, and you'll soon be able to fly through it on your own much more quickly.

I remind you also that there are two thought process involved in writing gags. One is the almost instantaneous, computer-like procedure of rolling thoughts through your mind. The other is the more systematic and tedious research system. Admittedly, it is slow and routine, and some beginners may be tempted to bypass it and get right to the writing.

We've said a few times already and will repeat many more times—one failing of novices is quitting too soon. They quit too soon on preparation, on topics, and on jokes. I recommend that you be diligent with your preparation in the beginning. Write things out rather than skip over them. Eventually, you'll be able to shorthand many of these procedures, doing them mentally. You'll learn to work much more quickly—perform some of the routines mentally and rapidly—and you'll get to the jokes sooner. But at the beginning, this is not advisable. Even today, if my deadline permits, I still prepare all my monologue work before getting around to writing any jokes. The quantity and the quality are always improved by it.

Vic Braden, a famous tennis authority, told me that as a youngster he used to fantasize about playing on the Davis Cup team and having those great coaches whisper words of tennis wisdom to him between games. He used to watch big matches and wondered just what secrets the coaches whispered to their players. Eventually, he earned a spot on the Davis Cup squad, and between games the coaches would whisper to him, "Bend your knees" or "Keep your head down." Their only secret was, "Be well schooled in the fundamentals."

Enough sermonizing. You're ready to go to work. You've got a sharpened pencil or your computer is booted up. The blank pages are waiting. (Why do they always have to be so blank?) What's your first step?

Let's go back for a moment to my horrible nightmare: it was a nightmare because I had nothing to say. Your first job in writing is to find something to say.

Select a Topic

You have to select a topic. What are you going to be brilliantly witty about? It can be anything—current events, family life, social ironies, fantasy…anything at all. You simply need something to "unblank" that paper.

Where do you get that topic? Anywhere. You might read something ironic in today's paper. Look through magazines for something that intrigues your funny bone. Things are happening around your house that could be satirized. Listen to what other people are talking about—the "topic du jour."

> ✓ Sheldon Keller was a member of the famous writing staff of The Sid Caesar Hour. From there he went on to a spectacular career writing and producing many top-ranked television shows. He also taught writing classes at both USC and UCLA in Los Angeles. Sheldon once said:
>
> The one thing that always got me was that the students didn't want to work. You'd ask them to write and they'd have a million excuses on why they couldn't.

If you have a paying client, she will dictate the topics—but that's all right because she will sign your check. If you're free to select your own topic, be nice to yourself and try to make writing easier.

I'm sure you have some topic that inspires you. I generally find that I write best about some item that irritates me. Once I was driving along daydreaming about topics and the driver behind me became justifiably annoyed. He honked and nearly sent me through the windshield, it startled me that much. So I wrote an angry monologue about idiotic drivers who honk their horns for no reason. (Comedy writing can be therapeutic as revenge, too.)

From this point on, we will be proceeding in a step-by-step outline for writing a full monologue. Why don't you select a topic here and work through the next several chapters until you have a completed monologue of your own. For this first journey, don't be too ambitious. Select a topic you're reasonably certain you can be funny about.

Free Association

Now that you've selected your topic, allow your mind to consider anything and everything related to that topic. Don't attempt to be funny here. You're simply providing fodder for when you later start composing your jokes. You're not trying to be particularly selective, either. You don't have to pass judgment on the items that pop into your mind—simply write them down. Some may be useful in your writing, others may not. You won't be required to use each and every thing you jot down.

Let your mind roam freely and keep your pencil moving or your keyboard clattering.

As an example, suppose I had selected "owning a dog" as my topic. My list of free associations might read something like this:

Dogs: wet noses, cold noses, wetting on the rugs, chewing things, "Fetch," "Sit," "Heel," bringing pipe and slippers, bringing the evening paper, teaching tricks, biting the mailman, watchdog, scaring burglars, "Beware of the Dog" signs, "His bark is worse than his bite," chasing cats, shedding, begging for food, cleaning up after, cost a fortune to feed, chasing cars, burying bones, veterinarian visits, shots, in heat, neutering, human years and dog years.

That's all there is to this step. Another admonition—or rather, the same admonition offered once again: don't quit too soon. Push yourself at this step and get a few more relationships than you think you can get. Creativity comes with that little bit of extra effort.

This may seem to be a waste of time, paper, and computer ink cartridges, but there are benefits. A joke is a combination of two or more ideas blended into one. Generally you have a point of view and a related idea. This list can often provide both, but let's assume you have one or the other. The joke-writing process is to find the one you don't have. The list may provide it, or it may provide the springboard for finding it.

To illustrate, imagine that I want to say about my subject that I don't like dogs because they wet on the rugs. How can I say that in a funny way? Well, I might quickly run down my list of topics searching for some relationship. Well, one relationship with "wet rugs" is "wet noses." That might generate a line like this:

> *"I have a lot in common with this dog. He always has a*
> *wet nose, and I always have a wet rug."*

How about relating it to "bringing pipe and slippers."

> *"This dog wets on the rug so much that instead of bringing my slippers when I get home, he brings me my galoshes."*

Perhaps we can get a tie in with "scaring burglars."

> *"We can always tell if there's a burglar walking around the house. You can hear the rug go squish, squish, squish."*

Without the list to refer to, these gags probably would have taken much longer to write, if indeed they ever would have popped into my mind at all.

The list can trigger a point of view or a related idea. After you've worked with it a few times, you'll see the benefits much more graphically than I can ever describe them to you.

Organized List

After you've allowed your mind to roam freely and you've jotted down a list of free associations, you try to stimulate your mind to find even more relationships that might be used for jokes.

This step is actually a patterned list of free associations. It's more organized. List people, places, things, events, words, clichés, and phrases that are similar or related to your subject, and a list of the same categories that are opposite. The opposites are, of course, related to your topic by their total difference.

I recommend that you make up a sheet of paper that is blocked off for these categories. That way you'll always have the areas clearly in front of you. I've enclosed a preprinted sheet as an example, but you can design your form any way you desire.

On my preprinted form I've listed a few of the ideas that I might jot down in each category. Your list should be much more extensive, because the same old caution applies—don't quit too soon. Work and think until you get a fairly representative number under each division. Some topics will be easier to analyze than others, but I recommend getting at least seven items in each section.

TOPIC OWNING A DOG

		PEOPLE	PLACES	THINGS	EVENTS	WORD, PHRASES, CLICHES
SIMILAR		Pluto Lassie Pavlov Veterinarian Dog next door	Kennel Dog house Pound	Leash Paper on floor Fireplugs Favorite tree Dog food	Dog days 1st litter When burglar broke in	His bark is worse than his bite. Fetch, sit, heel, stay Man's best friend.
OPPOSITES		Cats Dog catcher Mailman	Stores that don't allow dogs The bedroom	Other pets Dog's natural enemies Dog's prey	Cat show Alcoholics Anonymous meetings (AA people are dry – dogs are wetter)	I'm afraid of dogs. I don't trust dogs. I'm a cat lover.

The joke-writing benefits are exactly the same as we discussed with free associations. The added advantage of this list is that it focuses your mind on specific areas. When you channel your thinking, your mind becomes much more productive. The more ideas you have to work with, the more and better jokes you will eventually generate.

Let's take a paragraph or two to reflect on what we've just done. Your first project was to freely associate any ideas you could think of that applied to your topic. You may have had some difficulty coming up with many ideas. However, being wary of quitting too soon, you continued. When you finally finished, you thought you had every conceivable thought related to your subject. Then you categorized your thinking. You organized it more, and again you came up with related and opposite ideas. It may have been a struggle for a while, but you completed the project. Your second list should have many more items on it than your first list. Several of them will be duplicates, but quite a few will be new items.

The point is, by organizing you thoughts and funneling your efforts, you were able to come up with new associations, even though you were probably convinced after the first effort that there were no more ideas related to your topic.

All you did differently in the second project was channel your thinking. Rather than think of anything that was associated, you thought of any THING that was related, any PLACE that was related, and so on.

It should be apparent to you now that preparation and organization work.

Take heart. We're getting closer to that moment when you can start writing jokes. Admittedly, it's taking us longer than it really ought to go through this procedure step by step because you have to spend a lot of time reading my commentary. With subsequent writing ventures, you'll whip through these preliminary steps in no time. All we've actually done so far is make two different lists.

That, however, is the good news. The bad news is that we have one more procedure to go through before we get to the fun part—the actual writing of the jokes.

Subdividing the Topic

In Chapter 9 I mentioned that for our purposes a monologue is considered to be twenty-five to thirty-five jokes long and promised to explain why I arbitrarily chose that length. Here are my reasons:

First, it forces you to do your preparatory work. Two or three dozen gags on one topic is a considerable task. Most of us keyboard jockeys would rather attack the joke writing, finish it, and dismiss it. Were we to do that, we might write only six to eight jokes, which we might be satisfied with. However, since we began with a more challenging quota, we have to do the preliminary research to make the task accomplishable.

Second, it doesn't permit you to quit too soon. (Have you heard that before?) Writing can get a bit tough after writing the first five or six inspired jokes. The obvious jokes have been neatly typed, the inspired ones also, and we swear that there is nothing else funny about this particular topic. The goal of twenty-five to thirty-five jokes compels you to continue, and you'll surprise yourself with some of the clever material you can generate after you've guaranteed yourself that it couldn't be done.

Third, it makes your efforts more marketable because there is enough material there for the buyer to edit and still be left with a workable routine.

Fourth, the volume allows you to be more selective. If you're writing a finished presentation, you can edit down to your best gags and be sure that you'll have enough.

None of the above logic, though, makes writing a monologue any less formidable. Here's a technique that will help, though. It's easier to write five or six jokes on a given topic, than it is twenty-five to thirty-five. The secret, then, is to subdivide your topic into five or six subtopics and write half a dozen jokes on each subtopic. The result: a twenty-five to thirty-five joke monologue.

You arrive at your subtopics by *analyzing* your main topic. You note facts about it…you question it…you pull it apart searching for its components. Thinking of a topic, you generally have one or two half-written jokes somewhere in your head. Those may generate subtopics. Review your extensive list of related subjects, both your free-association and your organized list. You probably have several good subdivisions in there.

My main topic was "owning a dog." I broke it up into the following subtopics:

    a) General (this is a catchall division allowing me to do one or two jokes that lead into the routine.)

   b) Wetting on the rug (notice that came from the free-association list)

   c) How big the dog was

   d) Dog biting the mailman and other visitors

   e) The dog chewing things around the house

Subdividing in this manner allows me to do a full routine on owning a dog. These are not the only subtopics about owning a dog; they're not the best, either. They are simply the ones that I chose to stimulate my mind to write thirty-five jokes about owning a dog. (Another benefit of this device is that if I were assigned tomorrow to write a routine on owning a dog, I could select different subtopics and write another full routine about the family pet.)

This division into subtopics is probably the most important part of writing a monologue—with the exception of writing the jokes. It will determine the tone of your monologue and the ease with which you write it.

Remember how much more productive your free-associating was when you organized and channeled it? The same applies here. If your subtopics are creative and well-thought-out, your jokes will be better and easier to write and your monologue will be more original.

Since you have already selected a topic, try now to think of areas that apply to it, but also strive to make them different and inspired.

Once you complete that, we can move on to the jokes. (Ain't this fun?)

- *11* -

Getting the Jokes Flowing

All of our work to this point, with the exception of some of the exercises, has been preparatory. That's necessary. Boxers spend months preparing for an important fight. Football teams drill for the entire season. Baseball players are continually sharpening their skills. But that moment of truth always arrives—they have to face the opponent.

You've now hit that moment of truth. Your opponent is the blank sheet of paper. It's a formidable foe. And, it's your battle to fight alone since neither the book nor I can write the jokes for you. However, we can do a little bit of coaching from the sidelines.

By now you should have a topic, a comprehensive list of references, and a set of subtopics. You now need to convert them to a series of twenty-five to thirty-five gags (as we discussed in Chapter 10) that we'll later work into a monologue.

There is no need to write the routine in chronological order; just get them down on paper for now. If you can sit at your computer and begin with joke number one and proceed to joke number thirty-five, and it's easier that way, then do it. That's a tough assignment, though.

The extensive preparatory work we've been doing has all been toward one goal—to make the joke writing easier. Now we'll take advantage of that.

I recommend that you make an easy-to-read list of your subtopics and keep them in front of you while you're writing your gags. Keep a running tally of how many lines you've done on each subtopic, but don't limit yourself in any way with this scorekeeping. It's simply to stimulate your mind to write more and better jokes.

The first joke-writing process is to roll thoughts and ideas through your mind with computer-like speed, selecting those two or three related items that you can word into a joke line. Your mind will be operating almost with a will and direction of its own. You merely step in when it stops and type out the joke that it has presented to you. At times this process will feel like aimless daydreaming—that's when the mind generates gags so quickly that you'll hardly be able to write or type fast enough to harvest the ideas. If your mind likes a certain subtopic and delivers more than the five- or six-line quota, allow it to continue. I've had subtopics that were so fertile, I gathered enough gags from them to be monologues on their own. Then I expanded the other subtopics and created another routine from them.

Sometimes, though, after hitting a few good lines, the mind stops and needs more direction from you. That's when you can turn to your running tally sheet and say to your creative self, "We need more lines on this subtopic," and allow it to wander again, focusing, though, on that specific subtopic.

If you remain reasonably faithful to your subtopics, you will eventually generate your twenty-five to thirty-five gags that are all related to the main topic. In Chapter 12 we'll discuss how to routine these into a smooth-flowing monologue.

Right now your priority is to generate the gags that will go into your monologue.

Inspiration probably produces the best and the quickest jokes. Set down any topic and gags that pop into your head out of thin air. Accept them and put them on the paper—even if they don't fall into any of your subtopics. Don't be overly concerned. You may even create enough material to complete an entire monologue totally different from the one you started on. I know this has happened to me occasionally.

Inspiration is usually stingy. You'll get a few lines with no exertion, but generally not that many. Now you'll have to struggle to extract the lines from you mind. Following are a few techniques that might help.

Know What You Want to Say

Jokes are zany, bizarre, nonsensical, but in their own way, they have a point of view. They may be exaggerated, distorted, paradoxical, but they can be reduced to a certain logic. Most of them are saying something serious in a funny way. (There are some purely nonsensical lines, non sequiturs like, "It is better to walk with your back to the wind than to have your ear pinned under a manhole cover." I have no idea what that means, but it's funny and might get a laugh in a nightclub routine.)

As a gag writer, though, you are beginning from scratch and you need a starting point. In the mental joke-writing process you have one thought, and you're auditioning and selecting other thoughts that roll quickly through your mind. It's too much of a burden to roll two sets of thoughts through your brain and select two at random that will produce a gag.

Even the nonsensical line that we quoted above probably had a starting point in the mind of the writer. Imagine that the author said, "I'm going to create a completely nonsensical joke. I'll start with a traditional quote and come up with a funny-sounding phrase that has nothing to do with it."

The starting point for each gag is, "What do I want the gag to say?" The answer to that question doesn't have to be funny, but the joke you create from it will be.

In some of the exercises you did in Chapter 8, you captioned photographs. If 100 people captioned one particular photo, you would get 100 different gags. The starting point, though, was the same—the photo. If you're going to caption something, you obviously need something to caption.

A few examples may help make this clearer. In joking about filling out tax returns for the year, you may want to say that taxes are getting so high that it seems the government is taking almost all of (or maybe more than) everything you make. The resultant joke might be:

> "The IRS has come out with a new short form for taxes
> this year. It says, 'How much did you make?' 'Send it to us.'
> 'You can owe us the rest.'"

Or you might want to say that no matter what you make, the government arranges things so that you don't keep it. You might write:

> "I don't know why the government bothers with tax
> returns anyway. Why don't they just print all their money
> with a return address on it?"

Start with Factual Statements

We mentioned earlier that many gags are nothing more than straight lines that have been captioned. Some of the exercises in Chapter 8 deal with captioning. You'll find this a fairly simple creative exercise, provided you have the raw materials to work with. By listing a series of factual statements you'll have those raw materials. Then you begin rolling ideas, many selected from your reference compilation, through your mind until you strike a joke.

Again, the statements needn't be funny. They are the straight lines. They are merely getting you started in looking for the punch lines. In the Chapter 8 exercises you captioned pictures; now you're captioning "word pictures."

Finding factual statements in current events topics is a matter of extracting phrases out of newspapers, magazines, or from television reports. For example, as I write this, gas prices in the nation are soaring to all-time highs. The politicians are scrambling trying to solve the problem or offer some sort of *band-aid* to appease the public. One such gimmick was a proposal to issue a $100 rebate to ease the pain of high gas prices.

Here are a few factual statements about this proposal gleaned from the news media:

a) The GOP offers a $100 rebate to ease the pain of high gasoline prices.
b) Most voters feel the $100 rebate is not really practical.
c) There will be limits on who can collect the rebate.
d) The $100 will buy you gas for about two weeks.

Here are a couple of punch lines formed by simply captioning items **a)** and **b)**:

> *"The GOP is offering a $100 rebate to ease the pain of high gasoline prices. Big deal. It costs $116 in gas to drive to the bank to cash the check."*

> *"Most voters feel the rebate is not really practical. Why don't they keep the $100 and just send us all a new bike?"*

Sometimes you'll find that the factual statement prompts a punch line. Then you can vary the form. You needn't use the straight line and caption routine that strictly. This joke practically used item (c) as a punch line unto itself:

> *"Of course in order to qualify for the rebate you have to prove that your family is too poor to afford a car."*

This last gag was built by adding another element to factual statement (d):

> *"They plan to send a $100 check and one bullet. The money will buy gas for about two weeks. For the other fifty weeks, you'll just have to bite the bullet."*

Of course, the same device can also be used effectively on more general topics, too. For example, suppose you want to do some gags about a person who is a big eater. You might make some factual statements, such as:

a) This guy eats constantly.
b) He'll eat anything that's not moving.
c) He doesn't exactly *eat like a bird* (or does he?).

Here are gags that are built by adding captions to those simple statements:

> *"This guy eats all the time. He had two teeth pulled last week. They weren't decayed; just exhausted."*

> *"He'll eat anything that's standing still. He'll eat anything that's moving, too, only it takes him longer."*

> *"He eats like a bird. That means when he get hungry enough, he'll swoop down and scoop up an entire baby goat."*

Notice that in captioning word pictures, as opposed to using photographs, you can change words in the original statement in any way to make your punch line more effective.

There are no real rules in captioning factual statements. It's simply an aid to get your mind thinking along the right track. If breaking, bending, or manipulating any so-called rules helps you produce more and better gags, then go ahead and break, bend, and manipulate.

Investigate and Ask Questions

Once you have something to say or a factual statement you want to caption, you investigate it. Explore other areas of it. Why did it happen? Whom else does it affect? Who is pleased by it? Who is upset with it? What's the next logical step? There are limitless questions you can ask, and any one of them may prompt the punch line.

For instance, in the previous examples we stated that the GOP was offering a $100 rebate to assuage the hurt of high gas prices. I asked myself how much good that would do for a family. My answer was that it probably wouldn't get them very far. Hence the joke about it costing $116 to get to the bank to cash the check.

Sometimes, asking questions can open up a whole new approach or angle on a topic. For instance, once when a big earthquake hit the Los Angeles area, I did plenty of jokes about it. How scary it was—"It's pretty frightening when your bedroom goes down for breakfast before you do." How it affected the family—"Scientists say that pet behavior can warn you of an impending quake. That's true. The night before this one hit, our golden retriever took the car keys and drove to Arizona." But I also asked myself how the quake would affect the people of Hollywood. Did the "Desperate Housewives" become more desperate? How did it affect Tom Cruise? Julia Roberts? Jay Leno? George Clooney? Sylvester Stallone? All of a sudden I had a list of possible straight lines as long as Hollywood Boulevard. Come to think of it—how did it affect the people who cruise Hollywood Boulevard?

One of my favorite joke examples falls into this classification. (You'll notice from the punch line that this gag was written many years ago, but it remains one of my favorites.) A client called me to do some opening lines for her Las Vegas act. She had recently dislocated her shoulder and had to appear in Vegas wearing a large cast. The audience would be surprised and distracted by the cast, so she wanted some lines to explain it and dismiss it so that she could continue with her regular act.

The first thing I did was ask myself what sort of bizarre activity could have caused the accident. Here is the opening line that resulted:

> *"Ladies and gentlemen, I know you're wondering how I got this cast, Well, if there are any of you out there who have just bought the new book* The Joy of Sex, *there's a misprint on page 204."*

Exaggerate and Distort the Truth

Comedy is basically truthful. Phyllis Diller once wrote in the margin of some material I had written for her, "Honey, if it's not true, don't send it to me." Although comedy is based on truth, it's not often that true statements generate jokes without some sort of tampering by the humorist. One way to highlight the truth of a statement is to exaggerate or distort it out of its true proportions.

This is the same principle that caricature artists employ in making their drawings. They isolate a few features and distort them to false prominence. The resulting likeness isn't anatomically correct, but it doesn't destroy the recognizability—many times it enhances it. Some celebrities are easier to recognize from a caricature than they are from a photo.

Humorous exaggeration serves the same purpose, sometimes stating a case more powerfully than brilliant oratory.

The trick here is to allow your mind to play with the dimensions and the colors and all the physical attributes of the mental image until you create a funny picture. Sometimes you might even exaggerate and extend an idea out to its ultimate. For example, Steven Wright says, "I've been doing a lot of abstract painting recently. It's extremely abstract. No paint, no brush…I just think about it."

Remember that we discussed in Chapter 3 how flexible the mind can be in distorting images and accepting them as reality. Audiences will accept distortion and not quarrel with your proportions, so long as you're funny.

David Brenner used to do gags on himself exaggerating the size of his nose. "I thought it was a third arm."

How's this line from Bob Monkhouse for an exaggeration? "My Dad only hit me once…but it was with a Volvo." It's hard to visualize, but we allow our minds to do just that.

Joan Rivers once said of an overweight celebrity, "She has more chins than the Hong Kong phone book."

Steven Wright has a gag that illustrates distortion. "I put instant coffee into the microwave. I almost went back in time."

This line by Carol Siskind also distorts time. "I'm a bad cook. I use the smoke alarm as a timer."

Use Standard References and Expressions

Once I was doing an after-dinner speech before a group of personnel executives. During the meal I overheard two executives talking. One said something about running a reference check and they both chuckled. I asked what that term meant and they told me it was a process the company went through with some of the people they were about to hire. The term may be standard now, but at that time, I had no idea what it meant.

When I started my talk I said, "Your president called me and asked if I could speak tonight. I said I could and he said, 'I'll get back to you as soon as we run a reference check.'" That joke got a big laugh and applause and I don't even know what I said.

It always amazes me how two computer programmers can talk to one another and be perfectly intelligible, while a bystander might think they were talking a foreign language. All businesses have a jargon peculiar to them. Those phrases and expressions, if they're not too inside for your audience, make valuable fodder for your joke mill.

Also, almost any topic has a series of references connected with it. I have done hundreds of football monologues and every one probably has "Gatorade" in it at least once. If you're working for the military, you'll probably refer to eating something or other "on a shingle."

There are innumerable general slogans and phrases familiar to everyone. When Barry Bonds was having trouble because of the steroid accusations, he told the sports reporters that his life "was a shambles." David Letterman said "He shouldn't be surprised at that. It says right on the side of the steroid package—'This product may cause shambles.'"

Most well-known advertising mottos can be used in gags, like "Come fly with me," "We try harder," "Got milk?" You can probably think of many more. The nice thing about them is that some advertising writers somewhere are creating more for us even as you read this.

There are many popular catch phrases that may come in handy, too. I used to love to do "six-pack" jokes.

> *"I'm all ready for my golf game. I've got a scorecard, a pencil, and a six-pack of erasers.*

And for a while practically everybody adopted the "industrial strength" slogan for their gags.

> *"I won't say I'm gaining too much weight, but my doctor put me on industrial-strength diet pills."*

Create Formula Jokes

We mentioned formula jokes briefly in Chapter 7. These are gags that follow a standard pattern, for example, when Johnny Carson hosted *The Tonight Show* from New York, he would mention to the audience how cold it was. The audience on cue would shout out, "How cold was it?" Then the formula joke—"It was so cold in New York that on Times Square the flashers were only describing themselves."

There are limitless numbers of joke formulas. There is no way all of them could be listed in this chapter, but by listening you'll be able to pick up several for yourself and then plug in your own references. It's joke writing that's akin to painting by numbers.

There's a *translation* formula.

> *"Vegetarian: That's an Indian word meaning 'lousy hunter.'"*

There's a formula that goes "You know you (fill in the blank) if..."

> *"You know you have to lose weight if you step on one of those speaking scales and it says, 'Come back sometime when you're alone.'"*

Jeff Foxworthy, with his redneck routines, has made good use of this form.

✔ While ROUND TABLE was interviewing stand-up comedian Max Alexander, he got a sales call from a memorial park. The conversation after that phone call went like this:

ALEXANDER: *Somehow they got my name and number and called and asked if I'd made plans. I told them, "I'm going away for the weekend, but if any long-term plans come up, I'll call." Then he said, "You know if you sign before you make plans for a funeral, it's cheaper." It's like the airlines. Fourteen days in advance is required.*

ROUND TABLE: *Do you have to stay over a Saturday night?*

ALEXANDER: *Yeah, yeah, excellent. You see? There's a bit. You see how we created a bit of material there? That's how it works.*

> *"You know you're a redneck if you go to the Cousin's Picnic just to meet women."*

> *"You just might be a redneck if you've ever worn a tube top to a wedding."*

These tips should get you started cranking out those twenty-five to thirty-five gags. It may be difficult at first, but it gets easier the more you do. Again, I caution you that these suggestions are not commandments—they're ways to stimulate your creativity. Use them one at a time or all together—whichever way gets your mind shoving ideas through your brain so that you can get those jokes on paper.

Once you get the gags written, we'll move on to organizing them into a smooth-flowing routine.

- 12 -

The Art of Routining

If you've written twenty-five to thirty-five jokes on one topic, that's commendable. Many of my writer friends say that they don't enjoy writing but are proud of having written. Humorist Peter De Vries said, "I love being a writer. What I can't stand is the paperwork." So to have authored nearly three dozen gag lines on a given topic is something you can be proud of. However, it is not yet a monologue. It's like building a house and you've just had the bricks delivered.

Importance of a Logical Flow

Now you have to arrange those jokes in a logical order so that they will glide smoothly, like a narrative. There are few things more tedious than reading or listening to a collection of disconnected one-liners. Yet it's exciting to read a funny story or listen to a skilled raconteur. Everything is flowing to a natural conclusion—to a high point—and each joke pulls you along with it.

Good routining also improves your lines because it allows you to be more concise. Each joke you write is not only complete unto itself but can also serve as a setup for jokes to follow. Consequently, the gags that follow won't need as elaborate a setup. Later in the chapter, we'll proceed step by step through a sample portion of a monologue and see how this applies.

Routining enhances the overall comedy effect by taking advantage of the natural peaks and valleys of comedy we discussed in Chapter 9. When the late Johnny Carson delivered his opening monologues on *The Tonight Show*, he would sometimes kid about these peaks and valleys, but they actually do exist. They have to because each joke suffers in comparison to its neighbors. Each gag in a comic's routine cannot have the same degree of *funniness*. If each did, it would become monotonous. The softer jokes can make the strong jokes seem stronger, and some of the strong jokes can be used to help the softer ones. Also, some of the weaker jokes help the stronger jokes by providing the setup for them.

David Letterman, in his opening monologue, is not afraid of the valleys of comedy in getting to the peaks—the punch line. Letterman takes his time with the setups because he knows he has a solid punch coming that will justify it.

In working with the legendary monologist Bob Hope for many years, I learned how he would take advantage of this "peaks and valleys" phenomenon. If you can find some of the opening monologues from his specials, watch and study them. You'll notice how each topic builds to a crescendo and how Hope would extract laughs from weaker jokes based on that crescendo.

It reminds me of a crowd watching a fireworks display. There is anticipation as they watch the little speck of light propelled into the sky. There are "oohs" and "ahhs" as it explodes into a giant ball of light. There's even a thrill in watching the glowing particles of light drift back to Earth. That's the way your comedy routine should operate. Just as varied rhythm in a fireworks display adds excitement, so your peaks and valleys should be staggered. Naturally, we want more peaks than valleys, but so long as we must have the valleys, we might as well take advantage of them.

Assembling the Routine

There are no hard and fast rules to assembling a routine. It's pretty much a seat-of-the-pants operation. Comedy is so subjective that in a group of six or eight jokes, few people will agree which is the "biggie" you should build to. However, the mechanics of routining are fairly simple.

Start by dividing your jokes into their separate subtopics. Now try to determine a logical progression of subtopics. Sometimes this is predetermined for you. If you're doing a routine about taking your wife to the hospital to have a baby, you won't talk about how bad traffic was on the way until after you've done the gags about packing her suitcase. Other times, though, the subtopics do not fall in any logical order. Then it's totally up to your discretion and good comedy judgment.

You can use either of these two methods for arranging gags, or invent your own.

This first method takes more time, but generally produces better results, especially if the monologue isn't cut and dried as far as the logic of its progression goes. I cut each of my jokes into separate strips of paper and then lay each subtopic out, in a logical order, from first to last joke.

This makes the gags physically easier to arrange because they're unattached. I keep rearranging them until I hit the order that satisfies me. Then I staple them together in readiness for the final retyping.

In the second method, I go through my entire collection of jokes and decide on the progression of subtopics. Then I go through and put a large circle in the margin for each joke that applies to subtopic one. Now the particular jokes I want are easily visible and I go back to those jokes and arrange them in logical order, numbering them within that circle as I go.

When I have arranged all the jokes in subtopic one, I circle those gags that apply to subtopic two, number them, and keep repeating the process until every gag is numbered. Then I retype from gag number one to the end.

This system is more difficult because it doesn't lend itself as easily to modification. Once you put that number in there, you really aren't inclined to erase it and foul up your progression. When the gags are physically separate—as on individual strips of paper—modification and rearrangement is much simpler and convenient. I also find with this second method that I'll invariably miss a gag or two that should have been placed earlier in the routine. Then I have to devise some scheme of renumbering.

I recommend method one—the cut-and-staple procedure—unless you're working by an open window on a windy day.

With today's computers, though, some of you who are more adept at handling software may be able to find you own efficient system of "cut and paste" that works as well as anything else. Not being a computer wizard, I'll leave those systems to your own ingenuity.

Blending the Gags Smoothly

Regardless of which system you decide on, though, once you get the gags rearranged, you'll discover that many of them don't fit together properly. You wrote each joke as a separate entity, and you probably wrote them in no logical order. Now that they're in a sensible progression, some of the rough edges have to be smoothed out. You may have too many similar joke forms too close together. You may have a joke with an elaborate setup that is no longer needed. You may have a good beginning joke that needs a setup. All these problems can be taken care of with some minor rewrites.

To illustrate, suppose you have these two jokes together:

> *"I'm such a grouch in the morning the milkman will never come near the house. He mails us our milk."*

> *"I knew a guy who was such a miserable grouch that at his funeral, the only pallbearers they could get were six guys who had never met him."*

Obviously, the two jokes are about different people, but that can easily be adjusted. Also, though, the setup lines are too similar for jokes that come this closely together. You might rewrite the gags like this:

> *"There's a guy in our neighborhood who is such a grouch, the milkman is afraid to approach his house. He mails the milk to him."*

> *"At his funeral, the only pallbearers they could get were six guys who had never met him."*

Now they're about the same person and we've dropped the redundant setup, but that leaves the second line a bit vague. So we could rewrite it with a new setup, but one that's different from the first.

> *"There's a guy in our neighborhood who is such a grouch, the milkman is afraid to approach his house. He mails the milk to him."*

"Nobody liked this guy. At his funeral, the only pallbearers they could get were six guys who had never met him."

As I mentioned earlier, you simply can't do a routine of six or eight jokes that all begin with "This guy was such a grouch that…" However, if the joke is valid, the setup lines can be adjusted or even dropped without affecting the humor content of the gags. This will become apparent as you reread your newly routined monologue.

Filling in the Blank Spots

You may also become aware of gags *that are not* in the routine. You'll see places where you feel lines should be but aren't. For instance, suppose you're doing a routine about your lazy friend, and the bulk of the lines are about his inactivity around the house, except for one line about his sloth at the office. That should prompt you to do a few lines about his work that lead up to that line.

Here it's not a simple matter of rewording. You have to get back to the keyboard and generate a few more lines.

Transitions between Subtopics

Probably the most glaring omissions will be in going from one subtopic to another. Often those segues can seem abrupt. One effective way to smoothly blend from one subtopic into another is to use a joke that combines some element of each subtopic. That way you'll be able to introduce your new subtopic and proceed with your new jokes.

As an example, let's go back to my routine about owning a dog. One subtopic was how big the dog was and another about his biting people. After doing several jokes about the animal's size, I could use a line like the following:

"Do you have any idea what a dog that size eats? …Mailmen."

Now I've introduced the premise that the dog might bite people. I'm free to do more jokes about other people the critter has chomped on.

Tying It All Together

For clarification, let's go through a portion of a monologue, starting with the roughly written first draft and on to the final routine. (This routine was written about a new road in the Philadelphia area called the Schuylkill—that's pronounced "Skoo-kill"—Expressway. At the time it was considered a precarious roadway by the locals.) I'll discuss the reasons for the arrangement and for some of the changes we made along the way. Since this is admittedly a seat-of-the-pants procedure, it might happen that you would have arranged the gags in a much different order. That's fine—in fact, it might be worth your while to try that.

Here are the gags as they were first jotted down.

1. *A safe journey on the Schuylkill Expressway...that means you finish in the same car you started with.*

2. *There are always accidents on the Schuylkill Expressway. I saw a twelve-car pileup there the other day. Twelve-car pileup...that means a woman signaled for a left-hand turn and eleven people believed her.*

3. *The Schuylkill Expressway...that's a road that takes you from South Philadelphia to Valley Forge in twenty-five minutes flat...whether you want to go or not.*

4. *It's the only road in the world that you can travel on from one end to the other without once leaving the scene of the accident.*

5. *If you want to speed your travel time on the Schuylkill Expressway, just move to the rear of the ambulance.*

6. *Actually our Schuylkill Expressway is a famous road. It has been cited by religious leaders all over the world. It ranks second to World War II as a cure for atheism.*

7. *I can always tell when I'm approaching the Schuylkill Expressway. My Saint Christopher statue gets down from the dashboard and climbs into the glove compartment.*

8. *Schuylkill Expressway...that's an old Indian term meaning "White man drive with forked steering wheel."*

Now let's go back and arrange this monologue in logical progression and discuss some of the reasons. I'll put the order of the jokes in a circle to the left of the gag. I'll also use an alphabetical system for this so that we don't confuse the new numbers with the numbers of the gags that I'm using for this illustration.

Ⓐ **1.** *A ~~safe journey~~ (Pleasant trip) on the Schuylkill Expressway...that means you finish in the same car you started with.*

Ⓕ **2.** *~~There are always accidents on the schuykill Expressway.~~ I saw a 12-car pile-up there the other day. (The way it happened was) ~~Twelve car pile up...that means~~ a woman signaled for a left-hand turn and ~~eleven~~ (11) people believed her.*

Ⓑ **3.** *~~The Schuykill Expressway...that's a~~ road ~~that~~ (that) takes you from South Philadelphia to Valley Forge in twenty-five minutes flat...whether you <u>want</u> <u>to</u> go or not.*

Ⓔ **4.** *It's the only road in the world that you can travel on from one end to the other without once leaving the scene of the accident.*

Ⓖ **5.** *If you want to speed your travel time on the Schuylkill Expressway, just move to the rear of the ambulance.*

Ⓗ **6.** *Actually our Schuylkill Expressway is a famous road. It* *has been cited by religious leaders all over the world. It ranks second to World War II as a cure for atheism.*

Ⓓ   **7.** *I can always tell when I'm approaching the Schuylkill Expressway. My Saint Christopher statue gets down from the dashboard and climbs into the glove compartment.*

Ⓒ   **8.** *Schuylkill Expressway...that's an old Indian term meaning "White man drive with forked steering wheel."*

I'll go through my new arrangement and changes to each joke, discussing them as we go.

A. This joke seemed to be the only one that had potential as an opener. Joke number 8 did also, but it seemed kind of abrupt to begin with a definition before doing a small joke about the road.

I changed it to "pleasant trip" because it might be easier to get to the routine that way. "I had a very pleasant trip over here on the Schuylkill Expressway ..."—then do the joke line.

B. I simply changed the format because otherwise my first three jokes would all have been the definition formula.

F. The first sentence was no longer necessary because the preceding jokes already established the road has a few accidents. This is a case where a joke is made more compact by routining.

In this gag, I dropped the definition formula because it has already been used enough in this short routine. It varies the routining a bit without hurting the gag.

G. This gag feels out of place in the routine. It either needs more jokes to establish the emergency procedures along the roadway or it should be dropped. Let's drop it.

H. To me, this is the biggie that we've been building to. Now if it's as good as I expect it to be, then we might be able to add a joke or two after it to capitalize on the laugh this joke will generate. So I created the following trail-off jokes.

"Some of the potholes on there are big enough to be foxholes, anyway."

"The Pope blessed it, but he won't ride on it."

Now let's see how this section appears in its final form.

I had a very pleasant trip over here on the Schuylkill Expressway. A pleasant trip on the Schuylkill Expressway... that means you finish in the same car you started with.

That road takes you from South Philadelphia to Valley Forge in twenty-five minutes flat...whether you want to go or not.

Schuylkill Expressway...that's an old Indian term meaning "White man drive with forked steering wheel."

I can always tell when I'm approaching the Schuylkill Expressway. My Saint Christopher statue gets down from the dashboard and climbs into the glove compartment.

It's the only road in the world that you can travel on from one end to the other without once leaving the scene of the accident.

I saw a twelve-car pileup there the other day. Twelve-car pileup...that means a woman signaled for a left-hand turn and eleven people believed her.

Actually our Schuylkill Expressway is a famous road. It has been cited by religious leaders all over the world. It ranks second to World War II as a cure for atheism.

Some of the potholes on there are big enough to be foxholes anyway.

The Pope blessed it, but he won't ride on it.

The only thing remaining now is to generate a blend or transition line to our next subtopic. Let's assume that we'll be doing material about your driving problems with the local police next. We would then invent a line that has something to do with the expressway but also included the police. It might be one like this:

"Actually the Schuylkill Expressway is a safe road. Very few people ever get tickets on it. The reason is the police are afraid to drive on it."

Adding the Finishing Touches

Earlier we said having the jokes written was like having a bunch of bricks delivered to a construction site. It allows us just as much latitude, too. The resultant house might be ranch style, colonial, or split-level. The humorist can do whatever she pleases with jokes, also, arranging them in any progression or form. It is important, though, to give them some flow because it makes them easier to read or to listen to. If you're trying to sell them, you want that buyer to be interested while reading. If you're presenting them yourself from the lectern or the stage, boy do you want that audience to be captivated.

I've cautioned you many times not to quit too soon. Until now that admonition applied to the quality of each joke and the quantity of all the jokes. Now it applies to the overall quality of the monologue. After struggling through three dozen lines and arranging them into a routine, don't think you're done with it. Now is when it needs some masterful strokes.

An artist friend of mine used to say that anyone can paint a picture, but it takes an artist to touch one up. I was privileged many times to see what he meant. Students brought in paintings for his criticism and advice. To my eye the artwork looked good, but the master would take a brush and make a few almost unnoticeable strokes—and the painting would be transformed. It would suddenly have a new energy, vitality, and reality.

The same applies to comedy. Certainly composing and arranging thirty-five comedy lines is praiseworthy, but you still have to add those deft brush strokes that change it from a good monologue to a work of art.

One producer I worked for had a devastating put-down. Eager writers would bring in their latest efforts for his appraisal, and he would glance over it and say, "This isn't writing. It's typing." Going over your routine one more time with a critical eye will guarantee that it will be "writing."

Below are a few of the weaknesses that you should be aware of along with a recommended cure for each. But remember that comedy is a subjective art. In each individual joke, what one critic thinks is a weakness you may see as a strength. I've already mentioned that I have written gags that I loved and found out later that I was the only one who did love them. You have to be the ultimate judge of what leaves your computer. Before you can satisfy anyone else, buyer or audience, you have to be content with your material. So reread it, pencil in hand, and be aware of some of these possible shortcomings.

Jokes that Are too Direct

Often comedy writers hit on a good combination of ideas and simply write the ideas down. The joke is funny, but it's not funny enough. It doesn't test the audience. There's not enough of a surprise element, and consequently, the joke appears obvious.

Now is a good time to discuss the nature of laughter and why it exists. Although I don't classify myself as an expert, I did read one hypothesis that has helped me when formulating successful jokes.

This theory states that laughter originated as a cry of victory. Early cavemen would be involved in life-and-death struggles. Once the battle was decided, the victor would be relieved of tension and let out a scream of glee. It seems to be valid if you compare this life and death struggle to any competition, especially sports.

In most sports, you see that laughlike cry of triumph. But you're wondering what that has to do with comedy. Well, humor can be considered a duel of wits. The comic throws out a straight line and everyone knows a joke is coming. The audience accepts this as a challenge and immediately begins formulating gags of their own. Before they have had a chance to get too far, the comic offers his punch line. The audience laughs because the tension of the battle is ended—the comic gave them the solution to the riddle.

Then there are jokes that we call "groaners." When the audience hears them they groan instead of laugh. Why? Because the punch line was a weak one. They know that if they had enough time, they would have come up with a better one. These are the gags that are too direct, or too obvious. They're more statements than jokes.

The ideal joke tosses out a straight line and issues a challenge to the listener. Then just at the right time, its logic defeats the listener. A good punch line should make the listener stop for a fraction of a second, think, and then say, "Oh yes, I get the connection."

In editing your monologue you want to find those areas where you can make the audience think for that split second. You want to eliminate those gags that are pure statements.

Here's a nice comedy line about marriage from a humorous speaker, Anita Milner:

> *"My husband and I celebrated our thirty-sixth wedding anniversary. You know what I finally realized? If I had killed the man the first time I thought about it, I'd have been out of jail by now."*

It's a lovely, irreverent line that says something in a unique way and hides the surprise until the last minute. But let's take that same idea and do it as a statement, turning it into a joke that is too direct.

> *"My husband and I just celebrated our thirty-sixth wedding anniversary. I should have killed the guy the first time I thought about it."*

You can readily see that the line lacks power now. It might get a laugh because it has a certain amount of shock value, but it will not be nearly as effective as the earlier version.

If there is any joke in your routine that appears too blatant, take some time to figure out a way of saying the same thing by implying it. Say it by *not saying it*. It should improve the humor content.

Jokes that Are too Obscure

Now let me do another version of that same joke to make a point:

> *"My husband and I just celebrated our thirty-sixth wedding anniversary. You know, I could have been out of jail by now."*

Now this gag makes no sense. It's too obscure for the audience to figure out.

This is the flip side of the previous admonition. It's the total reverse of it. In this case, the two comedy ideas are so far from obvious that they become untranslatable.

Rip Taylor used to use a line in his nightclub act after a joke of his would get a minimal response. He would say, "You're gonna think about that one when you get home and LAUGH." You do want your audience to think for a fraction of a second before catching your punch line, but you don't want them still thinking about it while they're motoring home. It's dangerous.

I went to a Hollywood restaurant once with a writer friend and the waiter was a part-time comedian who insisted on doing his act for us. When my sandwich arrived, there was a small chunk out of the piece of bread. It looked like someone had taken a bite from it. I showed it to the waiter and said, "Did someone take a bite of my bread?" He said, "Oh no, we're just playing hockey in the kitchen." I had no idea then and I have no idea now what this waiter was talking about.

Surely, in the waiter's mind there was some comedic connection between a missing bit of bread and a hockey game. However, he failed to convey the relationship to his listeners. Consequently, he had no joke. (He also had no tip.)

Here's another example. This joke is from Tom Dreesen:

> *"I'm dating a homeless woman. After a date, I can just drop her off anywhere."*

It's a bizarre line that implies that since she doesn't have a home, he can't really take her home. He can take her anywhere at all. The audience picks up on the irony immediately.

However, suppose I rephrase it as follows:

"I'm dating a homeless woman. Saves gas."

Now the audience pauses, searches for the meaning, and can't find it. How does it save gas? Why would dating a homeless woman be easier on your gas budget? The idea is intact. He saves gas because he doesn't have to drive her home. Anywhere he drops her is home. But a vital step is left out which makes it too difficult for the listeners to make the connection.

As the comics used to say, "I just tell 'em, folks; I don't explain 'em." No joke will work if you have to furnish a detailed explanation with it.

Spend some time reviewing your gags and make sure your meaning is clear. Sure, make the audience think a bit, but be certain that eventually they'll *get it*.

You must also be sure that your meaning is clear to each particular audience. Earlier I quoted a gag in which I used the inside term "reference check." It worked beautifully, but only for that particular crowd. That gag cannot be incorporated into a standard act, because no one else would know what it meant.

This phenomenon occurs occasionally in television writing. Our West-coast based staff will write a funny takeoff of a commercial, but on investigating we find that we can't include it in the show because the commercial is regional. Viewers on the East coast wouldn't know what we were talking about.

You have to be careful that all your phrases are universal, too. I've written a few jokes with the word "genuflect" in the punch line. I was surprised to learn how many people don't know what "genuflect" means. I thought I had written some beautiful jokes and the audience looked at me like I was from another planet.

Jokes that Are too Wordy

Shakespeare said, "Brevity is the soul of wit." That still applies today. Be stingy with your words. Say only as much as you must to effectively convey your idea. Why? Because each straight line or setup that you offer the audience is a promise of a punch line to come. Your audience begins anticipating the reward at the end of it. The longer you make them wait, the more you have to deliver. If it's too long, they're all sitting there a bit impatiently thinking, "Boy, this had better be good." Why create that kind of pressure for yourself and your jokes?

Here's a wordy joke about buying a puppy:

> *"My husband went out and bought a puppy. When he got it home, it wet in the living room. It wet in the dining room. It wet all over house. He calls it a puppy; I call it a bad kidney covered with fur."*

That long setup is unnecessary. Everyone knows what puppies are famous for. There's a great old joke where someone says:

> *"I just got a dog."*
> *"Does it have papers?"*
> *"Yeah, but he never uses them."*

Everyone understands that joke even though there was no mention of the dog having accidents in the living room, dining room, and all over the house.

The worst problem with verbiage in a gag, though, is that it telegraphs the punch line. It robs the joke of its surprise. Because the puppy example dwells so long on the dog's bad habit, the audience sees the punch line coming. They anticipate it. And you also risk giving them so much time that they just might compose a better punch line than the one you deliver. Make your point, but don't beat it to death.

Sometimes you'll find that a punch line needs a lot of setup and try as you might, you simply can't cut down the words. Here I offer two options: A) make sure that the punch line you deliver is worth the extended buildup; B) cut the buildup by delivering part or parts of it in smaller, softer jokes. Here's a case where you might note that you have to add jokes to make your routine flow a bit more smoothly. Each joke you write can also act to set up those to follow.

As an example, let's refer back to a joke we discussed in Chapter 9. It's a good gag, but the setup is awkward and long. It reads:

"Most of you know that Doc Wilson and his wife have seven lovely children. And all of Doc's friends know that he is constantly fiddling with his pipe. I spoke to his wife of twenty-eight years before the banquet and asked her if that annoyed her—that her husband was constantly playing with that pipe of his. She said to me, 'No, Gene, not at all. After seven children, I'm for anything that keeps his hands busy.'"

There are a lot of words used to get to that punch line, but they're necessary to explain the humor. Let's explore now how we can get across the basic premise of the joke with shorter gags.

"Doc Wilson and his wife, Eileen, were married twenty-eight years ago and to this day she is the love of his life—well, after his pipe, of course."

We get a laugh here and we let our listeners know that Doc has been married for twenty-eight years and that he is fond of his pipe.

"Together they've raised seven wonderful children. Well, Eileen took care of the children. Doc, of course, was always busy taking care of his pipe."

With this gag we let the people know that Doc is usually playing around with his pipe, that he spends a lot of time caring for it.

With a couple of simple jokes, we've now established all that we need to get our "biggie" across.

"I asked Eileen before the banquet tonight if it annoyed her that her husband was constantly playing with that pipe of his. She said to me, 'No, Gene, not at all. After seven children, I'm for anything that keeps his hands busy.'"

The gag is now cleaner. It's less wordy. Most important, the audience didn't have to sit through a long buildup to the punch line. Instead, they chuckled through it. They get less impatient that way and become more tolerant and more receptive to the joke.

✔ Jay Leno began his comedy career in the colleges and coffee shops around Boston and built his career into hosting the prestigious Tonight Show on NBC. He says:

> The biggest mistake you can make as a comedian is wasting people's time. You take people on this long winded tale, and then it doesn't go anywhere.
> When I see a guy who has a story and the punch line just ends with an obscenity, what good is that?

Jokes that Don't Please You

This is kind of a catchall, cop-out category, but it is valid and important. Since comedy is a seat-of-the-pants operation, you have to trust your seat and your pants. You must listen to your own instincts.

Sometimes a gag will seem to fit all the criteria, but it still won't feel right to you. Others may say, "It's a great joke. Leave it alone." Still you feel dissatisfied with it. That discontent may come from your knowing that you have a better joke in you. Listen to your inner voice and spend more time improving line. You just may end up with a ten-carat gem.

- *13* -

Shortcuts to Humor

As author and reader, you and I must now to come to a meeting of the minds. I can tell you about comedy writing. I can tell you how to prepare your manuscripts. I can prepare your mind for writing humor. I can help you market yourself and your material. But I can't write the jokes for you. Forgive the unflattering metaphor—you're the proverbial horse that I've led to water, but I can't make you drink. It's up to you to write your own jokes.

I'm not so naïve as to think that my advice will magically produce fantastically funny lines the first time you sit down at the computer. You shouldn't be that naïve either. (I feel it's safe to tell you that now because you're probably too far into the book to ask for your money back.)

If, after having tried a few of the exercises you've discovered that comedy writing is not that easy, then you've learned a valuable lesson. It's also a lesson not all comedy buyers have learned.

I'm always amazed at how easy people in the comedy business think good comedy is to produce. Many a star thinks nothing of poking his head into the writers' office and saying, "Hey guys, I'm doing a banquet tonight. Can you write about fifty or sixty lines for me during lunch?" It shows a complete ignorance of the creative process. These are some of the same people who complain how exhausting it is for them week in and week out to read lines written in a script. Fred Allen, the radio humorist of many years ago, helped write most of his own material. I gained a great deal of respect for Allen when I heard this anecdote:

Fred Allen had come to the studio one day and heard another performer throwing a tantrum over the script he'd been handed. "These writers are trying to ruin me," the star bellowed. "This material stinks. I can't go on the air and say this stuff." But Allen asked him, "Where were you when these pages were blank?"

> ✓ Bob Mills is a former attorney who turned to comedy writing. He began writing for Dinah Shore, spent two seasons working on Dean Martin's TV show, and then joined Bob Hope's writing staff in 1977. He talks about attacking the blank page:
>
> I read a lot about writers' block, but I find when you're doing this for a living on a day-by-day basis, it becomes so automatic that you really don't think about it. That isn't to say that some days you aren't funnier than other days, but you know what's required and when it's required, you just get it done ... somehow. Besides, professional writers have a sure-cure for writer's block that they can take out and look at any time they feel the need. It's called "THE MORTGAGE."

Some instructions require very little input from the beginner. If you purchase a tape recorder, the owner's manual will tell you to push this key to record and that key to play back. After you've read the manual once you're an expert tape recorder operator. That's not true with comedy writing. Even with detailed guidelines, you must supply some thought, some creativity.

This book has now taken you to the point where you should understand the mechanics of writing jokes and routining monologues. Now comes the time for your originality. Most professional writers concede that the only way to learn to write is to write, to write, and to write.

If you have faithfully labored through the exercises and diligently experimented with the recommendations and not been totally satisfied with the results, don't be discouraged. As with any undertaking, it takes effort and practice. Writing good humor requires a considerable amount of imagination and a great deal of discipline. My suggestion is to relax, have fun with it along the way, and be delighted with the improvement you'll begin to notice.

OK, so you've got your references neatly listed, and you've formed some ironic combinations. Now how do you make the jokes funny?

Shortcuts to Humor

Following are a few ideas that I (a little presumptuously) call "shortcuts to humor." I've found these help draw out the humor in a situation and also help to intensify the comedy.

You can use these in conjunction with all the suggestions you've learned so far in this book. They are more a slant or an angle that a joke can take. Using this list can help you generate humorous combinations, or it can provide the wording for two ideas you already have. Here they are:

- Reflect the truth
- Relax tension
- Shock
- Attack authority
- Involve the audience
- Just be funny

Reflect the Truth

Truth is stranger than fiction. It's usually funnier, too. People love to recognize the truth in humor. You've seen impressionists come forward and do the voice of some celebrity. People howl and applaud even if the performer said nothing funny. Why? Because they *recognize* the celebrity.

Steven Colbert emphasizes truth in his political satire. He tells his listeners often, "You can't make this stuff up."

That's the value that you can bring to a joke when it's not only funny but also truthful. The audience perceives that truth and identifies with it. It sparks a laugh.

In my banquet speech, I often tell a story about watching my daughter perform in a kindergarten talent show. I mention that "my wife and I sat very patiently while the…uh…*nontalented* children performed." It always gets an appreciative laugh because the parents in the audience recognize it as true—they know that they have felt the same way at children's recitals.

Anytime you're stuck for an ad lib, say something truthful. It will usually produce a laugh. For example, suppose you're asked to say a few words at some function or another. You could say simply, "I don't normally do much public speaking. Right now I'm scared to death." The audience will support you with laughter. They appreciate the truth.

Or you could say, "I'm not considered much of a public speaker. For the next few minutes, you're going to see why." Again the truth will bring you laughter.

Some stand-up comics use this technique to thwart hecklers. I saw one comic doing his act when someone in the audience shouted out. He approached that person and apologized. He said, "I'm sorry, I didn't mean to talk while you were interrupting." The audience recognized the truth, laughed, and it quieted the heckler.

Any time you're stuck for a punch line, look to the truth. There's generally humor embedded in it.

George Carlin does some wonderful routines with words. He loves to analyze and play with the idiosyncrasies of language. Basically, though, he is dealing with the truth of the statements. He is seeing a literal meaning in them that most of us overlook.

> *"The stewardess asks, 'Would you like to get on the plane now?' 'No thanks, I'd rather get in the plane.'"*

Or...

> *"Then the stewardess announces, 'We're preparing now for our final descent.' Oh God, I hope not."*

We laugh because we recognize the truth in these comments—and also the dumbness of them. We're laughing at ourselves because we use and accept these statements as true without realizing what they literally mean.

Truth can also be exaggerated or extended out to its logical conclusion and you needn't limitd yourself to reflect only facts. Your true pronouncement can be distorted, twisted, extended or shortened—played with in any way so long as it remains recognizable.

Steven Wright comments on an observation that the theory of relativity believes that time and space are the same thing. He says:
> *"Scientists first began noticing this when Albert Einstein kept showing up three miles late for his appointments."*

Relax Tension

Nothing eases tension in an audience so effectively and easily as comedy, and a tense situation can give you the greatest straight lines, a phenomenon especially useful for ad libs. Should something upset an audience, almost any line will get laughs. If a waiter drops a tray of dishes while an entertainer is onstage, the crowd has been upset, tension has been created, and the audience is waiting for the comedian to relieve it. In a situation like that, the performer can get laughs by saying or doing almost anything.

I remember watching a very funny comic perform one night, but his biggest laugh was unplanned. He was working in a small club that had rented its upstairs for a private party. In the middle of his act, the folks above must have started dancing a polka. The noise coming through the ceiling was frightening. The comic said, "What's going on up there?" Even that innocuous line got some laughs from the crowd. Then someone from the audience volunteered, "It's a wedding party." The comic said, "Can't they wait till they get home?" Boffo laughs.

Relaxing tension is such a surefire device for getting laughs that some comics even create their own stressful situations. I watched an entertainer perform once, and in the middle of a song, he began choking and said, "I think I swallowed a fly." He called offstage, "Can you get me a glass of water, please?" The water wasn't produced, the star kept coughing, building the tension. Finally the performer said, "Oh, never mind. I'll just let him walk down."

If you perform your own material, sooner or later something upsetting will happen. People drop things, lights blink on and off, sound systems go crazy, hecklers shout out the wrong thing. It can be annoying, but it can also be a sent-from-heaven straight line. You'll fare best if you treat it as a setup and provide an off-the-cuff punch line. Remember, it won't be that difficult because, as I've said, in situations like these almost any line will get a laugh.

Once I emceed a company awards banquet held early in the evening, right after work. The sound system wasn't working properly, and each time I approached the microphone it whistled shrilly. I backed away and it stopped. I approached it and it whistled. I backed away. It stopped. When I approached it again, it whistled. The audience was laughing heartily at my misfortune. Finally one of the technicians noticed the problem and adjusted the system. At last, I took the microphone without its rebelling. My opening line was, "Well, when you hold a banquet at six o'clock, a guy doesn't always have a chance to shower first."

The audience loved this because they appreciated the situation was totally beyond my control. This annoyance was making me appear the fool, yet I took the joke and played it back on myself. That dismissed the incident and we could get on with the show.

As a writer, you can create your own tension and then provide a punch line that relieves it.

I heard a speaker one time who was doing a pro bono performance. He began by taunting the host association about how little he was being paid.

> *"It's nice to be here with the (name of association). This is a cheap group.* (Remember the previous section? This got a laugh just for being a true statement.) *I'm ashamed to tell you how much I'm getting paid for this gig. Let me give you a hint, though. I did a show earlier tonight and got $400. Now I'm doing this one. When you average them out, I'm getting $200 a show."*

Shock

Shock humor literally jolts the audience into laughter. It can be accomplished in a variety of ways. Robin Williams is a brilliantly inventive comic—some say a *comic savant*—yet part of his humor comes from acting bizarre and wacky onstage. It startles the audience and they respond with laughter.

Dirty jokes, too, rely on shock value. If you dissect an off-color story, you may find that there's nothing inherently funny in it, except that someone would use those words in public.

Comedian Lewis Black has a hilariously funny act, yet many of his punch lines get added impetus by his use of indelicate language.

Insult humor, too, depends on shock value for its laughs. We're astounded that anyone would say something so outrageous to another person. So we laugh.

A few years ago, actor Hugh Grant was involved in an embarrassing scandal. The incident involved an enormous amount of press humiliating Grant and endangering his career. His first public appearance afterward was on *The Tonight Show*. As soon as Grant took his seat next to the desk, Jay Leno leaned forward as said, "What the hell were you thinking?"

There's nothing intrinsically witty in that line, yet the pure shock of it brought loud and sustained laughter from the studio audience. The line was quoted in many newspapers the next morning. It was funny because it was so audacious.

Part of a comedian's entertainment value is that he can say things that normal people either can't or won't say.

Attack Authority

This really is an offshoot of shock, except that it's a bit gentler. Basically, it's insult humor, but the comic is on much safer ground because chances are the audience will side with him. He's ribbing someone who the audience agrees deserves to be kidded—the boss, for example.

It was this technique that Bob Hope used so successfully when entertaining servicemen and women overseas. He always appeared to be more one of the enlisted men rather than one of the generals.

At the beginning of my career when emceeing retirement and twenty-five-year parties where I worked, I always got a nice response from the audiences when I kidded the higher-ups—the supervisors or the managers.

> *"The boss of our department is a tough guy. It's hard to tell whether he's managing with his heart or his mind—they're both made of stone."*

> *"Our department manager has the personality only a mother could love—provided she didn't have to work for him."*

I got my early comedy-writing experience doing roasts for fellow workers at the place where I was employed. I became the unofficial "Toastmaster General" at our plant. I kidded the guests of honor, but I was also gentle with them.

Although it may seem contradictory, there is a way to do insult humor, make it funny and enjoyable, and not antagonize anyone if you apply the following guidelines:

- Kid about things that are fabricated, or obviously not true. At one party I kidded a guy who prided himself on his drinking prowess. I said, "When he retires we're going to light a permanent flame in his honor. We're going to set fire to his breath." This line was funny, yet acceptable, because this man didn't *drink* excessively; he *talked about it* excessively. There is no way I would do that line about someone who had a serious drinking problem.

• Kid about things people kid themselves about. The joke above illustrates this point well. This man liked to joke about his drinking feats. I went along with him.

• Kid about things that are of no consequence. I'll stick with examples from these company roasts because a writer walks a fine line here. We were ribbing people who were good friends, and we didn't want to hurt them. One supervisor had a powerful telephone voice and could be heard all over the office. A speaker said of him, "He's the only fellow you can hang up on without losing volume." That line doesn't belittle his work, his personality, or his family—it kids him about something that doesn't really matter.

By using these guidelines and a bit of common sense, you can do insult humor without really insulting anyone. A safe rule of thumb, though, is when in doubt about a joke, drop it. It's easier to write a new joke than it is to get new friends.

Involve the Audience

Your listeners will always enjoy humor more if they are made a part of it. Localizing your comedy always multiplies its humor content because the audience members feel like they're sharing the stage with you.

On the banquet circuit, I'm often invited to play golf with the president of the host association. I make that a part of my opening remarks.

> "I played golf in the tournament today with your president, Charlie Lastname. We rented a golf cart but we didn't really have to. Where Charlie hits the ball, it's easier to take public transportation."

It's poking fun at one of the audience's own. It's kidding someone they know. It gets laughs.

Instead of using jokes that begin with "Two guys were walking down the street," find out the names of some people in the audience who fit into the story, and tell it about them.

You can also localize by using the names of places in the area... suburban towns, eating places, the local mall. All of these devices bring the audience into the performance.

Anything you can do to bring your audience into your routine will enhance the comedy.

Just Be Funny

Obviously, this category is designed to get me off the hook for anything I omitted in the preceding ones. It's meant to convey the message that if you have something that's funny, it doesn't have to fit into any particular category. Just use it.

Steven Wright, one of the most inventive comedy writers of all time, has a line that defies categorizing that reads:

> *"When I was a kid we had a sandbox in our back yard that was filled with quicksand. I was an only child... eventually."*

Kathleen Madigan had a line in her act during the time when the book *Final Exit*, a controversial book on how to commit suicide, was first published. She talked about being in a bookstore checkout line behind a customer who was buying it.

> *"This guy was about to pay $19.95 for a book on how to commit suicide. I said, 'Hey man, I'll stab you in the head for five dollars.'"*

Again, it's a line that only falls into the category of being funny.

Some of my writing colleagues thought that the classic Abbott and Costello routine, "Who's on First," was weak. They felt that it was impossible to have a team with such outlandish names. It was too much of a coincidence and it was unbelievable that the double meaning could run that long. History has proved that it's one of the most successful comedy routines of all time. Even if it does violate a few rules of logic, it follows the most important rule of comedy—it's funny.

Remember a joke is something that gets a laugh. If you have an idea that's *just plain funny*, write it.

- *14-*

Writing to Your Audience

There is only one ultimate judge of comedy and that is the audience. The rest of us are merely guessing. Some of the pros are better guessers than others, but even the best cross their fingers and hope that the audience responds.

Making People Laugh

Carpentry is an exact science. It can be creative, but it's always exact. If you take out a tape measure and mark off the distance from point A to point B, that's how long the board must be if it's going to fit. Comedy is not exact. You can't measure how long a pause should be or exactly how to make a voice inflection in order for it to work and produce a laugh. It's a seat-of-the-pants operation.

When I speak about comedy to writers or performers, I usually ask them the following two questions:

- What is a joke?
- What does every entertainer have in common?

I suggest that you think about those questions and try to answer them for yourself before going on.

Here's my take:

What Is a Joke?

Surely there are learned and technical definitions of a joke, but my homemade one is practical and applies—a joke is anything that makes people laugh. It can be a series of words, a look, a shrug of the shoulders, even a moment of silence—but if it makes people laugh, it's a joke.

What Does Every Entertainer Have in Common?

All entertainers must have an audience. They cannot perform without one. Some people might contend that a filmmaker doesn't have a crowd in the editing room or that an author writing a book does it alone. True, but all of them are working for the benefit of an audience...eventually. No one would make a movie if it were never to be shown, nor would anyone begin a book that was to have no readers.

The answers to these two questions are very important because they highlight *people*. A joke makes *people* laugh. An entertainer performs for *people*. The audience is supreme.

An audience is tremendously important in humor because it becomes an active participant in the performance. There is no humor until audience members get involved. You've heard the question, "If a tree falls in the woods and there is no one around to hear it, does it make a noise?" I don't know if it makes a noise or not. I do know, however, that if you tell a joke and it gets no laugh, it's not a joke. There is really no comedy until the listeners ratify the comic's input with laughter.

A comic once told me how much he envied singers. He thought they had the easy life—they could sing the same song over and over again, and they had free access to the greatest material in the world. Any novice vocalist can sing Cole Porter or Lennon and McCartney. But where does a young comic get top-notch comedy material? The same comedian complained, too, that a bad singer still gets applause after the song is done. But telling a bad joke doesn't get automatic laughs.

The audience doesn't need to participate in a song. A vocalist can warble away and the crowd is free to talk to one another at their tables; when they realize the song is coming to its conclusion, they generally turn politely and applaud. Certainly, some singers pull an audience into the performance, make them stop talking, and get them involved in the show. They're great entertainers, but the point is that even bad singers get polite clapping. A comedian, on the other hand, *needs* the attention of the patrons. The audience must listen, and laugh spontaneously. Otherwise there is no humor.

Never forget that true humor is a partnership between the humorist and the audience. Sadly, many writers and performers overlook this. To this day, I'm confused by the comics who came offstage and complain that , "Nobody could make that crowd laugh." I wondered why people would get dressed up (they used to at one time) and come to an expensive nightclub in order *not to be entertained.*

If You Ignore Them, They Won't Laugh

As a writer, you have to acknowledge the audience's importance to your writing, and take that into consideration when you create a joke or

Joan Rivers talks about audiences:

The audience tells you what you can and can't do immediately. And what they'll laugh at and what they won't laugh at, you'll know very quickly... if you've got the right audience.

Legendary comedian Bob Hope had this take on the subject:

I've worked for every kind of audience. I used to do a joke about working for Chicago gangster audiences back in the '20s. I said, "This one audience there was so tough, if they liked you they didn't applaud; they let you live."

I have done a few command performances and I performed at the White House. One time I stayed overnight in the Lincoln Bedroom. When I woke up the next morning, I freed all my writers.

I've also done state fairs and worked for soldiers right on the battlefield.

I tailor my material to whichever crowd I'm working to. You have to. You have to give the people what they want to hear, what they're thinking and talking about.

That's why having writers come along on the military trips was so great. They'd talk with the guys and girls in the camp and get some good topics for me to kid about on stage.

But basically, I think people are people. When the Queen laughs, she sounds pretty much like someone at the state fair with her kids holding her hand.

All people love to laugh.

routine. You have no choice. If you ignore them, you won't get to know them—their likes and dislikes. Your humor won't appeal to them. If it doesn't, they won't laugh. If they don't laugh, you have no product.

If you want to make a fortune from gold, do you go out and simply start digging holes in hopes one of them will uncover a rich vein? Certainly not. The earth is a participant in this venture. It will eventually supply wealth, but you must study the earth, discover where gold is likely to be found—then dig to hit the mother lode.

The humorist must regard the audience as a participant, because it is this relationship that will supply the reward. Therefore, the writer must study the audience and find out where mirth is to be mined.

Once I delivered a banquet talk to a convention of insurance people. In my opening I said, "It's easy to tell that this is a convention of insurance salespeople. On my way here tonight, I stopped in the lobby and asked someone how to get to the banquet hall. He said, 'You go down this corridor and turn to the right but God forbid anything should happen to you, how's the little woman going to get there?"

This audience howled because the gag hit them right where they work.

At another large convention, the ceremonies officially opened with the president of the association riding into the meeting hall on a beautiful white horse. The keynote speaker got howling laughter and appreciative applause from this audience when he capitalized on this situation by saying, "That was an historic moment when your president rode in here on that beautiful white stallion. I understand it's the first time you've ever had a complete horse at this convention."

Paula Poundstone is a funny, inventive comedian. If you watch her television specials, you'll see how powerful audience participation can be. She usually starts a conversation with someone in the audience, kids them, banters with them, and scores big laughs with that device. The audience-reaction shots show how much the people relish having Paula Poundstone conversing with *one of them.*

Do Some Research

As a writer, how do you capitalize on audience participation? Again, we're back to the preparatory work. You have to become something of an investigator.

Once, while writing for Bob Hope, our troupe was going to do a show at Lajes Field in the Azores. We had written material that would apply at that base. However, because of high winds, we were not permitted to attempt a landing there. We turned around and flew two hours to Rota, Spain. We would do our show there instead.

Hope asked me to write new material about the base at Rota, Spain. How could I find out about this base when we were 35,000 feet in the air. Actually, it was easy. Several of the military people on the plane had served at this particular base. I spoke with them and came up with a routine that played beautifully that night. Why? Because it was about this base and the people serving there.

You must do the same sort of research into your audiences. If you can't analyze them yourself, ask other people. Question the owner of the night club or the officers of any association you might be addressing. Ask people who live in the city you may be visiting. Interrogate any one who can provide you with insight.

This is basically what you want to know about your audience:

- What applies to them?
- How does it apply to them?
- What do they know?

What Applies

If you have two jokes of equal value, the one that applies to your audience can get ten times the laughter of the other. It's worth doing some research.

Find out what the people you're going to talk to are talking about themselves. What's happening in their city? If you're talking to a business or professional group, what is happening in their line of work?

If you're doing material for a college campus, find out who the big sports rivals are and what happened in the rivalry this year. Did this college win or lose? Was it a decisive victory or a close call? Find out the good restaurants and the real dives. What's the name of the notorious necking spot?

If you or your comic client are visiting a city, what are the headlines there? Has the mayor been up to anything strange lately? What's the weather been like? How are the local teams doing this year?

If you're working for a particular group of people, uncover some of the inside politics. What is the topic of conversation among the members of the group?

I once did a show for a group of insurance people in Vancouver, British Columbia. I casually mentioned to one of my hosts that I had never seen so many unusual license plates. He laughed and explained that in British Columbia, insurance agents distributed auto licenses and they all took care to get the unique numbers for themselves. At the banquet I mentioned that you could tell it was an insurance agents' convention—outside was a parking lot full of the most beautiful license plates in Canada.

That was an accidental discovery, but writers shouldn't generally rely on serendipity. Ask someone in the organization to supply you with some newspapers, bulletins, or his own ideas about what's going on with in the organization.

How It Applies to Them

If you're doing material for a convention of farmers, you can write jokes about the President's farm policy, right? Right, but you'd better find out how it affects the farmers and what their position is on the policy. If they're pro and you do jokes that are con, you might be in trouble.

If you're working for a college that is de-emphasizing football, you'd better find out where the students stand before you compose your gags.

Some folks may argue that this makes you a fence-straddler; it sounds like a wishy-washy position to take. But it really isn't. You're simply trying to find the mind of the audience and then use that to make your gags work. Often, you can tell the same joke in a slightly different way to generate a response.

Here's a joke I've heard that can be told at either a Republican or Democratic gathering:

> *"A man asked a politician why he was a Republican and*
> *he responded by saying, 'My daddy was a Republican, and*
> *his daddy before him.' The man asked, 'If your daddy was a*
> *jackass and his daddy before him, what would that make you?'*
> *The politician replied, 'A Democrat.'"*

Simply reverse the parties and you have a joke fit for either group. You're not really taking a stand pro or con, you're just kidding.

Here's another example. Let's suppose Alpha Manufacturing Company and Beta Manufacturing Company are fierce competitors. This is a story you can tell at a convention of Alpha employees:

> "A very rich gentleman wanted to get his three sons started with business of their own, so he asked the oldest son what he wanted. The boy said he wanted an oil company, so the man bought him Exxon. The second son was a bit younger. He said he liked movies, so the man bought him MGM. The third son was much younger and he loved Mickey Mouse. He wanted anything that was Mickey Mouse, so the man bought him Beta Manufacturing."

Obviously, the story works just as well when you're appearing before Beta employees—provided you remember to change the punch line.

There are other ways of manipulating a joke so that it doesn't reflect back on you. In writing a newspaper column, I have to maintain political impartiality, otherwise I'd lose half my readers with one offensive gag. Impartiality can be accomplished by using such "handles" as "it's rumored that…" or "Some people say that…" "Some Democrats are wishing that…" "Some Republicans are hoping that…"

The bottom line is, as a humorist you're involved with an audience. What does it benefit you to do lines that won't amuse them? Either convert lines so they're less offensive or drop the routine and write a different one.

In any case, it pays you to find out which way an audience thinks on each issue you're going to speak or write about.

What They Know

Once I was writing for a certain comic and I ad libbed a joke line. He didn't laugh. I explained why the joke was funny and even quoted the newspaper article that I had read about this particular topic. He said, "Gene, let me explain something. When I do a joke on my show, I like to have people know what the hell I'm talking about."

That's pretty good advice. Even though it may seem obvious, it's often overlooked.

One danger in asking people in an organization what's going on is that they may tell you, you'll write up a fistful of good jokes—then you find out the night of the banquet that the only people who are aware of what you've been told is going on are the president and corresponding secretary of the organization. The general membership never heard of it.

Sometimes a line that makes perfect sense to you may be completely unintelligible to a different audience. You must either know the frame of reference of each audience or use universal references that are understood by all.

In writing topical one-liners for comedians who travel all over the country, writers in Los Angeles get most of their inspiration from the L.A. papers. However, they'd be wise to check to make sure the rest of the country is aware of the topic.

Most of the above cautions apply to specific audiences. What do you do when you're writing for a general audience? You have to work to general frames of reference. You have to come up with ideas that the entire nation is aware of.

Leno and Letterman do monologue material each night that has to appeal to the entire country. Dave Barry publishes humorous essays that deal in generalities that apply to almost all the readers. Bill Cosby reminisces about childhood. His topics are universal to anyone who was once a youngster.

The gags are much easier to come by the more particularized your audience is, but the same principles apply even if your audience is potentially the whole world.

- 15 -

Keeping a Comedy Notebook

I recall an incident from early in my comedy career that taught me a valuable lesson about writing. One Saturday morning I woke around seven o'clock, dressed, and rushed over to my tennis club for my weekly five hours of doubles. Normally, I would shower afterwards and relax by watching whatever inane sports I could find on television. This particular Saturday, though, I had to hurry and do a newspaper column that was due. I couldn't think of a single topic to write about.

This is typical of most writers: When the deadline nears, the mind goes blank. However, the reason I was so rushed this day was because I wanted to watch the Wimbledon matches on television. John McEnroe was playing brilliant tennis in this tournament, but also was generating a lot of controversy because of his "bad boy" antics. The front page of the morning newspaper showed a photo of McEnroe being the "brat of Wimbledon." All that the club members talked about during our tennis recesses was the mischievous monkeyshines of McEnroe at the sedate and proper Wimbledon tournament.

But I couldn't think of anything to write about. All this was right in front of my nose and I couldn't think of anything to write about. McEnroe at Wimbledon cried out for satire and I didn't see it.

The lesson I learned is that a large part of comedy writing is preparation. It won't write the jokes for you, but when the time comes to compose the gags, preparation will make your life easier, and you'll finish your assignments much sooner.

Had I prepared that Saturday morning, I could have written an entire newspaper column while luxuriating in my bubble bath. In fact, twelve gags on McEnroe's Wimbledon antics might have been dashed off in the six-minute drive from the tennis club to my home. Had I been truly alert, the twelve gags might have been written for me by my colleagues as they discussed Wimbledon during our tennis breaks.

We've talked a great deal about preparation, but most of it has been devoted to preparing the topic. A joke, as we all know by now, is a combination of two different ideas—which needn't necessarily be on the same topic, so long as they are related in some way. In fact, relating a standard topic to a current news item gives it a particular zest. It makes the joke as fresh as that morning's headlines.

Ideas are the raw material that jokes are made from. You can *never* have too many of them. Also, you can never *remember* all of them. You can't trust your faculty of recall to serve you well as the deadline nears. My overlooking the McEnroe topic is sad testimony to that.

While blocking this chapter out in my head this morning, I visited my barber. While I was there, his phone rang almost constantly. The barber had to keep assigning different times to his many customers. There was no way he could keep each appointment in his head, so he kept an appointment book by the phone and jotted down each reservation as it was made.

Why then should gag writers expect to keep all their ideas in their heads ready for immediate recall any time they need them? They can't, but many of us try.

It's only logical that any and all ideas that you come by should be jotted down for future reference. They may generate entire topics, or they may provide the punch line for a joke you need. In any case, it is much

---

✔ Drew Carey talks about how he gets ideas for his stand-up act:

I take ideas from the paper. Not the political stuff necessarily. If there's an ad for furniture, I might write down couches and TV. That's just an example; I don't have any couch material.

Another thing I like to do if I'm really stuck is go to the funnies. This really helps me. I go to the funny pages and I don't take the joke, but I take the subject. Like, say, the subject is a mother and daughter fighting. You put that down as a subject to write about, just for the topic. Getting topics is the hardest thing.

more dependable if they are written down than if they are simply assigned a corner of your brain. There they are too easily misplaced or overlooked.

I keep a notebook of current topics. Each day, while reading the papers, I jot down items that have special prominence. They may be selected from the front page, the entertainment section, the sports page, the business section, or even the comics. During the course of the day, I engage in conversation with a number of people. I might jot down any topic that many people are talking about. This could be a new movie under discussion or a TV show that everyone watched. I also might jot down ideas I get from watching TV news or talk shows.

At the time of this writing, my current topics include the following:

> The popularity of and the controversy over *The DaVinci Code* film.
>
> *American Idol* is the most popular show on television.
>
> Barry Bonds has been accused of using steroids and is currently trying to surpass Babe Ruth in lifetime home runs.
>
> White collar crimes are news with two Enron executives just convicted in a much-publicized trial.
>
> Vice President Dick Cheney accidentally shot a friend during a hunting outing.
>
> The FBI is once again digging to try to locate the remains of Jimmy Hoffa.

In addition to newsworthy topics I might keep a list of everyday observations. Certain things that are noteworthy might happen to me while I'm driving on the freeway. Salesclerks in department stores may be more rude or more cheerful than usual. Anything that strikes me as noteworthy is…well…it's noted.

Now with all this ammunition I'm much better prepared to write a column or compose jokes. My notebook is an invaluable resource that provides a tremendous amount of fodder for either individual gags or a premise to write about.

For example, the idea about the controversial film *The DaVinci Code* prompted these comments:

> *"The premise of* The DaVinci Code *is that Jesus and Mary Magdalene married and had a child. They think it might*

be that kid who hit over .900 one year in the Jerusalem Little League."

"Some people claim the film is blasphemous, yet it still took in $24 million on opening day. It could've taken in $48 million except that half the people waiting in line to get in were struck by lightning."

Sometimes, after you keep your comedy notebook for a while, you can combine elements from it. For instance, Barry Bonds's alleged use of steroids might be consolidated with an item related to baseball that was in the press a while back. When baseball great Ted Williams died, his son had his body delivered to a cryogenics lab to be frozen. Those two items prompted this line:

"Baseball purists are up in arms that Barry Bonds could become the home run king even though he might use steroids. If Ted Williams heard about this he'd be turning over in his freezer."

Your notebook can take any form you choose. Mine is a simple pocket-sized loose-leaf book that I keep on my desk. As ideas present themselves, I simply enter them with a date and short capsulization. Some writers keep a handheld PDA for their notations or tap away on their laptops. I worked with one writer who kept a large sheet of paper taped to his office wall on which he made his entries. This way all topics were visible with a glance. No page-turning was necessary. As topics became too dated to use, he simply crossed them out with a single line. You may develop your own handy system. Any procedure is acceptable so long as it works for you.

One writer I know keeps a voluminous, well-organized list. He has a section devoted to television commercials. In another section he lists celebrities and a brief notation on what has made them newsworthy recently. In a separate section he lists popular movie titles and comments on them. He lists both the box-office smashes and the worst flops. He keeps tabs on the latest TV shows and how they do in the ratings. He also keeps notes on the shows quickly cancelled. He has a section of newsworthy quotes from famous people.

This isn't a tremendous amount of work, because once you do the initial research it's a matter of making a few entries each day. A collection like this, though, can be a terrific time-saver.

Notebook to the Rescue

If I were to ask you right now to write fifteen spoofs of television commercials, you would probably be hard put even to think of that many memorable commercials, let alone write jokes about them. But by simply turning to the right page in the notebook, you'd have all your research already done for you.

Sometimes in writing about certain topics, television shows become straight lines. For instance, when a writers' strike hits, it's logical to do jokes on how that would affect current shows. It's hard to keep attuned to what's on TV these days with the hundred of channels available. I would have to check the onscreen guide or scroll through the program listings before I could begin the gag writing. It is much easier if you keep the most popular shows listed in a notebook.

These are only the obvious applications of such a notebook, but there will be some inspiring fringe benefits, too. A notebook can provide brilliant ideas for gags on topics that don't seem to have any relationship to some of these lists. But when you find that relationship, you create a truly original gag.

A comedy writer's notebook will make each of your assignments a bit easier. In the long run, it will make your comedy writing faster and better. As we've said so many times, you learn to write by writing. Each time you write you learn more about writing. Your mind becomes accustomed to it.

The lists in your notebook will act as a prompter to teach you to associate ideas and to do it fast. That's what the ideal humorist does.

Someone once asked Mel Brooks's Two-Thousand-Year-Old Man who he thought was the greatest comedy team in the history of film. Brooks answered:

> *"I would have to say Wilt and Neville Chamberlain. What a hysterical team. Neville would read the Nuremberg Pact, then Wilt would stuff him through a basket."*

What a weird combination—Wilt and Neville Chamberlain. You imagine how many different names went through Brooks's mind before hitting that one?

I've worked with many comedy writers who have astoundingly quick minds. When a straight line is delivered, they can select a name from history that fits perfectly into the punch line. These gagsters are innately brilliant, but some of their mental dexterity comes from having done it over and over again.

Woody Allen's off-the-cuff remarks always amaze me. An interviewer once asked Woody what gave him the biggest thrill in life. He said, "Jumping naked into a vat of cold Roosevelt dimes." Where did that idea come from? Another questioner asked what his greatest sin was. Allen confessed, "Having impure thoughts about Art Linkletter."

We should all aim for the comedic brilliance of a Woody Allen or a Mel Brooks. If you haven't attained that mental quickness yet, start by keeping a writer's notebook.

- 16 -

Sketch Writing

Although I began my comedy writing career as a gag writer—a guy who supplied funny lines to funny people—eventually I had graduated to sketch writing and then sitcom writing. It was a difficult transition because the tendency among one-line writers is simply to string a series of jokes together to form a sketch, but sketch writing is not that easy.

Certainly a sketch is a collection of jokes, but it is much more. Remember the bricks metaphor from Chapter 7? Gags are the bricks from which sketches are fashioned, but a pile of bricks at a construction site doesn't make a decent dwelling. You can't simply mortar the bricks together, either—that just forms a collection of glued-together bricks. You need a master plan to build a house. The building blocks must be assembled in an orderly, well-designed fashion. I suppose the difference between a gag writer and a sketch writer is like the difference between a mason and an architect. Nevertheless, you'll find it's easier to learn the sketch form, and you'll be better at it, if you're schooled in the basics of joke writing.

What Constitutes a Sketch?

Professional writers say that a sketch needs a beginning, a middle, and an end. That definition doesn't tell me much because anything that occupies time and space has a beginning, a middle, and an end, and a good sketch should do a great deal more than just occupy time and space. The beginning-middle-end precept is merely a simplistic way of saying that a sketch has to be more than a collection of gags.

A good sketch needs

- A premise
- Some complications
- A resolution (or ending)

Thus we arrive at the cliché beginning-middle-end. Let's take a look at each part of a sketch.

A Premise

Just as the starting point for joke writing is having something to say, likewise the starting point for sketch writing is having some sort of story to tell—that's your premise. It may seem axiomatic that your sketch should have a story to tell, but even solid writers sometimes forget it.

Many times ideas that are pitched for sketches are not premises at all. For example, a writer may suggest, "Our star is a funny guy. Let's dress him up in a cowboy suit and it'll be hilarious." That's not a premise; it's a costume. If you dress this funny guy in a cowboy outfit and put him in front of a camera, he still has to *do something*.

Another writer may suggest, "This lady is really funny. It'd be wild if we just make her the head of the complaint department in a large store. Crazy things will happen." That's not a premise; it's a place. Who will she be dealing with there? What will her attitude be?

Something that just seems to lend itself to crazy antics isn't enough to make a sketch. The craziness has to be programmed and directed. There has to be a reason for it to take place. It must have impetus that leads it in an orderly progression. It needs a premise.

Let's say you do dress your comedy star as a cowpoke and he gets in trouble with a vicious gunfighter who gives him just till noon to get out of town. Then when he tries to book a ticket on the noon stage, the clerk behind the desk makes him go through all sorts of security checks and whatnot. As the hour gets nearer and nearer to twelve o'clock, you have a reason for some wacky things to happen. You have a premise.

Suppose the lady we put behind the complaint counter has a long line of unhappy customers waiting, but the first person in line is her husband. His complaint is that he wants a divorce. You have the beginning of a sketch. You have a premise.

Before you begin to write a sketch you should be able to explain what it will be about and have it sound interesting in one or two sentences. That's a hint that you've found a beginning—a premise. A gambler who is threatened by a vicious gunslinger with a life or death situation and then has to hurry a slowpoke ticket clerk tells us a lot more about a sketch than "dress a funny guy up in a cowboy suit."

When writing your sketch, you should get to your premise quickly, and it should generally be delivered almost like a punch line. It should be concise, clear, and explain what the sketch is all about. I call this the "Uh-oh Factor." It's that point in the sketch where the action is moving along nicely, and then suddenly you introduce a plot point that causes the audience to say "Uh-oh, what are they ever going to do now?"

This idea was illustrated graphically in those now classic *I Love Lucy* shows. In almost every one of them there would be that moment where audience members would actually shout out "Uh-oh" when Lucy began her shenanigans. Remember the famous "chocolate factory" episode. Lucy and Ethel had a job to do that seemed simple, but as soon as we noticed that the belt was speeding up and the chocolates were coming more quickly, we all said, "Uh-oh." There should be that moment in your sketches.

I once did a sketch for Peter Sellers and Lily Tomlin. They were two strangers seated side by side on an airplane in flight when suddenly the

> ✓ Carol Burnett not only performed in countless sketches during the eleven-year run of The Carol Burnett Show (1967–1978), but she also read and approved most of them. We asked her what she looked for in a script. She said:
>
> Well, I look for it to just be funny. That's certainly a good enough reason to do something, because belly laughs are very healthy.
>
> I also—if it's not that flat-out funny—would like to look for what is it about. Is it about something? Are we saying something? Not that I want to preach or give messages. There's a lot going on in today's society and in the world that we can comment on. We did that with Eunice. We were commenting on certain kinds of family life in a funny way but in a very truthful way.
>
> I guess I look for truth. There's got to be truth even when you get a pie in the face. You don't arbitrarily throw a pie in somebody's face. There's got to be a reason behind it. So I think truth.

151

pilot announced that their plane was in serious trouble and he doubted if they would make it safely to an airport. After some general hysteria, Sellers turned to Lily Tomlin and asked if she were sitting in the right seat. "What difference does that make at a time like this?" she wanted to know. Sellers said, "Because I think your life is flashing before my eyes."

The audience immediately responded with "Uh-oh, what an embarrassing situation this could be."

Now this sketch was about something. It had a beginning. It had a story to tell. It had a premise.

Some Complications

Once your premise is set forth, you have to make something happen. If your premise has presented a predicament, the audience is going to want you to try to solve it. If you've postulated a goal to be accomplished, you have to introduce some complications to that goal.

For instance, the cowboy that we introduced earlier has to do something to get the clerk to move more quickly so that he can get out of town before the gunslinger takes aim. The husband who wants a divorce from the department store complaint lady has to try to find some way to get that agreement from her.

Obviously, you can't pose a premise and then jump abruptly to the ending. The complications keep the viewers intrigued, interested, eager for the resolution.

Sometimes your complications can be episodic, a series of joke situations that happen one right after the other. One sketch I wrote for *The Carol Burnett Show* featured Tim Conway and Harvey Korman as Revolutionary War soldiers surrounded by the enemy. They had a solitary cannon. Harvey proposed that he would decoy the enemy into the open and Tim would then destroy them with one perfectly timed and aimed cannon shot. Harvey charged into the enemy lines and Tim discovered that the cannonball was bigger than the mouth of the cannon. ("Uh-oh...Harvey's in trouble now.") Harvey came back into the picture a little worn for his ordeal. He got the cannonball into the cannon, then charged courageously back into the enemy lines. Now Tim tried to clean the cannon and lost the brush. Then he didn't have a match. Then he tilted the cannon and the cannonball rolled out. And so on and so on.

All the complications I could think of were wedged into this sketch and could have been used in any order.

Sometimes your complications are progressive. Those are sketches in which plot point A causes or leads to plot point B, which leads to plot point C, and so on. The gags, unlike those in the previous example, are in a strict progression. They are connected chronologically. An example of this type of sketch is one where people are threatened by a gunman and a cohort comes in and gets the drop on the gunman. The situation appears to be solved. Then someone else comes in and gets the drop on the guy who got the drop on the gunman. And it continues on and on...but the action must be in a logical, chronological sequence. The gags are not interchangeable.

The complications and the plot points within a sketch can be almost any sort that you can invent. The point is that your premise has to be strong enough to drive and sustain the action.

We had a delightful premise on *The Carol Burnett Show* that stymied the writing staff for a while. The story line was that two gentlemen are vacationing in Hawaii. One has lost ten dollars and is brooding over it. The other tries to reason with him, saying it's silly to ruin a costly vacation because of a ten-dollar loss. The brooder says, "That's easy for you to say. It wasn't your ten bucks." So the second man takes ten dollars from his wallet and sets fire to it. "Now," he says, "we've both lost ten dollars. Let's forget it and have a good time." The brooder relents, cheers up, and takes a pack of cigarettes out of his pocket and says, "Hey, look, I found my ten dollars."

Although the writers loved the premise, the consensus was that there was no place to go with it. Once the man discovered his ten dollars the sketch was over. We needed to devise enough complications to keep the sketch going. Eventually, we did find a natural progression of events that made for an amusing sketch. It's printed in its entirety at the end of this chapter so you can see for yourself how it turned out. As an exercise, take the premise and play with it to see if you can come up with enough complications to sustain the sketch. (Here's a hint: solve the immediate problem and search for a complication to that. Then solve that difficulty but find another problem it can cause. Keep going till the ending.)

A Resolution

Endings are usually the hardest part of sketch writing. It's like jumping off a building—the jump and the fall are relatively harmless. It's the sudden stop that does the damage.

A sketch is like an elongated or acted-out story joke. If you've ever told (or listened to) a joke, you know that the most important part is the ending. If you have a weak ending, you have a weak story. So it is with the resolution of a sketch.

Resolutions take the most effort in writing and are the cause of most rewrite time in a variety show office. If you ever want to be believable as a head writer on a variety show, all you need to do is look pensive and say after reading a sketch, "The ending could be a little stronger."

My writing partner and I would often write two endings for our sketches and hand in the *weaker* one with our first draft. That way, when it was returned for a stronger ending, we had one already prepared and hidden in our desk drawer.

The big problem is that the ending has to be surefire. It has to get the big laugh. Along the way, you can permit mediocre gags to slide by because if one doesn't provide the laugh, the next one will. However, you only have one ending. It had better work.

A good ending should progress naturally out of the sketch's action. That poses trouble for the writer, because the ending should be a logical conclusion of the sketch—and yet not be predictable.

For instance, in the cannon sketch discussed earlier in this chapter, the ending should deal with the cannon. Perhaps Harvey finally takes Tim, stuffs him into the cannon, and fires him at the enemy.

A poor ending would be after doing this entire sketch about the troubles of firing the cannon, Tiger Woods walks onto the set with a golf club, does a *hilarious* line about a lost golf ball, and walks off to tremendous laughter and applause. You've got a star, a great joke, and an audience convulsed with laughter—but you don't have a resolution for your sketch.

To generate the ending, review the plot points of your sketch. Discover which way they go, then reverse the direction, twist the thrust, extend it, bend it, break it...do something unique with it, but have the ending be a natural result of the sketch itself.

Your ending should also tie the sketch into a neat little package. It should almost be so definitive that the sketch couldn't go any further even if you wanted it to.

Trying to be definitive can get you into trouble, however. A recurrent problem we had on the Burnett show was that many of the sketches ended with death. A character would get shot accidentally, or someone would be bumped out a window. This is because in sketches containing comedic physical abuse, any physical shtick you write can be topped—you can always write another disaster after that one. The only ultimate is death. We used to make certain that the sketch deaths were genuinely comedic and not in bad taste—but we still tried to find endings that didn't require some character's demise.

Your endings need a finality to them. The audience must know that the sketch has ended and be satisfied with the resolution.

An exception to this is the kind of ending that flip-flops a sketch back on itself. In an ending like this, the last line of the sketch is actually the beginning of a new sketch. For example, in a sketch about a strange psychiatrist who torments his patients, the guy finally breaks down and tearfully admits that he's crazy and can't help himself. The patient leaves and the shrink composes himself, goes to his desk, and says to his nurse, "Send in the next patient, please." You know that he's going to do the same thing all over again.

Sometimes when this device is used, the (hypothetical) new sketch is magnified by the ending. For example, you have a woman who can't train the family dog. The entire sketch is about the woman chasing the dog and both of them destroying the house. Finally the woman finds a way of getting rid of the dog. She sits and rests, and just then her husband comes home with a gorilla on a leash. You know she'll have the same problem only ten times worse.

These types of endings work occasionally, used sparingly. They're cheating, because the audience realizes that you haven't really resolved the predicament—you simply start it all over again. It can be as annoying as being asked a riddle, and when you give up and demand the answer, simply being presented with another riddle.

You must be careful, too, that your ending doesn't destroy the sketch. Trick endings will sometimes do this. Often writers spend so much time working on the ending that they forget what the sketch is about. Suppose that you have a hilarious sketch about a husband and a wife who are attacked by little green men. They shoot and throw things at the attackers. When the green men leave, the husband says to the wife, "Our kids really have a good time with Halloween, don't they?" Even if that were a riotous ending, it would destroy the credibility of the sketch. The parents wouldn't fight so violently if they knew those were their own kids dressed for Halloween.

After you decide on your ending, reread the sketch with that ending in mind, to be sure it's compatible with the body of the sketch.

One sketch ending we had to rewrite on *The Carol Burnett Show* points out how difficult endings can be and how strange sketch logic can become—and also how you can get the joke you're after if you don't quit too soon.

This sketch featured Carol Burnett and Tim Conway as husband and wife in a motel room. After going to bed and turning out the lights, Carol felt a huge bug in the bed. Tim had to get up and do something about it. The audience never saw the insect, but the thing kept becoming more and more of a threat and Carol became more and more hysterical. Finally, after a lot of good comedy, Tim managed to get the insect out of the room. But now Carol was sad that they took the creature away from his family. Maybe the bug had children that were waiting for him to come home to them. Carol forced Tim to go out and get the insect and bring it back.

Here's where we needed the ending. The writers' first choice was that as soon as Tim stepped outside the door, we heard a squishing sound—end of the insect.

Most of us objected to this because it was too cruel. This is what's strange about sketch comedy logic—each week we shot Tim, pushed Harvey out windows, threw people off cliffs, but we couldn't kill a bug that was too small for the eye to see. It sounds weird, but it made sense.

Understand, it wasn't the censors who objected to this. It was the writers themselves who refused to write it in.

Now another peculiar phenomenon occurred. Some of the writers wanted to get the rewrite over with and they began to argue for killing the insect. "Nobody cares about bugs." "We never see him on camera." "We kill people on the show, why can't we kill an insect?" (What a sad commentary that writers would sacrifice an innocent insect just to get home in time for dinner.)

Finally, someone threw the perfect ending that broke up the entire room. We typed it and it was one of the best endings we ever had. (Well, at least it got us home before dinner.)

The ending: Tim went outside the room, then came back and reported to Carol that the insect had joined a bunch of other insects, probably his family, and that they all looked happy and contented. Carol bought that story and was delighted. As Tim walked around the bed to climb back in, he turned his back to the camera, and we saw a four-foot lizard clinging to his back.

Idea Sources

Where do you get ideas for sketches? Who knows? F. A. Rockwell wrote a book entitled *How to Write Plots That Sell.* This volume was first published in 1975, but you can probably still find a copy in good bookstores or on the Internet. It's well worth having. There may be more modern books on how to plot out novels and screenplays, but this one deals specifically with various way of stimulating the mind to come up with usable plots.

A staff writer has an advantage over a freelancer in that he or she can brainstorm sketch premises. Most variety show staffs spend many hours en masse "pitching" ideas. ("Pitching" is where we just throw random observations to the room for discussion, hoping some workable ideas will result.) Most of the writing is done by individual teams, but a good deal of the pitching or brainstorming is done with eight or ten writers in a room.

The premises can be launched from any springboard. Some of the sketches we wrote were based on off-color jokes that we transformed into family-hour sketches. The basic premise for the ten-dollar bill sketch you'll read at the end of this chapter resulted from a hassle I had on an outing with my children. One of them was upset about losing a few dollars of her own money. To smooth things over I set fire to a five-dollar bill. Then my daughter found her "lost" money and I was left brooding because I had wasted five bucks of my own cash for nothing.

Most of the staff's ideas came from everyday occurrences dressed up in sketch form. One writer mentioned at a pitch session that he had gone to a restaurant the night before. His waitress was always accompanied by another young woman who said and did nothing. She just followed the waitress around. This writer asked what was going on and the "speaking" waitress said, "Oh, she's my puppy." That was their word for someone who was being trained.

We all loved this idea and kicked it around. The resultant sketch was that one of our performers was holding up a bank, but the teller took a good deal of time to hand over the cash he demanded. Why? Because she was training a new teller. Our performer said, "What a coincidence. I'm training this young man to be a bank robber." At the end of the sketch a policeman bursts into the bank and gets the drop on the robbers. However, they get away because the policeman was training a new officer.

A sketch, like a joke, is a combination of two or more ideas. It must be written more delicately, though, because you're asking the audience to invest more time in it. Remember that the longer you go, the better the payoff has to be. Sketches go for some time, so they have to entertain along the way and have a strong punch line.

In the history of television, two shows stand out as epitomizing the sketch format. One was Sid Caesar's *Your Show of Shows*, which aired from 1950 until 1954. (Another show which was basically the same format—so I'm considering it the same show—aired from 1954 until 1957. It was titled *Caesar's Hour*.) The other was *The Carol Burnett Show*, which was broadcast from 1967 until 1978.

There are other fine examples of sketch writing, notably *Monty Python's Flying Circus, The Benny Hill Show, Saturday Night Live, In Living Color*, and occasional sketches on the late night talks shows with Jay Leno, David Letterman, and Conan O'Brien.

Nevertheless, I've selected sketch examples for this book from *The Carol Burnett Show* for several reasons.

First, because this show was such an outstanding model of the genre.

Second, because sketches from this show are readily available on DVDs (as are some sketches from the Sid Caesar shows). You can not only read the scripts as presented in this book but also see how the sketches were performed.

Third, because as the coauthor of these sketches, it was easy to obtain permission to reprint them.

The sketches reproduced here are:

"The Hollow Hero"
"Root of All Evil"
"No Frills Airline"

I also want you to take note of the writing style and the format. Study these sketches and enjoy them.

THE HOLLOW HERO (from episode 75)

(Carol Burnett, Harvey Korman, Tim Conway and extras)

MUSIC: PLAYON
SOUND: CROWD ROAR

(ON A PARADE GROUND A LINE OF BRITISH SOLDIERS ARE STANDING AT ATTENTION. ONE SOLDIER (BIRL) IS STANDING IN FRONT OF THE QUEEN (CAROL) WITH THE KING (HARVEY) BY HER SIDE. SHE PINS A MEDAL ON HIS CHEST. THEY SHAKE HANDS. CAROL AND HARVEY NOW MOVE ON TO THE NEXT SOLDIER (TIM). SHE MAKES A SMALL GESTURE TO HIM AND SMILES.)

(SHE TAKES THE MEDAL FROM HARVEY. SHE STARTS TO PIN IT ON TIM'S CHEST.)

> CAROL
> Private Newberry, for your distin-
> guished heroism, in the face of the en-
> emy, far above and beyond the call of
> duty, we, as your King and Queen, are
> proud to present to you, in the presence
> of your fellow countrymen…

(INDICATING THE AUDIENCE WITH A QUEENLY SWEEP OF HER ROYAL HAND)

> …gathered here and the millions of
> viewers at home…the highest honor this
> nation can bestow…the Perks Medal-
> lion.

> TIM
> I don't want your medal.

CAROL

(NOT SURE SHE HEARD RIGHT)
I beg your pardon?

TIM
I don't want it.

CAROL
What?!!!

TIM
Stick it in your ear.

(CAROL GIVES HARVEY A PUZZLED LOOK. "WHAT DO I DO NOW?" HARVEY PULLS HER BACK GENTLY AND THEY BOTH TURN SO TIM CAN'T HEAR THEM)

HARVEY
What did he say?

CAROL
He said, "Stick it in my ear."

HARVEY
Don't do it.

CAROL
I shan't.

(THEY TURN BACK TO TIM)

You must take the medal.

TIM

(PUSHING IT BACK AT HER)
No.

CAROL

(PUSHING IT BACK AT HIM)
Yes.

TIM

(PUSHING IT BACK AT HER)
No.

CAROL

(PUSHING IT BACK AT HIM)
Yes.

TIM
No.

(HARVEY CLEARS HIS THROAT TO ATTRACT HER ATTEN-
TION. SHE LOOKS AT HIM. HE SHAKES HIS HEAD VERY SLIGHTLY
AND CAROL STOPS. CAROL STEPS ASIDE AS HARVEY STEPS IN
FRONT OF TIM. HE GIVES HIM A FRIENDLY SMILE THEN LOSES
HIS TEMPER AND GRABS HIM BY THE LAPELS)

HARVEY
Listen you...you...

(CAROL CLEARS HER THROAT TO ATTRACT HARVEY'S AT-
TENTION AND THEN SHAKES HER HEAD. SHE THEN MOTIONS
HIM WITH HER HEAD TO COME BACK WHERE THEY CAN TALK
PRIVATELY. HARVEY LETS TIM GO AND HE AND CAROL TURN
THEIR BACKS TO TIM)

CAROL
Let me handle this.

(HARVEY NODS WITH DIGNITY AND BACKS AWAY. CAROL
AGAIN APPROACHES TIM)

>   Young man, every soldier wants a
>   medal.

>   TIM
>   I don't. I want a pony.

>   CAROL
>   A what?

>   TIM
>   A pony...you know...a little horse.

(HE GIVES HER A LOOK LIKE SHE'S STUPID. CAROL LOOKS AT HARVEY AND GIVES HIM THE MOTION THAT THEY SHOULD TALK PRIVATELY. THEY TURN THEIR BACKS TO TIM)

>   CAROL
>   He wants a pony.

>   HARVEY
>   A what?

>   CAROL
>   A pony...you know...a little horse.

(SHE GIVES HIM A LOOK LIKE HE'S STUPID)

>   HARVEY
>   How about if I have him beheaded?

>   CAROL
>   Good idea.

(THEY TURN BACK TO TIM)

>   CAROL
>   Young man, how would you like to
>   have a pony with no head?

HARVEY

(TO CAROL, QUICKLY)
Psssssssst.

(HE GIVES HER THE MOTION WITH HIS HEAD. THEY TURN
AWAY FROM TIM AGAIN)

I meant have **him** beheaded…not the

pony.

CAROL
We can't do that.

HARVEY
Why?

CAROL

He's the biggest hero this country has

ever had.

HARVEY
What did he do?

CAROL

He saved the lives of his entire pla-

toon by swallowing a live hand gre-

nade before it went off.

HARVEY
Really.

CAROL

Really! That brave man has no inter-

nal organs.

                        HARVEY

    (NOT BELIEVING HER)
                Get out of here.

    (SHE MOTIONS WITH HER HEAD AS IF TO SAY "WATCH." SHE
    TURNS BACK TO TIM AND OPENS HIS MOUTH. SHE THEN YELLS
    DOWN INTO HIS THROAT)

                        CAROL
                Hello!

    (ECHO)
                        Hello…hello…hello…hello…

    (HARVEY MOTIONS HER BACK WITH HIS HEAD. THEY TURN
    AWAY FROM TIM)

                        HARVEY
                I say we give him the pony.

                        CAROL
                Right.

    (SHE CLAPS HER HANDS TWICE REGALLY. A SOLDIER (STAN)
    BRINGS IN A PONY AND STANDS AT ATTENTION WITH THE PONY
    IN FRONT OF TIM)

                        Private Newberry, for your distin-
                        guished heroism in the face of the
                        enemy…far above and beyond the
                        call of duty, we as your King and
                        Queen, are proud to present you with
                        the highest honor this nation can
                        bestow…a pony.

(TIM LOOKS DOWN AT THE PONY FOR A LONG BEAT THEN BACK AT CAROL)

                    TIM
          I don't want that pony.

                    CAROL
          I beg your pardon?

                    TIM
          I want a blue one.

                    CAROL
          You what?

                    TIM
          I want a blue one...you know, like the
          sky.

                    CAROL

(WAVES PONY OFF)

(STARTING SLOWLY AND BUILDING TO NEAR HYSTERIA)

          You're crazy. You know that? You're
          crazy. We're standing out here in the
          hot sun trying to give you a medal
          ...engraved and everything. You
          don't want that...you want this...
          then you don't want this...because
          you want that. I'm out here busting
          my royal bustle trying to please you
          and you say you don't want this
          pony 'cause you want a blue pony.

> Well, lemme tell you something, you
> hollowed out little creep…there's no
> such thing as a blue pony.

TIM
In that case, I'll take the medal.

(CAROL LOOKS LIKE SHE WILL HAVE A STROKE. THE FRUS-TRATION AND RAGE SLOWLY RISES WITHIN HER. HER HANDS COME UP AND SHE STARTS TO GO FOR HIS THROAT)

HARVEY

(STOPPING HER)
Pssssssssst.

(HE MOTIONS FOR HER WITH HIS HEAD. CAROL STOPS HER ADVANCE ON TIM AND JOINS HARVEY WITH THEIR BACKS TO TIM. HARVEY WHISPERS SOMETHING IN CAROL'S EAR)

(CAROL NODS AND TURNS BACK TO TIM AS HARVEY, WHIS-TLING AND BEING AS NONCHALANT AS POSSIBLE, SNEAKS AROUND BEHIND TIM, GETS DOWN ON HIS KNEES, AND CAROL SHOVES TIM BACKWARDS OVER HARVEY)

SOUND: BODY FALL

(HARVEY THEN GETS UP, LEAVING TIM SPRAWLING ON THE GROUND. HE ESCORTS CAROL OFF STAGE WITH REGAL DIGNITY)

MUSIC: PLAYOFF

(APPLAUSE)

ROOT OF ALL EVIL (from episode 91)

(Dick Van Dyke, Tony Randall, Vicki Lawrence, Bartender)

MUSIC: PLAYON

(DICK AND TONY ARE STITTING AT A BAR. BOTH ARE DRESSED IN HAWAIIAN SHIRTS, THEY'RE IN THE MIDDLE OF THEIR VACATION. TONY IS DEPRESSED)

DICK

You're gonna spoil our whole Hawaiian vacation over that lousy ten bucks.

TONY

Look. I don't like losing ten bucks of my hard-earned money no matter where we are.

DICK

Now that is dumb. That is really dumb. You spend all this money to come over here and it's wasted because you lost a lousy ten bucks.

TONY

Sure...but if it happened to you you'd probably cut your throat.

DICK
It would not mean **that**...

(SNAPPING HIS FINGERS)
>...to me.

>TONY
>It would if it was your ten bucks.

>DICK
>Ten bucks isn't what this is all about. It's the fact that you're letting it bother you, and letting it ruin our vacation.

>TONY
>I guess if you lost ten dollars, you'd just forget about it.

>DICK
>Absolutely right.

>TONY
>Like hell you would!

>DICK
>All right.

(DICK TAKES HIS WALLET OUT AND REMOVES A TEN DOLLAR BILL)
>I just wanna show you something.

(HE HOLDS UP A TEN DOLLAR BILL)
>This is a ten dollar bill, right?

>TONY
>Yeah.

>DICK
>Watch this.

(HE TAKES OUT A CIGARETTE LIGHTER AND SETS FIRE TO THE BILL)

> TONY
> Hey, what are you doing?

> DICK
> Just watch.

(THE BILL GOES UP IN SMOKE)

> There. Ten dollars of my money up
>
> in smoke.

(HE LETS IT BURN OUT IN THE ASHTRAY)

(BRUSHING HIS HANDS WITH FINALITY)

> . . . doesn't bother me in the least.

> TONY
> Boy, you really are a nut.

(HE TAKES OUT A PACK OF CIGARETTES)

> Hey . . .

(HE TAKES A BILL OUT OF THE CELLOPHANE AND SHOWS IT)

> There's my ten dollars.

(DICK JUST STARES AT HIM IN DISBELIEF)

> Sure, I remember putting it in there
>
> so I wouldn't lose it when we were
>
> playing miniature golf.

(NOW TONY FEELS BETTER)

> Aw, now I can enjoy Hawaii...come
>
> on, let's go shoot some pool.

                    DICK
            Hey...how about giving me the ten
            bucks?

                    TONY
            What for?

                    DICK
            I just burned my ten dollars.

                    TONY
            You wanna set fire to money, that's
            your problem.

                    DICK
            But I did it for you.

                    TONY
            Thank you. Now let's go before all
            the tables are gone.

                    DICK

    (VERY GRUMPY)
            I'm not going anywhere.

                    TONY
            What's wrong with you?

                    DICK
            I'm out ten bucks is what's wrong
            with me.

                    TONY
            Didn't you just tell me that ten bucks
            doesn't mean anything?

DICK

Yeah.

TONY

Well, now I'm telling **you.**

DICK

Wait a minute. That's different. I didn't do something stupid like lose the money.

TONY

Oh, you did something smart, like set fire to it.

DICK

All I know is that you were out ten bucks, now **I'm** out ten bucks.

TONY

All right, tell you what I'll do . . . you're making such a big stink over this, I'll split the difference. I'll give you five bucks.

DICK

(HE DOESN'T LIKE THAT IDEA)
Five . . . ?

(BUT HE DECIDES TO SETTLE FOR IT)
Okay.

> TONY
>
> Let me get change for the ten. Bar-
>
> tender.

(BARTENDER (DON) COMES OVER)

(TONY HANDS HIM THE BILL)
> Can you break this into fives for me?

> DON
> Sure.

(DON TAKES THE BILL AND GOES TO THE CASH REGISTER)

(HE NOW TURNS BACK AFTER CLOSING THE CASH REGIS-
TER)

(COUNTING OUT FOUR BILLS)
> Here you go...five...ten...fifteen...
>
> twenty...

(DON MOVES OUT OF THE PICTURE)

(TONY AND DICK SIT THERE FOR A BEAT LOOKING LIKE THE
CAT THAT ATE THE CANARY)

(BOTH ARE WONDERING IF THEY REALLY GOT AWAY WITH
THIS. NEITHER ONE IS MOVING TOO MUCH FOR FEAR THEY
MIGHT BLOW THE WHOLE SCAM. TONY EVEN MOVES HIS
HANDS A BIT TO COVER THE MONEY, VERY DISCREETLY SO
THAT NO ONE LOOKING CAN TELL THEY GOT MORE THAN
THEY SHOULD HAVE GOTTEN. A SMILE CROSSES BOTH THEIR
FACES)

(TONY NOW PICKS UP THE MONEY. DICK STARTS RUBBING
HIS HANDS TOGETHER IN ANTICIPATION OF THE WINDFALL)

TONY

(HANDING DICK ONE BILL)
There's your five.

(HE FOLDS THE REST AND PUTS IT IN HIS POCKET)

(DICK IS DUMFOUNDED)

DICK
Hey . . .

TONY
What?

DICK
Where's the rest of my money?

TONY
I gave you five.

DICK
Yeah, but you got fifteen.

TONY
It was my ten.

DICK
Oh no, it was my ten.

TONY

(DUMPING THE ASHTRAY)
There's your ten.

DICK
Forget that ten. You just got twenty

from the bartender. The fifteen you
got in your pocket and this five.

(DICK LAYS HIS FIVE ON THE BAR)

TONY

Hey, you're the one that was saying
money didn't mean anything.

DICK

It didn't then. It does now. You owe
me five bucks.

TONY

You know you're ruining our whole
vacation with this money thing.

DICK

I want another five.

TONY

If I give you another five, can we forget the money and just have a good
time?

DICK

Put another five down there and I'll
never mention money to you
again…believe me.

TONY

I don't know why I'm doing this…

(HE TAKES ONE OF THE FIVES OUT OF HIS POCKET)

...but anything to keep you quiet.

There.

(HE PUTS THE FIVE ON THE BAR NEXT TO DICK'S OTHER FIVE)
Now can we just be friends and have

a good time?

(HE HOLDS OUT HIS HAND FOR A HANDSHAKE)

DICK
Okay, buddy.

(THEY SHAKE HANDS)

(WHILE THEIR HANDS ARE CLASPED, DON COMES INTO THE PICTURE)

DON
Hey, I gave you ten dollars too much

before.

(HE TAKES THE TWO FIVES OFF THE BAR AND MOVES OFF)

(DICK QUICKLY GRABS TONY'S HAND)

DICK
Give me five dollars.

TONY

(TRYING TO WRESTLE HIS HAND FREE)
Let go of me, will you?

DICK
Give me five dollars.

TONY

It's **my** money.

DICK

It's not your money. It's my money.

(VICKI, AS A BEGGAR LADY, COMES IN WITH A HANDFUL OF SCRAGGLY FLOWERS)

VICKI

Flowers for your lady. Help the poor.

TONY

Wait a second. Here's the answer.

Let's give the ten bucks to someone

who really needs it.

DICK

Good idea. I'll go along with that.

TONY

(STARTS TO HAND VICKI THE MONEY)
Here you are, my good woman.

DICK

Hold it. Hold it.

TONY

Now what?

DICK

You want to be the big man, don't

you? I should give her five dollars of

that money.

TONY

(HANDING DICK THE TWO FIVES)

>Here, give her the whole thing if you want.

DICK

(HANDING HER THE MONEY)

>This is for you, dear. May this make your life a little fuller in these troublesome times.

VICKI

>Oh, thank you, sir...thank you...

(SHE BEGINS TO SOB A BIT AND THROWS HER ARMS AROUND DICK, HUGGING HIM AND PATTING HIM)

(SHE TURNS AND LEAVES)

(DICK IS DELIGHTED WITH HIMSELF)

TONY

(A LITTLE BIT SURLY BECAUSE THE MONEY IS GONE)
>Are you happy now?

DICK

>Yes, I'm very happy. Nothing is as rewarding as generosity. In fact, I'm going to continue that generosity. I'm going to buy you a drink. Bartender...

> DON
> Yes, sir?

> DICK
> Two more here, please.

> DON
> Right.

(DICK REACHES INSIDE HIS COAT FOR HIS WALLET. IT'S NOT THERE. HE FEELS AROUND A BIT. THEN THE AWARENESS COMES OVER HIS FACE)

> DICK
> She took my wallet…and my watch
> …stop, thief.

(HE RUNS OUT AFTER HER)

(DON BRINGS TWO DRINKS, SETS THEM DOWN, AND HOLDS UP THE CASH REGISTER TAPE)

> DON
> Hey, you got a double star on your
> receipt. Both these drinks are on the
> house.

(TONY LOOKS AROUND TO MAKE SURE DICK CAN'T SEE, AND POURS DICK'S INTO HIS OWN GLASS)

(HE RAISES HIS GLASS TO DON)

> TONY
> Cheers.

MUSIC: PLAYOFF

(APPLAUSE)

NO FRILLS AIRLINE (from episode 70)

(Carol Burnett, Harvey Korman, Tim Conway, Extras)

VICKI (Introduction)

Not too long ago, many of the commercial airlines introduced a new low cost fare which was nicknamed the "No Frills Plan." Simply put, it meant that you gave up some of the little extras like movies, cocktails, stereo, and if you wanted lunch, you had to bring your own. Tonight, we'd like to bring you **our** version of the "No Frills Plan."

MUSIC: BRIDGE

(SET: INT. AIRLINER)

(EXTRAS CROSS THROUGH)

(HARVEY IS BEHIND THEM, FOLLOWED BY TIM. THEY ARE BOTH CHECKING THEIR BOARDING PASSES AGAINST THE SEAT NUMBERS)

HARVEY

Two A...Two B...Three A...Three B...Here I am.

TIM

Hey, there's mine. I'm right in back of you. I'm in the no frills section.

HARVEY

(NOT INTERESTED)
Fine.

TIM

Save a lot of money back there. And
you know what they say. The back
of the plane gets there the same time
as the front.

HARVEY
That's wonderful.

(HARVEY STANDS IN AISLE AND STARTS REMOVING COAT.
AS TIM SQUEEZES BY HIM, HE TRIPS)

TIM

(LOOKING DOWN)
Ooops. Watch it. That rug ends right
there.

(HARVEY OPENS THE OVERHEAD COMPARTMENT AND
STARTS LAYING HIS JACKET OUT IN IT AS TIM STARTS REMOV-
ING HIS JACKET)
Of course, you don't get any food or
anything...

(HOLDING UP A BROWN BAG)
...that's why I brought this. Besides
I never saw a meal yet worth forty
bucks. But everything else is the
same.

(HE OPENS HIS OVERHEAD COMPARTMENT TO PUT HIS JACKET AWAY. IN IT WE SEE A SPARE TIRE. A JACK AND A LUG WRENCH FALL OUT. HE CATCHES THEM JUST IN TIME AND SHOVES THEM BACK IN THE COMPARTMENT)

Well, we don't have to worry about

a flat.

(HARVEY SITS AND TIM SITS WHILE HOLDING HIS JACKET IN HIS LAP)

(LEANING UP TO HARVEY)

It's not just the money, you know. It's

safer, too.

HARVEY

Good.

TIM

Never heard of a plane backing into

a mountain yet.

HARVEY

(PUTTING HIM IN HIS PLACE)

Do you mind…please.

TIM

(TO HIMSELF)

Harrumph…rich people.

(CAROL NOW ENTERS AS THE STEWARDESS. SHE IS CARRYING A PILLOW)

CAROL

(TO HARVEY)

Comfortable, sir? Would you like a

pillow?

HARVEY
Yes, please.

(CAROL PUTS THE PILLOW IN BACK OF HIS NECK)

CAROL
How's that?

HARVEY

(NOT SURE)

Well...it's better.

CAROL

(TO TIM)

May I take your coat, sir?

TIM
Oh, yeah...great.

(TIM GIVES HARVEY A SNOTTY LOOK. HE GOT BETTER SER-
VICE)

(CAROL TAKES TIM'S COAT AND FOLDS IT NEATLY, THEN
ROLLS IT UP IN A BALL AND PUTS IT DOWN BEHIND HARVEY'S
BACK)

CAROL
How's that?

HARVEY
Much better. Thank you.

(TIM NOW TRIES TO GET COMFORTABLE IN HIS VERY UP-
RIGHT SEAT. AS HE DOES THIS HE STRETCHES HIS LEGS OUT
INTO THE AISLE AND INTO THE NEXT SECTION)

CAROL

(TO TIM)

You're in the no frills section, right?

TIM

Yes, and you know what they say.

The back of the plane gets there the

same time...

(CAROL STOMPS ON HIS FOOT)

SOUND: CRUNCH

CAROL
Then get your feet off of our rug.

TIM

(PULLING HIS FOOT BACK)
Yes, m'am. Sorry.

CAROL

(SPEAKING TO THE ENTIRE PLANE)
May I have your attention, please.

(SHE TAKES THE SAMPLE OXYGEN MASK FROM THE COM-
PARTMENT ABOVE HARVEY'S HEAD)

> Our cabin is pressurized for your comfort. It is very unlikely that there will be any sudden change in the cabin pressure, but in the rare event that this does happen our emergency procedure will be as follows…

(CAROL WHISPERS TO BONNIE)

(CAROL THEN BENDS DOWN AND WHISPERS IN HARVEY'S EAR. TIM TRIES TO LISTEN IN BUT CAN'T)

TIM

(TO HARVEY)

> What did she say? I didn't hear that…what did she say?

(TIM STARTS MOVING UP TO HARVEY'S AREA AS HE SPEAKS. CAROL RETURNS)

CAROL
I said…"Keep you feet off our rug."

(SHE KICKS TIM IN THE SHINS)

SOUND: CRUNCH

(FORCING HIM TO RETURN TO HIS SEAT,HOLDING HIS LEG IN PAIN)

(SWEETLY TO HARVEY)
Is your seat belt fastened, sir?

HARVEY
Oh, no. I'll take care of it right away.

(HARVEY BEGINS FASTENING HIS BELT AS TIM STARTS LOOK-
ING AROUND FOR HIS)

CAROL

(TO HARVEY)
Thank you.

(CAROL STARTS TO WALK AWAY)

TIM

(STOPPING HER)
Ah...Miss...

CAROL
What????

TIM
My seat belt isn't fastened.

CAROL
Well, so?

TIM
In fact, I don't even have a seat belt.

CAROL
Noodge!

(SHE WALKS BACK TO TIM, REACHES IN BACK OF HIS SEAT
AND PULLS OUT A ROPE WHICH SHE QUICKLY WRAPS AROUND
HIS CHEST SEVERAL TIMES AND THEN MAKES ONE FINAL PASS
AROUND HIS NECK)

PILOT (VOICE OVER)
Stewardesses, prepare for takeoff.

(CAROL SITS IN A VACANT SEAT AND FASTENS HER BELT. HARVEY LEANS ACROSS TO WINDOW, TAPS ON IT AND WAVES GOODBYE TO SOMEONE, TIM WATCHES THIS AND IMITATES HIM. HE REACHES OVER AND STARTS TO TAP ON WINDOW. THERE IS NO GLASS IN HIS WINDOW AND HIS HAND GOES THROUGH)

SOUND: ENGINES REVVING UP FOR TAKEOFF

(AS TIM CONTINUES TO FEEL AROUND FOR THE VACANT GLASS, WE SEE SMOKE FROM THE ENGINE BEGIN POURING IN THROUGH THE WINDOW INTO HIS FACE. THIS IS FOLLOWED BY DUST, CANDY WRAPPERS AND MISCELLANEOUS PAPER. HE QUICKLY UNWRAPS THE ROPE THAT IS AROUND HIM, TAKES THE SEAT CUSHION FROM THE NEXT SEAT AND STUFFS IT IN THE WINDOW OPENING. HE NOW SETTLES BACK IN HIS SEAT AS BEST HE CAN AS THE PLANE TAKES OFF AND REACHES CRUISING ALTITUDE. CAROL UNFASTENS HER BELT, GOES BRIEFLY OUT OF SHOT AND COMES BACK WITH SEVERAL SETS OF EARPHONES IN PLASTIC BAGS)

(SHE GOES TO BONNIE, RANDY, SEATED IN FRONT OF HARVEY)

CAROL
Do you want to hear some music?

BONNIE
Yes, please.

CAROL
That'll be two dollars each.

(THEY GIVE HER THE MONEY)

CAROL

(TO HARVEY)

How about you, sir? Some music?

HARVEY

I'd love it.

CAROL

Two dollars, please.

(HARVEY GIVES HER THE MONEY AND SHE GIVES HIM THE EARPHONES. SHE NOW MOVES BACK TO TIM)

(TO TIM)

Would you like to hear some music?

TIM

(SURPRISED AND ANXIOUS)

Why, yes. Wonderful.

(HE HOLDS UP THE TWO DOLLARS AND CAROL BEGINS SINGING)

CAROL

(SINGING)

Off we go, into the wild blue yonder

...crash!!!

(TALKING)

That'll be two dollars, please.

(SHE TAKES THE BILLS FROM TIM AND EXITS)

> PILOT (VOICE OVER)
>
> Folks, if you will look out the right
>
> side of the airplane you will see that
>
> we are passing over the Grand Can-
>
> yon.

(TIME LEANS OVER TO HARVEY)

> TIM
>
> Well, so far your forty bucks got you
>
> over the Grand Canyon about a foot
>
> and a half ahead of me.

(HARVEY GIVES HIM A FROZEN STARE. TIM THEN LEANS WAY OVER AND STARTS LOOKING OUT OF HARVEY'S WINDOW. HARVEY SEES THIS AND LOOKS OUT THE WINDOW HIMSELF WHILE COVERING AS MUCH OF IT AS HE CAN WITH HIS HANDS SO THAT TIM CANNOT SEE. TIM SHRUGS, GIVES UP AND SITS BACK DOWN)

(CAROL NOW ENTERS WITH AN ARMLOAD OF PAPERS AND MAGAZINES)

> CAROL

(TO HARVEY)

> Would you like something to read,
>
> sir?

> HARVEY
> What do you have there?

CAROL

Well, I have **Fortune, Newsweek,
Time, Playboy, The New York Times**
and **The Wall Street Journal.**

HARVEY

Oh, good, I'll take **The Wall Street
Journal.**

(CAROL HANDS HIM THE PAPER. CAROL STARTS BACK UP
THE AISLE AWAY FROM TIM)

TIM

(CALLING HER)
Ah...Miss...

CAROL
What???

TIM
I might read a little something.

CAROL

Hokay. For the no frills section we
have **The Wichita Gazette, The
Opthamologists' Journal** and **The
Mushroom Growers' Weekly.**

TIM

Hmmm. Let's see what's happening
with those mushrooms.

(CAROL SLAPS HIM WITH THE PAPER WHICH HE OPENS)

HARVEY

Well, I think I'll get a little shut-eye.

CAROL

Oh, let me help you.

(SHE PUSHES THE BUTTON ON THE SIDE OF HIS SEAT. THE SEAT BACK GOES BACK INTO TIM'S LAP, CRUSHING THE PAPER AGAINST HIM SO THAT IT AND HARVEY'S SEAT ARE LITERALLY UP UNDER HIS CHIN. TIM CAREFULLY WORKS HIS FINGERS LOOSE FROM UNDER THE SEAT AND UP OVER THE TOP OF THE SEAT)

HARVEY

On second thought, maybe I'll have

a drink first.

(HE PUSHES THE BUTTON ON THE SIDE OF HIS SEAT, BRING-ING IT QUICKLY TO THE UPRIGHT POSITION. TIM IS PROPELLED UP AND OVER HARVEY'S SEAT AND DOWN INTO HIS LAP)

CAROL

(TO TIM)

No. No. No sneaking up here.

(TIM CLIMBS OUT OF HARVEY'S LAP AND GOES BACK TO HIS OWN SEAT)

TIM

Sorry. Just passing through.

(HE NOW SITS BACK DOWN)

CAROL

(TO HARVEY)

I'll be serving lunch shortly.

Would you care for the beef

or the turkey?

HARVEY
I think I'll have the turkey.

TIM
Hah…now you're going to

see what you get for forty

bucks.

(TIM TAKES OUT HIS LITTLE BROWN BAG)

By the time you get your

lunch, I'll be into my second

package of Twinkies…

(CAROL ENTERS AND PUTS THE TRAY OF FOOD IN FRONT OF
HARVEY)

Oh sure, it's fast, but is it good?

(HE SITS BACK AND TAKES OUT A SMALL SANDWICH AND
COFFEE IN A PAPER CUP WITH A LID ON IT. TIM JUST GETS IT
ALL OPEN IN FRONT OF HIM WHEN…)

PILOT (VOICE OVER)
Ladies and gentlemen, this is your

captain speaking. We're expecting

some very slight turbulence. I'd like

to suggest that you fasten your seat

belts loosely. Thank you.

> HARVEY
>
> Maybe you'd better take the food
> back.

> CAROL
>
> Oh, no, that announcement is just a
> precaution. We always check with
> the captain before serving.

(TIM STARTS TO TAKE A BITE OUT OF HIS SANDWICH WHEN HIS SEAT STARTS BOUNCING UP AND DOWN VIOLENTLY)

> If it were going to be anything seri-
> ous, we wouldn't even serve food
> and drink.

(TIM CONTINUES TO BOUNCE UP AND DOWN)

(DEMONSTRATING WITH HER HAND)

> It'll probably be just a little rocking
> motion or an up and down move-
> ment. You won't even feel it.

(TIM NOW STANDS UP WITH QUITE SOME DIFFICULTY BE-CAUSE OF ALL THE TURBULENCE. HE STEPS FORWARD INTO THE FIRST CLASS SECTION OF THE PLANE AND THERE IS NO TURBU-LENCE)

> CAROL
> What are you doing up here?

> TIM
>
> Miss, how come it's so rough back
> there and it's so smooth up here?

CAROL

Will you please get back in the no

frills section?

TIM

Yes, ma'am…

(AS SOON AS HE STEPS BACK IN HIS OWN SECTION THE TUR-
BULENCE STARTS UP AGAIN AND HE CAN HARDLY STAND UP.
HE MANAGES TO GET BACK IN HIS SEAT)

CAROL

Would you like a little wine?

HARVEY

Yes, good idea.

(CAROL EXITS. TIM STOPS BOUNCING UP AND DOWN, DE-
CIDES IT'S OVER AND BEGINS CAREFULLY WORKING THE TOP
OFF THE COFFEE CONTAINER SO AS NOT TO SPILL IT)

(CAROL RE-ENTERS WITH A BOTTLE OF WINE AND A GLASS)

CAROL

(SHOWING HARVEY THE BOTTLE)

Sparkling burgundy. Okay?

HARVEY

Perfect.

(TIM TAKES OUT A PAPER CUP AND HE AND CAROL START
TO POUR AT THE SAME TIME. AT THAT INSTANT, TIM'S SEAT
STARTS BOUNCING UP AND DOWN AGAIN, SPILLING COFFEE
ALL OVER HIM. CAROL POURS AND NOTHING HAPPENS. SHE
FILLS THE GLASS AND HANDS IT TO HARVEY. TIM STOPS BOUNC-
ING UP AND DOWN. HARVEY SWIRLS THE WINE IN HIS GLASS
AND TAKES A SIP. TIM WATCHES HIM, SWIRLS THE COFFEE IN

THE PAPER CARTON AND STARTS TO SIP. HE SEES THAT ALL THE
COFFEE HAS SPILLED OUT AND HE TURNS THE CARTON UPSIDE
DOWN. NOTHING COMES OUT)

(CAROL LOOKS AT HER WATCH)

CAROL

(TO HARVEY)

Say, you're not getting off at Chicago,

are you?

HARVEY

No, I'm going straight through to

New York.

TIM

I'm getting off at Chicago.

CAROL

Well, you'd better get your things

together and come with me.

(AS HE BEGINS GATHERING HIS BELONGINGS SHE PASSES
HIM AND GOES TO A DOOR IN BACK OF HIS SEAT. TIM GETS UP
AND FOLLOWS HER)

TIM

What time do we land?

(CAROL OPENS THE DOOR)

SOUND: WIND

CAROL

Land?

(SHE GIVES HIM A SHOVE OUT THE DOOR. HE GOES BY THE WINDOW WITH THE PILLOW)

MUSIC: PLAYOFF

(APPLAUSE)

- 17 -

Sitcom Writing

Sitcoms (short for situation comedy) are television shows, generally a half hour long, that have a story to tell. Some of the classics have been *I Love Lucy*, *The Dick Van Dyke Show*, *The Mary Tyler Moore Show*, *M*A*S*H**, and *All in the Family*. A few of the more successful recent ones are *Cheers*, *Frasier*, *Seinfeld*, *Friends*, *Everybody Loves Raymond*, and *Will and Grace*. Of course, each television season brings new hits which have the potential to join this distinguished list of classics.

A comedy variety show, by contrast, is made up of divergent sketches and characters, like the ones we discussed previously—*Your Show of Shows*, *The Carol Burnett Show*, and more recently, *Saturday Night Live*, *In Living Color*, and *Chappelle's Show*.

Most comedy variety shows are staff-written, while sitcoms, though they have writing staffs, buy many stories and scripts from freelancers.

Let's see how most freelance scripts are purchased for a sitcom. Everyone reading this will have heard or read of an exception to this scenario and exceptions do exist, but 99 percent of the shows assigned to freelance writers follow this typical pattern.

The producer's biggest problem at the beginning of each TV season is getting scripts working and finished on schedule. Many dependable writers graduate from the freelance pool. Several take staff positions on existing shows, others devote themselves to creating new pilots. Consequently, the producer generally has to discover new people to write scripts for his show.

The producer first reads many spec scripts submitted by agents.

Some even read unsolicited scripts. (A "spec script" is one that a writer creates without an assignment. It's written purely as a showcase for the writer's talent.) If a certain script impresses the producer, he will arrange a story conference with that writer.

The story conference is a meeting in which the writer presents several story ideas for a possible script assignment—in effect, a sale. This can be a frightening ordeal for the new writer. The author enters a room full of apparent adversaries—the producers, the story editors, script supervisors, and sometimes other colleagues of undetermined pedigree. There might be up to six people who refuse to be impressed with any of your accomplishments, and each of them probably has veto power. It's the writer's task to dazzle them with brilliance.

This meeting can be frightening for the staff people, too, because they are usually interviewing a stranger. They may buy a story from you and then be dependent on you to make their lives easier...or at least, to not make their lives more difficult. The ideal situation for them is to purchase a good story from you and have you turn in a well-written first draft within a reasonable time. However, they are never sure.

The meeting invariably begins with a bit of small talk, some bad jokes, occasionally a terrific joke, and then someone says, "Okay, what have you got?" That's the signal for the writer to start "pitching" story lines. "Pitching," in television jargon, is another word for brainstorming. Ideas are thrown to the creative minds to be discussed, discarded, changed, or simply ridiculed.

The well-prepared freelancer will have several storylines worked out for presentation. These may be presented orally or printed out so that the producers can read them or so that the writer may read aloud to them. There's no set formula. This is one of the few areas where producers try to make the writer feel comfortable. The freelancer should have some of this material on paper—even if it's only a paragraph or two—in order to leave a document with the potential buyers, if they show interest.

This can be the most discouraging part of the meeting. Let me present a playlet to show you exactly what I mean.

SETTING: Any television situation comedy producers' office. The room can be any size, but there will always be one less chair than is needed. Present will be two producers, two story editors, and two script consultants. One will be in tennis clothes, one in jeans and a T-shirt, one in expensive slacks and sweater, and all will have their feet up on the desk. We'll omit the small talk and begin with the phrase...

> PRODUCER A
> Okay, what have you got?

(SEVERAL OF THE BUYERS TAKE THEIR FEET OFF THE DESK AND SIT UP, LEANING FORWARD ATTENTIVELY)

> FREELANCER
> I have this one story where Carol and
> Marge are both dating the same guy,
> but they don't know...

> PRODUCER B
> Hold it. We have a story that's very
> similar to that in the works right now.
> What else have you got?

> FREELANCER
> Okay. I've got one where one girl is
> dating a bullfighter...

> PRODUCER A
> And the other girl is dating an ani-
> mal rights activist, right?

> FREELANCER
> Yeah...how did you know...

> PRODUCER A
> *Two and a Half Men* is doing a story
> with a bullfighter and an animal
> rights person. We can't touch it.

> FREELANCER
> Really?

PRODUCER B
What else have you got?

FREELANCER
I have a story where the girls find a submarine…

PRODUCER A
We've got a submarine story already.

FREELANCER
Okay, they're all sitting around in a diner…

PRODUCER B
Sorry. The network says we can't do any "eating" scenes.

FREELANCER
Okay, then. I've got one you'll love. Marge finds out she's going to need braces…

(SHE PAUSES, WAITING FOR SOMEONE TO VOICE AN OBJEC-TION. WHEN NONE IS FORTHCOMING, HER EYES LIGHT UP AND SHE CONTINUES WITH INCREASED FERVOR)

Now she really hates this at first, you see, but then she goes there and finds out she's in love with the orthodontist. But after the first visit he discovers that it's really Carol's teeth that need straightening. Marge tries to find ways of keeping Carol from visiting "her" doctor, and also some reason for seeing him herself even though her teeth are really fine.

(NOW THERE IS A LONG PREGNANT PAUSE. EVERYONE IS SEARCHING FOR A REASON TO SHOOT THIS IDEA DOWN. FINALLY...)

> PRODUCER B
> I like it.

(NOW THE AUTHOR REALLY GETS CAUGHT UP IN THE ENTHUSIASM. SHE SENSES THE SALE)

> FREELANCER
> I think it can be a really funny show. I've got this great scene in the dentist's chair...

> PRODUCER A
> I don't like dentist shows.

> FREELANCER
> Hey, I can make him a chiropractor. Yeah, that's even funnier.

> PRODUCER A
> How about if she falls in love with a ventriloquist?

> FREELANCER
> A ventriloquist?

> PRODUCER B
> That's good. Then we can do that scene we had to take out of the other show.

> FREELANCER
> A ventriloquist?

> PRODUCER A
> We have another meeting scheduled right now, but we like this. Try and

write up an outline of this same
show, except make the love interest
a ventriloquist. Okay?

FREELANCER

(WRITING RESIGNEDLY IN HER NOTEBOOK)
Right…a ventriloquist.

(SHE LEAVES AND EVENTUALLY WILL SHOW UP BACK IN THE
OFFICE WITH A FOUR-PAGE OUTLINE ABOUT A VENTRILOQUIST)

I admit that I exaggerated the story conference a bit, but they can
sometimes seem this bizarre. Nevertheless, this writer made a sale. Her
outline will be revised, probably extensively, and the notes reviewed
with her at a subsequent meeting.

She will then write a complete first draft, which again will be discussed during a meeting at which she's present. Then she'll turn in her
final draft.

This is the "final" draft for her only. After the second draft, she will
have no more to do with writing the script, but it will be changed considerably before it airs. Those changes will be made by the show's writing staff without consulting her.

Quite possibly, the story may be changed so that it's about a bullfighter
and an animal rights activist. Somehow they find a submarine and sit around
talking about it over hamburgers and shakes at a diner. Who knows?

This fictional playlet shows some of the problems that a freelance
writer has in selling a story to a sitcom. The author has no idea what
taboos the network or the show itself might have. I actually did pitch a
story once only to find that the network didn't want this particular star
to be shown eating on camera. The freelancer also has no way of knowing what stories are in the works or have already been taped.

When you consider a show like M*A*S*H* ran for many years and
produced about twenty-six shows each year, you have to figure that,
after a few seasons, the odds are against you coming up with anything
they haven't already done or considered.

Our playlet also demonstrates why it's best if the writer lives
near where the show is produced. (We'll talk more about that later in
this chapter.)

The scenario does have a happy ending, though, because the freelancer ends up with a sale. She got a story assignment for two reasons. First, the powers that be liked her writing style so they arranged a story meeting. Second, they liked one of her story ideas.

If you have an established reputation, it may be easy to get a story conference. Either the producers will be familiar with your work, or your agent will work hard to make them aware of your credits. If you don't have an established reputation, the buyer will want to see a sample of your writing. As a freelance writer, you'll either need an agent to market your talents or you'll have to send out spec scripts on your own to try to impress some producers. They'll want to know whether you can handle a storyline and dialogue before they contract with you for a freelance script. The relentless schedule of television makes producing a weekly series hectic. Even under ideal conditions, some say it is impossible. Consequently, no one wants anything that's going to make the task yet more difficult. The producers want reasonable assurance that any script assignment they hand out is going to be professionally executed.

For your spec script, you don't need to write for a specific show—any sitcom script will serve the purpose. Therefore, it's to your benefit to write for those shows that you enjoy and know well. Having watched a show regularly, you'll know the characters and it will be easier for you to write for them.

It's a good idea to pick from among the most popular current shows to write for. It makes the producer's task easier because he's also familiar with the show and the characters.

All producers read scripts in search of new talent, but not many of them like to. Most of them read into a script only until they find one or two glaring errors, then reject it, and move on to the next script. It's thus in your interest not to make any boo-boos. Since you're trying to demonstrate your expertise, your script needs to prove that you're aware of the everyday realities of television production.

Respect the Performers and their Characters

One fact of television life is that the producer has to do a show with stars. These stars attract an audience, they get paid handsomely, and they expect to be treated as the stars. They don't look kindly on newcomers stealing their thunder. It's incredibly difficult to produce a show that features a new character who is funnier than the regulars.

Producers often read scripts where writers create a new character who fits right into the show. The writing may be superb and the new character may be hilarious, but you simply can't do that to a cast—and keep your job.

Certainly, you've seen shows where a new character was introduced. You can probably think of several shows where that fresh character made such an impact that it led to a spin-off—a new show on the schedule starring that character. Generally, though, shows that highlight someone not in the regular cast are thought through by the production company and written by the staff. It's presumptuous for a beginner to try to create a spin-off with a spec script.

The best way to show off your writing skills with a spec script is by staying with the characters and the format of the established show.

Watch the Budget

Another fact of TV production is that there is never enough money in the budget to do the show. Budgets are constant foes to creativity; your spec script should reflect your awareness of this.

Study the shows you want to write for and notice the sets. Each show has a regular "family" of sets that they use. Certainly, you'll see additional sets being used periodically, but sparingly—not too many in one show. Some sitcoms will feature outside shooting, but again, sparingly.

Any new sets that are introduced cost money. They have to be designed and built. It's expensive, especially if they'll never be used on the show again. Keep your scripts as uncomplicated as possible as far as sets and shooting costs go. Try to limit your writing to the sets you've seen repeatedly on a particular show.

As a producer, I've made this mistake and turned in scripts that had so many sets they wouldn't physically fit on the stage we had to work with. I had to blush a bit and do some fancy rewriting before the show was taped. There is no way a writer can be aware of stage size or other particular limitations, but every spec script should show a general appreciation of the budget constraints of television production. If you're in doubt, play it conservatively. You want to avoid those errors that trigger the reader to discard your script and move on to the next.

Don't Destroy the Premise

Another cold fact of television existence is that the producer is paid quite nicely to put together a show each week and would like to continue producing that show for the rest of the season and for many more seasons to come. Therefore there is no percentage in offering a producer a script that is going to destroy the show.

That may sound stupid, but it really does happen. Writers will try to sell stories that will ruin the premise of a show; for example, if a writer pitches a story in which Ray Romano gets a wonderful job working as a sports writer for the *Los Angeles Times*. In order to take it, he and his family must move to L.A. This means they will no longer live close by the family—Mom, Dad, and brother Robert. That move will either drastically change the format of the show or end it entirely. Why would a producer think of buying a script that would terminate the show?

Note, too, that sitcoms usually wind up at the end of the half hour exactly where they started. Oh, predicaments may be introduced, but they're usually resolved in such a way that next week the show can continue on the same way it did this week. If your script is to show your talents—and be read—it had better respect that principle.

Maintain Established Characterization

A perennial complaint from comedy writers is that characters are too closely guarded by their creators. A classic line from an old show, *My Favorite Martian*, illustrates this. Dialogue in one script was criticized because "a Martian wouldn't say that." How on earth did this particular producer ever find out what a Martian would or would not say?

Nevertheless, the creators of shows, and the actors portraying those roles, have established characters that have personalities and prejudices and beliefs. Any dialogue you write should reflect that characterization, not oppose it.

You're trying to sell scripts. You're building a reputation so that you can eventually create shows and characters of your own. Until you establish that reputation, it's unwise to attack the windmills of television. If it ever comes down to an argument between you and the actor who portrays the character about what that character would say, believe me, the actor is going to win.

Remember, too, that you're not just writing gags now. In writing good sitcom dialogue, your joke-writing principles must be altered somewhat. The people you're writing for usually aren't inherently funny people like Robin Williams or Ellen DeGeneres. You are now writing for *characters*.

Williams and DeGeneres in doing their acts are on stage to make you laugh. That's what they do for a living. That is what their audience expects. Even outlandish setups seem logical from them. However, sitcom characters aren't onscreen to make us laugh. (The actors may be, but the characters aren't.) The characters are there to react to the situation in their own way. The writers try to make them react so that it will be funny and will make the audience laugh, but that is not the character's primary goal.

The difference may seem subtle and nitpicky, but it is very important. For example, some boxing enthusiasts argue that boxing isn't as violent as football. While the football devotees counter that the primary objective in boxing is to knock an opponent senseless but that football's violence is unintended.

A stand-up comedian is like a one-punch boxer who intends to "knock you senseless" with dynamite material. Everyone expects it, so that comic can throw his most devastating routines at you. The actor in a situation comedy, though, has to be more subtle. He acts. He is a character in a situation, and his dialogue and reactions must arise from that situation. *His* dynamite material has to refer to the circumstances.

Obviously, both circumstance and material have to be funny. From the writer's standpoint, though, the fun has to be approached from a different angle. Story, plot, and character are supreme in a sitcom, and they dictate the humor.

Make It Believable

In good sitcom writing, jokes move the story forward. They are consistent with the storyline and with the characters. The Marx Brothers film *Monkey Business* begins on shipboard with dialogue that says something like this:

> SEAMAN: *Captain, there are four crewmen trapped in the hold below deck.*
> CAPTAIN: *How do you know there are four of them?*
> SEAMAN: *They're singing "Sweet Adeline."*

The Marx Brothers' peculiar zaniness marked them more as comedians than comic actors. Their inimitable antics allowed them to violate rules. This particular line got a big laugh, so it accomplished its purpose, but let's study it in relation to our discussion of sitcom writing.

The line is unbelievable; it doesn't flow from the situation. If a panic-stricken crewman approached his captain with news of an emergency, the captain would want to know all the details. What is the exact problem? Could the emergency be controlled or would it spread to the rest of the ship. What was being done about it? But in this scene the captain asks how the seaman knows there are four trapped men. Why? Simply to set up the punch line.

In this instance, the joke took precedence over the situation. The Marx Brothers were unparalleled jokesters, so this technique was acceptable for them—but it should not be used in writing situation comedy dialogue. You shouldn't force even a good joke in where it doesn't belong.

Test this theory out for yourself by watching some sitcoms—both those you like and those you don't. Analyze them to see why you prefer some to others. You might be surprised to find that the jokes per se are just as powerful in one as they are in the other. The difference may be that the gags are sometimes out of place. They might be funny but unbelievable under the given circumstances.

Let's let the Marx Brothers off the hook by citing an example from a show that I produced, *Three's Company*. One particular episode illustrates how a good joke can be forced into an implausible situation:

Chrissy, one of the female leads on the show, is dating a policeman. Through some mix-up, she and Jack, the male lead on the show, manage to handcuff themselves together. Because the policeman Chrissy is dating has been guilty of other minor rule infractions, he may get in serious trouble if his superiors discover that civilians have his handcuffs.

When the policeman's commanding sergeant comes to the apartment, Jack and Chrissy, still handcuffed, hide in the bathroom. For some reason, the sergeant barges in there and Chrissy pretends she's showering—while Jack hides behind the shower curtain. The sergeant, embarrassed, excuses himself and exits. Conveniently (for the writers), though, he leaves his hat in the bathroom. As Janet, the other female character on the show, leads him to the door, he remembers his hat.

Here's the questionable scene (as if what has happened already made sense): The officer charges right back into the bathroom and almost catches the handcuffed Chrissy and Jack. Chrissy quickly grabs a towel while Jack frantically maneuvers to stay out of sight behind the towel.

The physical sight gags were hilarious. The audience, the final judge of comedy, agreed. What argument do we have with a scene that got loud laughter from the viewers?

Well, it's unbelievable. It strains credibility. Jack and Chrissy's situation is funny because they're in jeopardy, but sooner or later the audience is going to recognize that the jeopardy should never have happened. It was forced; it was unreal.

To begin with, the sergeant would never go into a closed bathroom without knocking. Circumstances didn't warrant it. (Let's excuse that for a minute, though.) Once he gets in there and finds a woman showering, the officer would NEVER go back in without knocking just to retrieve his cap. Janet was there with him. He could have politely asked her to retrieve his hat. Obviously, though, if Janet goes in, Chrissy and Jack have nothing to hide from her, so all their comic antics would be lost. It's the same reason the captain said in the Marx Brothers' film, "How do you know there are four of them?"

When you watch some of the current shows that you consider well-written, you will probably notice that the comedy appears natural and always seems to flow from the story.

Apply these guidelines to your own dialogue writing:

Map out Your Storyline and Scene: You'll know exactly where you're going and what you want to accomplish in each scene. This will keep your dialogue from rambling and your writing uniformly tight and compact. By following a road map, you'll discover that each line of your dialogue will be relevant and will have a purpose.

Ask Yourself What Normally Would Follow: Comedy writers are afraid of being predictable—yet that is exactly what you must be in writing dialogue. Well-defined characters should come across as real people. There is a predictability in the conversation of real people. If you question this, ask someone for directions. If they know the way, they'll tell you—and more often than not will include the phrase, "You can't miss it."

Your dialogue should convey that predictability. It can be done with ingenuity—that's the skill of the writer. But if someone breaks into a room and shouts, "My God, the maid has just been murdered," the next line of dialogue is not, "Where did you get those beautiful shoes?"

Ask yourself what the people in your story should say—and then write it for them.

Base Your Jokes on Characters and Situations: Once you know where your scenario is going, and what has to be conveyed to the audience, you can create your jokes, sight gags, physical shtick, or whatever. But remember that they must be consistent with the situation and must flow naturally from your characters. Analyze the situation and allow it to generate the humor. Resist the urge to force a joke in merely for the laugh.

Sitcom Structure

A situation comedy is basically is a story that has jokes in it, but *it's a story first.* When you sell a sitcom, you don't go to the producer and tell him jokes. You tell him a story. If the story works, the jokes will follow.

You must have a good, strong plot. What is a plot? It's a well-defined premise, with complications along the way, eventually resolving itself. That can also be called a good beginning, middle, and end.

That last phrase should sound familiar to you. It's basically the same formula we learned earlier for sketch writing. Sketch form is similar to sitcom, film, or novel form. The difference is largely in scope. With a sketch you generally investigate one incident and remain with it. With the larger forms, like a half-hour story or a ninety-minute film, you can write about other characters and events surrounding your main plot. The basic plot form, though, remains constant—goal or premise, complications, and a resolution. Beginning, middle, and end.

The premise is what your story is about. It's the goal your hero hopes to accomplish. It's the direction you start your audiences' minds along. At the beginning it generally seems attainable, fairly innocuous, and straightforward.

But then you introduce the complications—the obstacles to the goal. Obviously, without these you have a fairly weak story.It's the inventiveness of the complications that make a story both interesting and funny. To use a classic situation comedy show as an example, one episode of *The Dick Van Dyke Show* had Rosemarie, the show's perennial "old maid," going to dinner at Van Dyke's house. He has invited an old friend and Rosemarie is eager to impress this gentleman and perhaps start a romantic relationship with him. She dresses in a very sexy gown and mink coat and is determined to come on strong. However, when the gentleman arrives, we discover that he's now a priest.

The complication requires a solution, but often the solution can lead to other complications. For instance, Rosemarie's initial solution is to leave her fur coat on all through dinner so that the priest won't see her provocative dress. That presents the other complication—how to act nonchalant while eating dinner in a full-length mink coat.

These false resolutions can continue as long as they're funny or for as long as you have time. Some movies rely entirely on the process of complication and false resolution repeated over and over again.

Eventually, of course, the story must resolve. All the problems disappear and happiness is restored—but that's easier said than done. As we discovered in sketch writing, the ending can sometimes be the most difficult part. In writing a story you create a dilemma. Often, it's easier to create a complication than it is to untangle one—it's easier to mix up the pieces of a puzzle than it is to put them together.

Unlike the sketch ending, though, the sitcom ending needn't be as strong a punch line. Nevertheless, it does need to have certain attributes of the punch line. It must give the audience the feeling that the story was worth watching. It must be strong and believable enough to justify the half hour that preceded it. You don't want a groaner.

My writing partner and I once sold a sitcom script. The producers had worked with us before and trusted our judgment, so they gave us a certain leeway in creating the story. We had a beginning and a middle but no idea how the thing was going to end. (I don't always follow the advice I write in my books.) We had written ourselves into a corner because we created a dilemma from which there seemed no escape.

We got to our office one day and vowed to finish the script come what may. We had to find a resolution. I inserted a sheet of paper into the typewriter (we still wrote on typewriters in those days) and numbered it "Page 28."

Then the producers phoned us. "Send your script to us immediately," they said.

I said, "We don't have an ending yet, but we'll have it by end of day."

They said, "Not good enough. We just got word that we're cancelled. Send us whatever you have so we can pay you for the script."

We sent off the uncompleted script.

We never did find out how that story would end.

It's advisable to have a complete story mapped out in your head and outlined before beginning the dialogue. Writing is so much easier when you know where you're going.

In selling a story, though, the ending isn't that important. What will interest the buyers most is that first complication. If the problem you present is fascinating enough, they assume that jokes and a resolution will follow. Your sales pitch should present the goal and build to the interesting complication. They'll buy that.

Creating Ideas

Where do we find obstacles to the goal? The same place we find jokes—who knows? You can stimulate your mind pretty much the same way you do for jokes:

- Ask questions and make statements. What is the worst thing that can happen as your hero pursues his goal? Who else might get involved? What could possibly go wrong? The answer to these queries might present the plot points you're searching for.
- Analyze and dissect your situation thoroughly. The different elements and themes you uncover may trigger some plot complications you can use.

Writing a sitcom is like writing a short screenplay—you should know characterization and plotting very well. The field is much too extensive for me to touch on anything but the highlights in this volume, but there are many excellent books available. One book by Syd Field, *Screenplay, the Foundations of Screenwriting* ($16.00 paperback, Dell Publishing, 2005), is a well-respected how-to on screenwriting.

A Word of Encouragement; a Word of Caution

Before leaving this subject, I want to defend the industry so as to give you a realistic view of the selling of sitcoms for television.

Producers sometimes are bum-rapped for promoting a closed industry. It's not true. We need stories, we need ideas, and we need writers. We are open to all of them. Nevertheless, it's very rare that a story idea is purchased from anyone who doesn't live in the production company's immediate vicinity.

As I demonstrated earlier in the playlet, producers sometimes buy a show the author didn't intend to sell. He pitches one story, it's changed to something else, and finally he writes an outline about something he never even heard of before. It evolved from the meeting.

The outline he writes may go through the same metamorphosis, so that the author's first draft bears little resemblance to the outline, and the second draft may be even further removed from the first draft.

When the author watches the show on television, the only thing he may recognize is his name on the credits.

The writer is involved with and consents to many of these changes, and some happen after he is absent from the project, but the point is that producers don't buy a single story idea or storyline. They purchase an ongoing project.

Whether this process is the most efficient or not is irrelevant—it's just the way things happen in television. My partner and I once sold a script about a young boy minding a plant for a friend who was going out of town. The boy's parents mistakenly thought it was a marijuana plant and pulled a leaf off to sniff it. The producers objected to mutilating a plant the youngster was so fond of. We dropped that incident from our script.

When we saw the show on the air, one of the characters was so scared the police would find the plant that he ate the entire thing. We weren't permitted to pluck a single leaf, but in rewriting by the producers' staff, the plant was completely destroyed. That's how thinking varies from day to day.

Obviously, producers aren't going to pay top dollar to someone so far removed from the project that he or she can't participate. If they did, they would be buying an idea that's unchangeable, and so it's worthless to them.

The same principle applies to the purchase of variety show sketches, but for a different reason. There are strict rules covering payment for such purchases and they're not inexpensive. Most variety shows have a staff on salary, so there's no percentage in buying a single idea that may change many times when a group of writers is already being paid to come up with ideas.

You can write sketches, though, for other media than television—

for example, local theatrical or radio shows—whereas the sitcom can only be successfully produced on television.

Most writers dream of creating a new show and selling it to television as a series. That's done many times a year because each new season brings new weekly series. However, the odds are against this happening to a newcomer. Most pilots, because they are so expensive, are assigned only to writers and producers with proven credits. Again, it's an area of constant change. Hardly any pilot idea is purchased, scripted, produced, and put on the air without many network meetings and modifications. It's an ongoing process and the reputable professionals have to be close by at all times.

Then why even discuss sitcom writing if it's such an impossibility? Why should a beginning writer even attempt this form?

It's *not* an impossibility. I've had great success in handing out assignments to first-time sitcom writers, and many of the people my partner and I brought into the Writers' Guild are now scripting and producing weekly series. I simply feel that a writer can work more efficiently and wisely if she recognizes the percentages. A person can waste much energy trying to create a pilot for TV when the more prudent path is to write for established shows, create a reputation, and use that to eventually sell a pilot.

Second, a beginning writer should attempt the sitcom because all writing is beneficial. We learn from our work. Writing spec scripts— even those that won't sell—teaches you to write ones that will. And by writing, you'll have those showcase scripts that you'll eventually need if you're serious about writing TV sitcoms anyway.

Remember, the two best ways to learn your craft are to observe what others are doing and to practice. Watch TV, study what's being produced, and write.

PART THREE
BUILDING YOUR CAREER

"By perseverance the snail reached the ark."
—Charles Haddon Spurgeon

- *18* -

The Proper Attitude

The overriding question lurking behind every other question beginning writers ask is, "How do I get into comedy writing?" The answer is so simple and obvious that some readers may feel I'm trying to get off the hook with a pat answer. But I'm not. You get into comedy writing the same way you get into anything else you want in life—be good at it.

It's Not the Breaks

The way to succeed in anything is to be good at it and to keep getting better. Excel at what you do.

The golfing phenomenon Tiger Woods was a great amateur and now he's the outstanding pro, arguably the greatest of all time. How did he become that? Did he have connections? Did someone in his family know somebody who managed to get him in? Was it a massive PR campaign? Did he wrangle his way into notoriety with great charisma and personality?

No, he got to be a great professional golfer because he hits the ball far. He hits the ball straight. He hits the ball well. He outplays the greatest golfers in the world. He's good at what he does and he is determined to keep getting better. That's why he collects trophies and prize money.

The point is this: anyone with the skills of a Tiger Woods would have to be as successful as he is. That expertise can't be hidden.

In the early 1960s, there was a young athlete whom no one quite believed in. Oh, he was good. He had won an Olympic gold medal in his sport, but now he was a professional who wanted a shot at the heavyweight boxing championship of the world and not too many experts thought he was qualified.

Sonny Liston was then the reigning heavyweight champ. He was formidable, considered by many to be unbeatable. Nevertheless, this young upstart talked, shouted, and fought his way into a championship fight against Liston. Very few sportswriters gave him a chance. Hardly any of them picked him as the favorite in the fight.

Of course, Cassius Clay, who later changed his name to Muhammad Ali, did defeat Sonny Liston to become the world's heavyweight champion. He knocked him out again in the first round of the rematch. Then he became known as "The Greatest." Admittedly, this was by his own proclamation (he wasn't shy about his talents), but many boxing aficionados and fans since have agreed with that assessment. When did he change from the kid who had no chance to becoming, to many, the greatest of all time? He never did. He was good enough when he got the shot at Sonny Liston. He knew it, but the rest of the world didn't. He had to convince them, and convince them he did.

The proficiency of both Tiger Woods and Ali did their marketing for them. Their talent could not be denied. They both had to become the best in their respective sports.

Consider this for a minute, though. Imagine Tiger Woods saying, "I love golf. Boy, if someone could only get me into a professional tournament, I'd really practice hard and try to become the best in the world." Or picture the young Cassius Clay saying, "I don't want to work real hard unless I'm sure I'll be able to get a championship fight." You would never have heard of either of them. They had to be good to get the opportunity. They had to be good to get where they got and to stay there.

"How do I get to be a superb golfer?" Be good.

"How do I get to become a boxing champ?" Be good.

"How do I get into comedy writing?" Be good.

There's a myth that hidden somewhere in the United States are people much more talented than the big names. Someone somewhere can sing better than Barbra Streisand, but Barbra just got lucky. The guy in the next office is really funnier than Robin Williams, but no one has discovered him yet.

That simply isn't true.

I once worked on a television show where an entertainer who was not one of my favorites put on a private performance for everyone connected with the show. He hired a band and put on his entire nightclub act just for us. Frankly, this didn't thrill me. It was after a long day at work and I just wanted to go home. Professional courtesy, though, dictated that I stay. Well, by the end of the performance I had reluctantly to admit that he deserved the superstar status he enjoyed. He kept a jaded show-business audience enthralled for over ninety minutes.

Somewhere, someone feels that they could have had his success if they'd only had the same breaks. They're wrong. If they had had his showmanship, his talent, his vivacity, and his charisma, they wouldn't have needed *breaks*. Someone would have discovered them.

This point is very important for beginners to understand for two reasons: First, it tells you that you have to do the work. If Tiger were a mediocre golfer, but his uncle was a big shot on the professional tour, he wouldn't be famous today. "Connections" won't bring you success, either—talent will.

Second, it tells you that if you do perfect your skills, you won't have to depend on breaks—someone will discover you.

Breaks are tremendously overrated. They're nothing but everyday, ordinary circumstances. They don't officially become "breaks" until after the fact. Every name performer talks about his or her "big break." However, if that particular break didn't occur right then, it would have occurred later. If Cassius Clay hadn't gotten that contract to fight Sonny Liston, at another time he would have fought whoever was then current champ and still have been "The Greatest." A comic genius like Robin Williams would have become a major star even without *Mork and Mindy*.

To me, it's like taking a ride from point A to point B in the family car. You take a certain route and you arrive at point B. Then you say, "I turned left at 22nd and Siegel Street. If that corner had been roadblocked, I never would have arrived." Nonsense, you would have taken an alternate route. The same is true of so-called breaks.

Phyllis Diller Had this to Say about Breaks:

"People have a mistaken idea about breaks. There's no such thing as a break. If you're looking for breaks, you've got your eye on the wrong thing. Many folks turn down opportunities because they're usually disguised as 'hard work.' You'd be amazed at the number of people who won't go out on a limb, or progress, or change, and hurt a little for a while, to expand their powers. Most take the easy way, the comfy way. If you're not hurting a little, you're not growing."

Let me tell you about two young writers many years ago who read a magazine article on comedy writing that I wrote. They both corresponded with me and asked for assistance in their careers. Their material was promising, so I worked with each of them.

I asked the first writer to send me a set quota of material each week; this was a way of getting her to polish her skills with just a touch of encouragement from me. But the material never arrived. Excuse after excuse was offered along with promises that she would get on it next week or next month.

The other writer did everything I asked. In fact, he even wrote me back and said, "I've done all that. What do I do next?"

I didn't know. I'd never gotten this far before. I did give him some advice—and he followed it. His work improved and eventually I recommended him for an assignment on a television variety show. He got the job and moved on from there to a thriving career.

The second writer progressed from show to show not because I recommended him. I wish I could command that much respect in the industry. He was hired for job after job because he was good.

How do you get into comedy writing? Be good. It's not an oversimplification.

The next question, obviously, is "How do I go about being good?" You work as hard at your craft now as if you already achieved the success that you hope for. You write, listen, and you read as if you were the producer of a major television show. You perfect your skills now so that when the circumstances—not the breaks—present themselves, you can deliver.

I hope this hasn't made attaining a career in comedy writing sound easy. It's not. It's simply not complicated. There's a difference. If you come to me with a desire to play the piano, I'd advise taking lessons. That's not complicated, but it doesn't make your learning process easy.

Don't misunderstand this point, either. Once you're good, success probably won't be immediate. It takes a while for others to recognize your skills. To become successful you not only have to be good at what you do, you have to convince others. This demands perseverance. You'll have to show them over and over again before it finally sinks in. That's how you market your talent.

Acquiring the skill is the easiest part because you're totally in control. You depend on no one else. If it takes six hours of practice a day for three years to become a proficient jazz drummer, you can arrange your life to do that. Convincing others of your proficiency, though, can be frustrating because you're not in charge. They are.

Once, playing a silly parlor game, I learned a lesson that may benefit you. Some friends and I were taking a test that consisted of names of colors printed in contrasting inks—the word "blue" might be printed in red, and the word "yellow" in green, and so on. There were about sixty words in this list, and the test was taken by going through the list calling out the color of the ink, even though the word read a different color. Someone would time you, and your speed would supposedly tell something about your personality. Got the image?

Several of us took the test and I had a very fast time. When we read the results, the article said that my speed indicated I was careless with details. Naturally, I objected, but people said it was true because in going so quickly I probably made several mistakes. "I made no mistakes," I argued. They smiled patronizingly. Now I was a bit annoyed and determined to prove my point.

I took the test again with comparable speed while someone else checked my accuracy. He stopped me in the middle and said, "You just made four mistakes on this line alone." I said, "I'm not on that line. I'm on the line below it." Again, the patronizing smiles. Now I was getting angry. "If I can do this test in thirty seconds and this man does it in sixty seconds, how can he possibly test my accuracy?"

Finally, to prevent me from going into rage, my friends wrote down the correct answers on a separate piece of paper. I did the test at the same speed and made *no errors*.

You needn't applaud. I'm not telling the story to boast of my prowess at calling out colors spelling other colors. What I did learn was that often in life we will be evaluated and judged by people less qualified than ourselves. And that's frustrating.

You'll work hard at your craft. You'll assemble a showcase of your writing. You'll present it to someone who knows less about humor than you do. Authority doesn't always indicate ability or good judgment. You'll be rejected for the wrong reasons. You'll have to try again.

During your journey toward success, you'll receive many unjustified "no's." It's not really unfair; it's a fact of life. You must remember, though, that it only takes one justified "yes" to erase all those "no's." You don't have to have everyone accept your writing—just the people who know what they're doing.

Nevertheless, it's disappointing and irritating to have good efforts rejected. I almost blew my stack because somebody told me I couldn't do a puzzle in a newspaper. If you really want to make a success of humor writing, it will help if you approach the challenge with a realistic attitude.

It Won't Happen Overnight

Some aspirants have what I call "Send the Limo" syndrome. I recognize it because I had it for several years. Writers send a few pages of material out and sit home and wait for some Hollywood mogul to reply by sending a chauffeured limousine to whisk them away to Tinseltown. It's a fantasy we all have in the back of our minds.

It's not going to happen and you do yourself a disservice in expecting it because your disappointment could kill your enthusiasm. Your frustration could lead you to abandon a promising career when your first few queries don't bring dramatic results.

Any worthwhile career builds slowly and solidly. It will have its share of minor victories and slight defeats. It probably will not explode in a dazzling burst of triumph.

Why? Because first of all, if the person you sent your material to is at all important, he will have seen some pretty fantastic material before. He's not going to be knocked off his feet—not even if your writing is way above average quality.

Secondly, most of the people you will submit your material to don't really know good stuff when they see it. I include myself in that indictment. Remember that there are very few good judges of comedy. The rest of us are guessing.

I've read sketches and sitcom scripts I hated, then on tape night watched them go through the roof. I've read material that amazed me with its brilliance; on tape night it sat there like a lump.

I wrote a sketch for a variety show once that I was convinced bordered on genius. Seeing this masterpiece taped before a live, laughing audience was going to be one of the highlights of my career. I stood in the wings (so I could go onstage quickly when the audience called out,

"Author, author") and watched the sketch die a horrible death. I was crushed and confused—then convulsed with laughter when an old gentleman in the audience turned to his wife and said matter-of-factly, "It was a good idea."

We just plain, flat-out don't know, so an experienced comedy writer is reluctant to get too exuberant about any material, including yours, until it's been tested before the ultimate jury—the audience.

Why a Career Takes Time

Most prominent people in show business aren't in the habit of discovering new talent. They deal mostly in proven commodities. Las Vegas, for example, is the reputed show business capital of the world. Producers there don't look for new acts to put in their multi-million dollar showrooms? No. They bank on stars. They want a sure thing—established people with proven drawing power.

This same rationale applies to you and your writing. To impress a producer you have to be better than the known talent in your field. "Better?" you ask. That's right—*better*. Why? Well, let's look at it from the buyer's point of view. He knows what the certified talent can deliver. He's worked with them before and knows their output is good, consistent and on time, they are dependable, easy to work with, and will accept changes readily. You, on the other hand, are a question mark. He doesn't know if you can write fast, if you can deliver under pressure, if you can you take editorial criticism or meet deadlines. So long as you're *just as good as* the other guy, why shouldn't he go with the proven talent?

The only way you can gain an edge over this competitor is to be better than he is. Now you're offering the buyer something in exchange for the risk he's taking. You have to continue doing this until your reputation is established and you become the proven talent.

Be Realistic about What You're Worth

We all have to serve an apprenticeship and deal with the cold facts of life. Among those cold facts is compensation. Samuel Johnson once said that no man except a blockhead would write for anything except money. Now, money is one of my favorite rewards for hours spent at the computer keyboard, but a young career can sometimes be derailed by asking for too much too soon. During your apprenticeship, your skills will grow—as will your remuneration. But your skills should grow faster.

A novice writer may read in the paper that so-and-so makes a thousand dollars a page for his monologue material. Now a comic who works weekends for fifty dollars a night asks the young writer for some material. "Okay," the writer agrees, "but it'll cost you a thousand bucks a page." No sale.

First of all, any salary you read in the paper you should divide by two. We all lie. (Someday I hope to make as much money as I tell my friends I make.)

There's a show business story about that point which I'd like to pass on to you. A certain Hollywood writer was walking along Wilshire Boulevard and saw the movie he had written playing in a theatre. He casually walked in and asked the manager how the film was doing box-office-wise. The manager screamed, "This is the worst movie we ever ran in here. It's killing us. I may go absolutely broke." The writer said, "How much did you take in?" The manager moaned, "So far we did twelve dollars." The poor author was brokenhearted. He slumped over to Nate and Al's delicatessen for some lunch. While he was sitting there another writer came in and said, "Hey, I see your film is over at the Wilshire. How's it doing at the box office?" The guy said, "I don't want to talk about it." The other writer said, "Come on, I'm a good buddy. How's your film doing? You can tell me." The author said, "Okay. It did twenty-four dollars."

The moral of the story is that you shouldn't believe everything you hear or read about the money being paid to writers. Much of it is inflated. Besides, it's not really a true measure of what a beginning writer can or should demand. Some established comedy writers may be so successful and so busy that they discourage monologue assignments. They may charge exorbitant rates just to avoid being hired. That practice certainly isn't in the best interest of the beginner.

During your apprenticeship and while your career is growing, you'll need experience and credits more than you need top dollar for your work. If you work hard and constantly improve, the money will keep getting better. Perfecting your craft should take precedence over accounting figures.

Remember, the first step in marketing your wares is to be good.

- 19 -

Getting Your Career Going

Becoming a barber is not difficult. You find a barber school on the internet or in the Yellow Pages, enroll, take the required courses, get your certificate, and open your shop. Becoming a brain surgeon is just as uncomplicated. You study premed, then go to medical school, serve your internship, complete your residency, have your diploma framed, hang out your shingle, and subscribe to lots of magazines for your waiting room.

Yes, I'm making light of these professions and don't mean to offend any barbers or brain surgeons reading this book. I'm simply pointing out that there's no real mystery to taking up either occupation. The requisite steps can be outlined by any qualified counselor. Comedy writing is different. It's not an exact science. There's no diploma required and no licenses to be obtained.

Each new venture into comedy writing is a journey over uncharted land. No two professional humorists I've talked with have ever arrived at their careers by the same route. No two have ever followed any predesigned paths. There simply are none.

Your journey toward a career in humor writing will be an adventure, like the home computer programs that are listed as "adventures." These are disks that you insert into your computer; they place the operator in a situation. Then, by deduction and experimentation, you try to reach a destination or accomplish a goal. Aficionados tell me that some of these adventures take from nine months to a year to solve.

Your comedy-writing adventure may be like that. You already have a goal, but how do you accomplish it? Pretty much the same way as the home computer operator—by trial and error.

Do the Research

You first task is research. You'll want to know more about this business you're trying to enter. You'll want to read books on the subject, and magazines or newspapers that deal with comedy, and you'll want to talk to people who are associated with the industry.

The nice thing about the research is that it's all interlocking. It's like solving a jigsaw puzzle. Each time you find the correct place for a piece, you not only have solved that segment of the puzzle, but you've also given yourself information that you need to solve other segments. So you can jump into this research almost anywhere and it will lead you to the next logical step.

If you have a book on comedy, it may refer you to periodicals that deal with humor. Should you discover a periodical, it may suggest reading particular books. Suppose you know someone who deals in comedy? They may be aware of magazines and books you might be interested in. It all interlocks.

Suppose you know nothing. How do you begin your research? At the library. The librarian can be helpful in finding periodicals, associations, or books on your subject. However, sometimes you benefit more from doing the research for yourself. A glance through the reference section may uncover some books or ideas that neither you nor the librarian would have considered. A search through the library's online catalog may present new thoughts to your mind.

And, of course, the all-encompassing research tool today is the Internet. Get on and just start searching for any and all connections to comedy, humor, and comedy writing.

It's amazing how knowledge is intertwined and how quickly information can be compiled merely by starting somewhere. It's almost as easy as unraveling a sweater. Grab any loose thread and pull.

Where do you start? Anywhere. I recommend a publication that I started many years ago, called *Round Table*. You can contact our office at PO Box 786, Agoura Hills, CA 91376, or call (818) 865-7833. Of course, you can always check out details on the Internet, too, at www.writingcomedy.com. I subtitled *Round Table* as a gathering place for comedy writers and humorists because it's truly a dialogue form of publication. We encourage reader input so that subscribers may benefit from each other's experiences.

However, a copy of the weekly *Variety* may begin your research chain. It doesn't matter where you start unraveling the sweater so long as you keep on pulling.

Personal Contact

The dialogue aspect of your research is important. Your investigation will produce the names of many people who are in the comedy business. Call or write or e-mail and ask for an appointment. You may be surprised to discover how friendly and helpful these people can be …and want to be.

When I began my career, I toyed with contacting a gentleman whom I didn't know personally but knew of. I composed several letters—only to destroy them, thinking it would be presumptuous of me to write and ask for guidance. Finally, I worked up the courage and wrote. He responded with a phone call and we met a few days later. This gentleman became a true champion of my work, my mentor, the man who picked up my spirits when things didn't go well and my best friend to this day. He has been more responsible for my success than any other person. All as a result of a letter that I was afraid to write.

This gentleman was also influential in another important letter that I wrote. Phyllis Diller once canceled a scheduled interview appointment with him—he was a journalist—but left her home address so that he could send a list of questions she would answer by return mail. I sent a letter to that address, introducing myself as an aspiring comedy writer, and included several pages of jokes. Phyllis responded with a check buying many of my submissions.

This association helped launch my television writing career and gave me access to future clients.

I'm a big advocate of letter writing. Most people who are interested in the same things you're interested in delight in talking about them. Not everyone will answer your letters. Some will offer only a polite, noncommittal response. But some people you write to may become helpful pen pals and friends.

Of course, nowadays, you can substitute "e-mail" for "letter writing."

Don't Expect too Much

As we discussed in the previous chapter, your letter writing will produce better results if you are totally realistic in your approach. People are generally gracious with their knowledge and often are happy to share it with others. Many will even read samples of your material and might even offer constructive criticism. It's unfair, though, to expect much more of them.

All of us hope that someone will adopt us, sell our material, or get a job for us—but they won't, they can't, and they shouldn't. Why? Because those are *your duties*. No one else can really accomplish them for you. It's not only improper for you to ask that of someone else, it would be a disservice to you if they did.

Getting a person one job does her no good unless she has the ability to continue on from that one to the next. If you are that talented, your material will get the job for you.

✔ *Round Table* asked Phyllis Diller if it was easy nowadays to break into the comedy profession. She replied:

It's never been easy and it isn't today. But it can be done if you believe in yourself.

Sometimes new writers take actions parallel to entertainers breaking in and think they have to have loads of assistance. They have to realize the best helping hand may be at the end of their own arm. People fear going it alone. They want lots of help, somebody else to do all the work. People who think showbiz is all glamour sometimes think there's nothing to it—just walk out and be gorgeous, walk out and sing, or dance, or talk. Let me say this: Into all branches of show business—and that includes comedy writing—go years of work, experience, and training, or all three. When it looks "easy," you're looking at art.

Your letter of inquiry should ask only for an exchange of ideas and perhaps a request that they read some of your samples. Asking too much can turn the reader off.

Didn't I just say, though, that Phyllis Diller did all the things for me I've said a person shouldn't do? Yes and no. She did many nice things for me, but that was after we had worked together for several years. She knew what I could do—and had done.

Remember as a beginning writer, you're faced with the chore of finding out as much about the business as you can. Each bit of information you uncover will lead to several more pieces of knowledge. Some of this material will be tremendously helpful; some will have minimal value and some you'll discard. But it's an interesting adventure, one which will educate you and help your skills grow.

That's also why it's unfair for others to supersede this process. *To get the full benefit of it, you must go through it yourself.*

The Value of Networking

I used networking to get my comedy writing career going. I used it again when I began a career in public speaking. I knew little about the speaking business, so I began my research. I discovered a few books and newsletters on speaking. That led to other publications and eventually to some names. I wrote and called people I met through my reading. In short, I lunched and dined with many of the top speakers in the country. I was a guest in their homes and they in mine. Through the contacts I made, I landed many speaking engagements and spoke at the conventions of some of the major speakers' organizations—the National Speakers Association, The International Platform Association, and Toastmasters International. I went from knowing nothing at all to conducting workshops on humor in speaking in the space of one year.

Through this method of research, I met and spent three enjoyable days visiting with Doc Blakely, one of the top humorous speakers on the circuit at the time. He told me a touching story that applies to all of this. I would like to pass it on to you here (if Doc doesn't mind my paraphrasing).

> *When I first got interested in speaking I went to visit a man who lived near my hometown who was a fantastic and funny speaker. I told him I wanted to do that kind of work, too, and asked if he could help me in any way. He patiently listened to me and graciously listened to a tape of one of my talks. He seemed to like my work, so I asked if he could help me in any way. He asked what he would get in return. I offered him a price and he wanted more. I offered him a percentage of my income for a year and he still wanted more. Now I started to get a bit scared. I finally asked how much he wanted. He said, "You're going to make it as a speaker. You're going to work hard and be very good someday. When you arrive, some youngster is going to come to you and want help. My price for helping you is that you have to promise me you'll help that person, too."*

I love that story just as it stands, but there's an ending that makes it even more intriguing. This gentleman died not too long after helping Doc get started, and left a very young son behind. Many years later that boy—not knowing anything about this story—came to Doc Blakely to ask advice on becoming a speaker.

Rejection

Sometime during the course of your fact finding, you're going to have to submit some of your material for scrutiny. This can be a frightening experience because of the overwhelming fear of rejection. So much hard work and so much of yourself goes into your writing that it's painful to see it turned down. Yet we all have that fear because we've already admitted that we don't know comedy—we're only guessing. The guy who's reading it can always guess differently than the guy who wrote it. Even if we think it's funny, the reader may not.

A most terrifying experience is to sit in a room and watch someone read a sketch or monologue you've just written. Silence can take on a whole new coloration while that's happening. I always pick that moment to go out and get myself a cup of coffee or search for the nearest (or farthest) men's room.

It's also difficult to have to read someone's work who's sitting there gazing intently into your face for any expression of approval or rejection. It's always better to have the author leave his material with you so that you can read it, digest it, and think of some excuse for rejecting it besides, "It's simply not funny."

Most head writers abide by this unwritten law. They dance around a rejection with explanations like, "I don't think the characters really come alive," or "The premise is too unbelievable." Generally, they'll say anything except it's not funny.

Bill Cosby once did a routine about the corner bar his father would sometimes visit. He talked about his macho dad having a few drinks before heading home for dinner, and how he, a youngster, was sent to get his dad home. "Mom says you gotta get home right now or she's coming after you." None of the other men in the bar would say a word in ridicule. They all *knew they could be next.*

That's the way writers feel about saying, "It's not funny." Any of us, regardless of experience, could be next.

Facing possible or even probable rejection can frequently discourage a beginning writer from submitting material. It shouldn't. Shakespeare advised us well and succinctly when he said, "Doubts are traitors and make us lose the good we oft might win by fearing to attempt."

Rejection is part of any writer's life. It should be accepted and understood. Often a turndown is an economic reality, not a critique of your submission. Publishing houses, for example, can only produce so many books each year. For the sake of discussion, let's presume the one you send your novel to can publish twenty. Does it then follow that they will only get twenty quality submissions? Of course not. They will get many representative manuscripts. They will only accept twenty and reject the rest.

Rejection is also part of life, period. A painful duty of a television producer is casting. One actor is needed and fifteen hopefuls show up for auditions. The producer selects one for the role, but the others may be equally competent. In watching ballgames on TV, I often hear the cliché, "It's a shame one of the teams has to lose." It's a pity some of our manuscripts have to be rejected, but they do. If God didn't want us to receive rejections, He wouldn't have invented the self-addressed stamped envelope.

The beginning writer must also learn not to take rejection personally. It is not a comment on the quality of your material so much as it is a comment on the person judging your material. Yet again, we remind ourselves that we're only guessing. When you wrote your material, you made an educated guess that it was funny. Whoever reads it and dismisses it as unsuitable is guessing that it isn't funny. He may just be a lousy guesser.

All writers experience these setbacks. When I first started, I seriously toyed with the idea of writing but making my hobby collecting rejection notices. Some were truly disappointing; some were just funny. One stands out. I assembled several pages of monologue material and sent it to a very successful nightclub comic of the time, Joe E. Lewis. I received back a sheet of memo notepaper from the Fontainebleau Hotel in Florida that had written on it, "I already have a writer." Signed Joe E. Lewis.

As a cocky young jokesmith, though, I adopted an attitude that served me well through those apprentice years: I wasn't losing out when someone turned down my material—he was. Whether that arrogance later proved accurate or not didn't matter. It kept me going.

You must remember, too, that rejection is a negative and has no real meaning. It doesn't change anything you're doing. You still continue to strive for acceptance.

When Thomas Edison was struggling to perfect the lightbulb, he tried many substances unsuccessfully. Someone once asked him how many he tried, and Edison told him about three thousand. The gentleman said, "You tried three thousand elements and failed? You know no more now than when you started." Edison corrected him. "You're wrong. I know three thousand things that don't work."

Rejections are not obstacles to a career. They're simply things that don't work and can do us no harm.

Fearing rejection can do harm. It stops you from continuing. That's why it's essential to see how impotent rejection is.

Does anyone know or care how many filaments Edison tried unsuccessfully before finding the right combination? Whether it was one, three thousand, or one million is immaterial because the one success erased all the failures.

When people ask me who I've written for (and many times even when they don't), I say, "I've written for Bob Hope, Phyllis Diller, Carol Burnett, Bill Cosby, Tim Conway..." Wouldn't it be silly to say, "I didn't write for Henny Youngman, Joe E. Lewis, and thousands of others?"

To get your comedy career progressing, you're going to have to learn as much about your profession and your craft as possible. You're also going to have to expose yourself. Your precious material is going to have to be evaluated and judged, and it won't always get good grades. But that shouldn't dissuade you from continuing. Everybody doesn't have to like your material—just somebody who can write checks that don't bounce.

- 20 -

Practicing Your Trade

A woman went into a butcher shop and asked how much the veal cutlets were. The proprietor said, "Eight dollars a pound." The woman was astounded. She said, "What? I can get them across the street for six dollars a pound." The proprietor asked, "Then why don't you get them across the street?" "They don't have any," the woman said. "Oh," the proprietor said. "When we don't have any, they're only five dollars a pound."

I've remembered that joke from many years ago when comedian Myron Cohen told it on *The Ed Sullivan Show*. His skillful dialects did it much more justice than the printed page ever could. Nevertheless, there's a moral here: you can't sell what you don't have. You can't market your material until you've written it.

That seems fairly obvious, but I've found through experience that it isn't. I've periodically been able to recommend beginning writers for assignments. "Send so-and-so some samples of your work," I'd tell them. "Well, I can't," they'd reply. "I don't have anything."

Anyone you query or anyone you are recommended to will want to see samples of your work. There is only one way to get samples of your material and that is to write material.

My best advice to a comedy writer is to set a quota and stick to it. It needn't be a demanding quota, but it must be inflexible. In Chapter 3 we discussed the benefits of setting such a quota but let me repeat why it's an advantage from a marketing standpoint. By writing faithfully you'll build up enough material to assemble a showcase of your material. Perhaps more important, it allows you to select the best of your material as a showcase.

We writers like to feel that everything that rolls out of our printer is brilliant, but experienced writers know better. Some days it sparkles and other days it stinks. The percentage of sparkle to smell is what makes a good writer. Should anyone ask to see some of my work, I select some of the proven sketches from the Carol Burnett or Tim Conway shows or several of my favorite Bob Hope lines and proudly exhibit them. No way am I going to show them all the work I did. There are bombs in there. Heck, one sketch I wrote for *The Carol Burnett Show* was so bad that Joe Hamilton (Carol's husband and executive producer of the show) came on stage in the middle of the taping and said, "Stop doing this." Carol Burnett was so pleased that she kissed him, turned to the audience, and said, "He has just saved our marriage."

So build up a backlog of material from which to select a representative portfolio. Then continually update it. The only way to do that is to write, write, write.

Some of you may feel that this isn't a fair indication of your writing skills. Shouldn't the buyer be able to know how much you can write in a given period and how good that material is? Not really. The buyer wants to know how good you are. He wants to see your top material. He knows the facts of life—some days you'll be slow, some days you'll be bad. But if you prove you can write good material, he'll know that it'll be worth the wait.

Besides, the purchaser of comedy material can afford to be rather cold-blooded about your problems. He wants good, funny stuff. How long it takes you to turn that out and how much work it is for you are *your* problems.

Always present your best work and let the buyer beware. This lesson hit me recently. A producer friend called with a problem. He had fallen behind on scripts and needed some shows immediately, if not sooner. I went in and worked out a story with him and got an assignment for a script. He pleaded with me to have it completed and back to him the next day. That was out of the question—two weeks is the norm for a first draft. However, I did promise that I would work on it over the weekend and deliver it on Monday—a total of three days' work.

I wrote the script quickly and delivered it by messenger on Monday morning. Later a mutual friend asked the producer how he liked my script. "It didn't knock me out," was his reply.

This isn't sour grapes because I agreed with the producer. The script wasn't a knockout. I did see the rewrite his staff did when the show aired and it was terrific. However, the story points out that none of us considers the time or effort spent on a project. We all just consider the results. Is it funny?

Any time you're showcasing your wares, include only those you're most proud of.

Do It Yourself

While we're speaking of improvement, let me once again advise you to perform some of your material. Sometimes doing this can be extremely painful (when your material doesn't go over) but even then it is an invaluable lesson.

Even those who have no ambition to stand on a podium and deliver funny lines should try it once or twice. It will make your comedy writing that much better. There is no substitute for actual experience.

That's because, regardless of how much we study or how expert we become on a subject, we never really know it until we experience it personally. You should experience the feeling of telling a gag that, as the standup comics say, "kills." But you should also know the sinking feeling of delivering a line that "just lays there." You'll know how the comic behind the microphone feels. You'll gain a new respect for your craft and you'll be more dedicated to furnishing material that's as sure-fire as you can make it.

The legendary comic Jack Benny was once the manager of the Hollywood Stars celebrity baseball team when they played an exhibition at Dodger Stadium. He told his first batter to hit a home run. The batter struck out. Benny slammed his cap to the ground and left. He said, "If you're not going to follow orders, I quit."

This was the kind of fun that made this exhibition game a delight for the fans, but there is a moral: it's easy to give advice—even correct advice—but it's not always easy to follow it. Since you're going to be the strategist, the writer, the brains behind the comic, it'll serve you well to know the problems a comic faces.

To speak seriously about Benny's joke line, he might not have said, "Hit a home run" if he knew how difficult that assignment would be. I know I'm drawing conclusions from the absurd, but some writers do what Jack Benny did. They ask the comic to take their material and "hit a home run" with it when they really don't know how difficult a task that might be. That's why it's beneficial for them to step to the plate a few times.

There are certain practicalities that you can only learn from experience. Certain words are nearly impossible for a comic to say and maintain his rhythm. I learned from experience that I can't get out the phrase "shoulder holster" without fumbling over it. Other people have difficulties with other word combinations. If a comic says, "I can't say this joke as written," you have no right to quarrel with him and you won't if you've actually stood in front of an audience with a great punch line and said, "Shoulder holder...holder shoulster...holster shoulster..."

Once, for *The Tim Conway Show* I had written a series of blackouts about an Indian and a cavalry officer making peace. Each time they went through the ceremony, Tim, as the Indian, would do something accidentally to start the war up again. In one gag, Tim was holding a long spear. In moving to break it over his knee, he accidentally tripped the cavalry officer and stabbed him.

As we were taping this routine, Tim kept changing the joke. Finally, I asked him to do the gag as written because it was much funnier than the gags he was experimenting with. He handed me the spear and said, "Show me exactly what you want me to do." I took the long, heavy spear, stood in his place, tried to do what I had written—and discovered it was physically impossible. Naturally, I called the writing staff and got a new joke. I can't create when I'm embarrassed.

No one had more experience with jokes and with audiences than Bob Hope. Several of us writers sat with him in the London Palladium rehearsing a monologue he would do at a command performance for Queen Elizabeth II. He came to one joke in the monologue and took it out of the routine. It was my joke.

I said, "Why are you taking that joke out?" Hope said, "I don't want to do that in front of the Queen." I objected. "The Queen will love that joke," I said. (Like I know all the Queen's likes and dislikes.) Hope said, "Is that right?" I said, "Sure." He handed me the cue card with the joke written on it and said, "Then you do it."

If you absolutely, positively refuse to or cannot get in front of an audience to speak, then at least work with a collaborator who will face an audience. That way, at least you'll get some experience with audience reaction. But listen to the input from your speaker. If the material doesn't play well, your natural tendency will be to defend what you've written. Since you haven't stood before the crowd yourself, you may smugly blame the speaker for the wrong inflection or fault the audience for not being receptive enough. Don't. Smother your pride in favor of the lessons to be learned. Let your speaker tell you why your stuff failed and learn from it. You're intent on a writing career; you'll have plenty of times later on to defend your material.

Save Your Work

After you write your material, be sure to *save* it. Keep everything. Again, it seems that I'm belaboring the obvious, but many writers submit material for critique, read the notations, and then discard it. If you're serious about writing, you should preserve everything you write. Following are other reasons for archiving your material besides having it to show to prospective buyers.

✔ Impressionist Fred Travalena worked with many comedy writers to update and improve his routines. He offers this advice:

I would just say a word of business advice is not to go in for the financial kill. Go in there for the chance to write. Don't underestimate yourself either, but don't make it impossible. There are a lot of comedians who need material who are not wealthy guys. And a lot of times avenues are cut off for creative get-togethers, so to speak, because of a financial thing.

In terms of the new and upcoming comedy writers, don't give your material away, for sure. But don't make it impossible for somebody to build their future circle of references.

It Tracks Your Improvement

Keeping all of the material that you compose will be positive reinforcement that your writing is becoming more professional. Sometimes improvement is so gradual that we hardly notice it, and even believe it nonexistent. A look back at your earlier work can be vivid proof that you've learned quite a bit.

It Helps You During Dry Spells

Reviewing the good material you've written proves you can do it again. There are days when the blankness of the page can be overpowering. You don't feel funny. The topic isn't inspiring. You have better things to do than write foolish lines about silly things.

These are only three causes of writer's block. There are 8,452,327,261 other documented causes of it. Basically, it's fear that you can't do a good job on a project, so you subconsciously find ways of avoiding it. But re-reading some of your brilliant past work may show your subconscious you can do as professional a job on this assignment as you have done on others. Turn on the computer and destroy the whiteness of the page.

You Can Reuse Much of the Material

History does repeat itself. That's nice for the gag writer, because many jokes still apply the second time around. I learned this lesson early in my career. I was working for comedian Slappy White and wrote some jokes about the fight in which heavyweight boxer, Sonny Liston, knocked out Floyd Patterson in the first round. The one I wrote that I was proudest of was

> That fight was so short, when they raised Liston's arm I thought it was a deodorant commercial.

During the show that night, Slappy did not only that joke but also a whole routine on the fight. He had lines like

> I had a hundred dollar seat for that fight and Patterson, he sat down before I did.

> A guy asked me if I thought Patterson would ever fight again. I said, "As much money as I lost on this fight, when he sees me he'll fight again."

> But I'd like to see Patterson come back...and finish that first round.

I asked Slappy where he could get a whole routine that fast. He said, "Remember the Marciano-Wollcott fight?" I sure did. I watched that in my living room, went out to get a bottle of soda, came back, and the fight was over. (And that was before they had instant replay.) Slappy said, "Same jokes."

Your old material will prove useful even when the same jokes can't be used exactly. Chances are you'll be working on similar topics during your career. Inflation causes a controversy periodically. Stamp prices go up every so often. The stock market declines now and again. Going back over old routines may not actually provide usable jokes in these cases, but they will give you an idea on different slants to take with the topic.

You put in a lot of effort to create humor. You should preserve it all for future reference and possibly for future use. Naturally, the material you save is of little use to you unless you can find it again quickly.

I have a filing system that is simple and it's fast, requiring little maintenance or bother. Because it has served me well, I'll take a moment to pass it on to you. Feel free to use this one if you don't have a better one of your own.

My system is simply a chronological listing of my writing with an accompanying index. First of all, I break the writing down into the different contracts that I have. If I'm writing for Joe Blow, Jackie Lenny, and Lenny Jackie, I have three different indexes going. Make that four because I'd probably have one for "miscellaneous" or "general." Then each routine I do for each client is numbered from one to whatever. The first routine I write for Joe Blow is labeled JB #1, the tenth routine I do for Jackie Lenny is JL #10, and Lenny Jackie's fortieth routine becomes LJ #40.

Then I keep a separate loose-leaf book with an index for each client. As I write the routine, I list the number and what the material is about. A typical listing for Joe Blow might look something like this:

JB #10—How Grouchy My One Neighbor Is
JB #11—How Cheap My Brother-in-law Is
JB #12—How Demanding My Boss Is
JB #13—How I Don't Know How To Operate My Cell Phone
JB #14—Things I Hate About Driving

and so on.

I keep a copy of everything I write, either in a loose-leaf book or in a file folder. If I want to research past material, I read through the index until I find the appropriate number, turn to that page in the loose-leaf book, and there it is.

I follow the same procedure on most of the shows I work on. Each assignment is numbered and listed in an index, then filed accordingly.

It's a simple system because each routine is just noted and then filed as the next entry in a book. Once that's completed, it never has to be altered. It's there for when you want to find it.

I have a collection of over thirty volumes of monologue material containing well over 100,000 gags. I also have material from many different seasons of television writing. I can retrieve any material from this collection rather quickly.

I can't retrieve individual jokes with this system. I can only find the topics and search through all the monologues until I happen across a particular joke. But I can retrieve a particular sketch from a given show.

The benefit of the system to me is that it is simple and maintenance-free. The topic is written once in one place and the routine is filed once. It takes no more time than writing the title once in an index.

Remember, too, that this system predated the extensive use of home computers. Those of you who are more handy with the computer may be able to generate a system that is more comprehensive than this one and yet just as easy to use. (Be sure to back it up, though.)

The point is that your material should be saved and readily available to you. How you do that depends on your own ingenuity and, of course, the latest technology.

The essential step, though, is to get that material out of your archives and into the marketplace. That's what we'll talk about next.

- 21 -

Completing Speculative Work

Writing requires not only creativity and skill, it also demands discipline. Perhaps the discipline is even more important than the expertise. *A mediocre writer who is prolific will most likely be more successful than a brilliant writer who never gets anything typed.*

The question we ask in television is, "Can you put it on paper?" We may know people with brilliant comedic minds who are witty and inventive all the time. But can they put it on paper? Can they be witty and inventive when the deadline threatens? Do they have the discipline to put away the party comedy and turn out the material we need to plug a hole in the upcoming show? Hugh Prather, whose first book *Notes To Myself* sold over five million copies, has a quote that says it all—"If the desire to write is not accompanied by actual writing, then the desire is not to write."

Mr. Prather is harsher than I am on nonquota writers. These folks have a desire to write, but it isn't accompanied by actual writing. All of us who have ever wrestled with the blank page know that there are any number of excuses for not caressing the keyboard. There are pencils to be sharpened, desks to be straightened, drawers to be rearranged, and 1,532,653 other reasons to delay writing. But none of them is valid enough for us to abandon our efforts.

Yet some people do abandon their projects. One reason could be that the immensity of the assignment defeats them. This feeling is not unfamiliar to me because much of my work comes in spurts. I'll have nothing to do for some time and thoroughly enjoy it. Then I get a bunch of assignments at one time, each one with a demanding deadline. The inclination is to fret so much over the supposed impossibility of it that it really becomes impossible. But when I sit down and begin chipping away at it, it gets done. There's a proverb that says something to the effect that the longest journey begins with the first small step.

My family loses patience with me because I'm a terrible traveler. Some of my childhood traits remain with me—notably the one that prompts me, when we begin a long journey, to ask, "Are we almost there?" On a long drive, I'm constantly looking at the mileage indicator and figuring out how much farther we have to go. I destroy the enjoyment of the journey because I'm overwhelmed by the enormity of it.

Writers can react the same way. Presumably, we all like to write. Why then do we all worry about how large an undertaking is? We should rejoice that it's almost interminable. That means we'll have that much more opportunity to write.

Following are a few hints that I've used to help me get through a formidable task.

Convince Yourself that You're Being Paid

Television performers sometimes use any device to get their line changed. Writers don't like to change lines. It's an affront to our judgment and, more important, it means more work. So we have occasional conflicts. I remember one actor saying, "I don't understand my motivation for saying this line. I mean, I can't act unless I *feel* it. I have no reason to say this line. I mean, what's my motivation?" Our producer, bless his soul, said, "After you say it, you get a paycheck. That's your motivation."

A great incentive for getting work done is the money we're paid for it. Look back at the jobs you've performed in whatever you do for a living. Try to visualize your work in some measurable and visual form. See all your paperwork bound into books, your handiwork assembled on a loading platform. The accumulated work that you've done is astounding. You got it all done because a paycheck was dangled before your wallet each Friday. If someone asked you to do that much work starting now, you'd probably say it was impossible. Yet you did do it—because you got paid for it.

So pay yourself for the speculative writing you're going to do. How? Steal it from somewhere else. Let some of the labor you get paid for subsidize your labor of love. Let's suppose you work in a department store and earn ten dollars an hour. Assign that last hour of each work-day as your salary for writing two hours a night. All of a sudden, you're making fifty dollars a week for writing. Not bad. If you want a raise, give yourself the last hour and a half of work. Bingo, you're earning seventy-five dollars.

I'm making light of it, but this is not as silly as it sounds. You're investing in your future. It's the same thing people do when they put themselves through college. They work to get money to invest in themselves. In a sense, we all do it. We work not for money, but for the things that money can buy. If we want a color television, we buy it with the money we earn. If that set costs five hundred dollars and we make ten dollars an hour, we have in effect bought that TV with fifty hours of labor. Admittedly, it's a mind game. The important point is, if it works for you and helps you get your writing assignments completed, use it.

✔ Carol Burnett spoke to ROUND TABLE about having fun with the project you're working on:

The key is enthusiasm. The key is to try to have fun. I think that's something that I don't see very much in the faces of executives. They are very nervous about the money end of it and they forget why we all got into show business in the first place. It was because we wanted to have some fun, because it was a kick.

Select a Project that You'll Enjoy

I'm assuming that all these projects we're discussing are specula-tive. Since no one is paying you for this work, select only projects you enjoy. Then it becomes its own reward.

People don't expect to get paid for building model airplanes or doing crossword puzzles. They do them because they're relaxing and they enjoy them. Treat your project the same way. Do it because it's fun. Should it make money for you, that's profit.

Prepare Your Project

When I get on a plane, I assume the pilot knows where he's going. I'd be terribly annoyed if he came back while they were serving cocktails and said, "Does anybody know the way to Portland?" He should take care of details like that before he gets up in the air.

So should a writer who is tackling a large project. It's easy to get hopelessly lost in writing any work of any size. Even a short story can ramble aimlessly if it's not well outlined. As producers, my partner and I always wanted to see a detailed story outline before a freelancer could begin a half-hour script—not only because it gave us more control over the project, but because it also made the writer's work easier. The script would be completed much more quickly if the author knew from the start where the story was going and how it would end.

Begin by outlining your project in broad strokes. What form will it take? What will its point of view be? Conceive a generalized, overall vision of your venture. Then allow time to gather information. Be more specific and more detailed in outlining your undertaking. If you're attempting a screenplay or a teleplay, know what you need to cover in each scene and the plot points you'll introduce? If you're writing a book, rough out the chapter headings. Once you've gathered all the preliminary information, arrange it into a logical and coherent form. Set your scenes in chronological order, or arrange your chapter headings in some workable progression.

Be careful, though. Sometimes this planning can be used as an excuse to effectively scuttle the entire venture. It's easy to drag this stage of the project out for so long that the writing never happens. To prevent this, exercise even more discipline. Set a rigid time limit for this work and a daily or weekly quota to be met.

Set Your Goals and Begin Your Work

Everything in the world is reducible to bite-sized chunks. Every whole is the sum of its parts. So any large undertaking is able to be completed simply by completing lots of smaller parts. In fact, it's impossible to do anything other than completing it in parts. You can't give an hour speech. You can only say individual words that add up to sixty minutes total. You can't write an entire book unless you write one chapter at a time. In fact, you write characters that add up to words that form sentences making paragraphs begetting chapters totaling a book.

Accepting that, then, you have to divide your project into those bite-sized pieces. You have to break this enormous undertaking into workable sections. It's a mathematical exercise.

Now you divide what has to be done by the amount of time you have to do it in and that generates your quota. If you have a thirty-page story to write and ten days in which to write it, you have to write three pages of text each day.

Sometimes you'll have a deadline that dictates this division, but on speculative work you'll be able to determine your own deadlines. In that case, be nice to yourself. Don't make the workload so demanding that you overburden yourself. Make it realistic enough to keep your interest up. I like to allow myself room for tiny rewards. For instance, if I have to write three pages a day, I might struggle and do six in one day and take the next day off. Again, we're playing mind games, but whatever works, works.

Now you've finally arrived at that magic moment when all that remains is to sit at the keyboard and crank out creativity. All your excuses have been exhausted. You know where you're going and you know how to get there.

You can take the terror out of any project by reducing it to painless segments and enjoying each part of it on its way to completion.

- 22 -

Marketing Your Material

When visiting a very successful and well-to-do friend, I noticed a portrait of him in his office. In it, he had a stern expression and seemed to be sneering down at anyone looking up at him. When I kidded him about it he laughed and said, "I call that my 'I got mine—you get yours' portrait."

The same principle applies in marketing your material—each person must find his way by means of his own ingenuity and creativity. Humor is a very personalized art form. I may not like a certain comic even though I admit his talent. Someone else may have few technical skills but just be zany enough to get laughs from me. I may like some material I read and recommend it to other people who I think will like it equally as well. They may not. But other people who I suspect would dislike the material may fall in love with it.

All of this makes standardized recommendations almost impossible. Your task is to write good material—humor that satisfies you. You have to know it's good; then you have to find some influential people who agree with you. That's not an easy task no matter how expert your writing is. Most people don't buy talent, they buy results. It's the old chicken-and-egg riddle and job-and-experience dilemma. You can't demonstrate results until you get a chance to show your skills, and no one will give you a chance to show your skills until you've shown some results.

Take heart. It's not an unsolvable problem—we do have chickens, and people get new jobs all the time. More important, we have many talented new faces in comedy each year. However, there is no set formula for YOU. As we said earlier, a student follows certain required steps to become a doctor. But becoming a humorist requires more resourcefulness.

I'll sketch out some broad suggestions for you, but you'll have to pick and choose which will work for you and which won't. Be prepared for some failures. That's inevitable using a hit-or-miss system, but you'll learn from both your successes and your disappointments.

Here's an example to encourage you. Direct mail advertisers admit up front that their campaigns might only produce about a 2 percent return. That means 98 percent of the recipients reject the sales pitch. Yet many people in the business say that direct mail is the most efficient form of advertising. That 2 percent pays for the entire undertaking.

You'll have to do the same as the direct mail people. Concentrate on the positive and ignore the negative. In your mind you have to follow the advice of the old song and "accentuate the positive and eliminate the negative." Remember that one "yes" can erase thousands of "no's."

"All right, already," you're muttering to yourself. "How do I get started on this perilous journey?"

Give Your Material Away

One way to start *immediately* is to work for free. I love Samuel Johnson's statement that no one but a blockhead ever wrote except for money. It's not contradicting Johnson, though, to promote yourself so you can get around to making some money. A real blockhead is someone who withholds his services until he gets paid—and winds up withholding his services for the rest of his life.

I was walking a picket line outside Universal Studios during one of our writers' strikes. A young man introduced himself as a student in a Writers' Guild class. (At that time, to encourage new writers, the Writers Guild of America, West, the union all Hollywood TV writers belong to, offered free classes to beginning writers.) We struck up a conversation. He told me that he had written an outline for a screenplay that the teacher felt showed much promise. The boy received expert suggestions on his project and was told to rework it. I congratulated him. He said, "Yeah, but if they want me to do that much work, they're going to have to pay me something."

I went back to walking in circles holding a sign and knew that I could forget this lad's career.

Writing for free is a great educational tool. You can do it immediately and learn how the audience reacts. I say you can do it immediately because newspaper columnists will accept material from you if you let them know that you don't expect payment. A friend of mine, for instance, often puts humorous poems about local professional teams in sports journalists' columns. Local comics will gladly try out material for you—or at least read it over. The guy emceeing some shindig for the company or the lodge meeting will gladly take comedic input.

Aside from the educational aspect, you get promotional value. People will now know that you write humor. When someone wants to buy it, they'll know where they can get it.

My professional career actually started with giveaway material. A local TV personality wanted to write a column for the morning newspaper. I had sent him a query letter and some samples of my writing, which he liked, and I began writing for him purely on speculation. My letterheads were on his desk when a national comedian was a guest on his television show, and while they were in the office after the show, the comic read the material upside down, jotted down my phone number from the top of the page, and called me to write some material for his act. That led to my first paying contract and I was with the man for six years earning a nice part-time income.

You needn't donate all your time to charity, though. There's no sense having you mad at me or Samuel Johnson mad at you. Just be a blockhead for a little while.

Working into Magazines

First, try selling some of your material to the easier markets—the many small magazines, periodicals, and newspapers that publish a lot of humor, although they pay relatively little. Your chances of acceptance are considerably better here than in the high-paying, highly competitive markets.

But doesn't it make more sense, you ask, to start with the higher-paying, exclusive markets and then work your way down? The big ones just might accept the submissions. If they do, you make a lot of money. If they don't, you send it somewhere else.

Yeah, that makes sense, but there are some pitfalls. The rejection rate is tremendous and, despite your good intentions, that can become discouraging. You might surrender before getting to the markets that *will* buy your material. Also, if the stuff you're selling is topical, it won't last long enough to survive several rejections. I used to submit current material to Kiplinger's *Changing Times* magazine. At that time, they published an entire page of topical one-liners. The material had to be fresh and up-to-date. If they didn't buy my submissions that month, they were useless to me.

This isn't to discourage you from attacking high-paying markets. If you're good enough, you deserve to be and eventually will be in them. But at the beginning, it's a big morale booster to make a sale. The amount isn't as important as the acceptance. So pursue the smaller markets. Explore the prestigious ones, also, but not exclusively.

Finding the Comics

If you're writing monologue material, contact comics. Most of them depend on material to keep their careers alive. It's the lifeblood that keeps their acts vital. We all think, "Oh, they won't look at my stuff," but comics need material and it's not easy to come by. Most of them will look at your submissions. They may not *buy* them, but they'll look at them.

That's a generalization, of course. Some comics do their own writing or are content with the writers they employ. They won't be bothered reading material. You and I don't know who they are, though. So there's no harm in a polite query with a few samples included. The comic may say "no," but let him do it. Don't do it for him.

Here again, you might try the shotgun approach. Try several different strategies simultaneously to see which brings the best results. Contact local comics —they may not make as much as the big names, but they want to be just as funny. Landing a contract with a weekend comic might be your steppingstone to the next level.

How do you contact such a comic? Spread the word among friends that you'd like to write for him. It's amazing how easy it is to find someone sooner or later who knows the guy. He may be listed in the phone book. He probably belongs to the American Guild of Variety Artists (AGVA) and the local office might be able to put you in touch with him. Keep an eye on the entertainment section of the newspaper, and send a letter to or call the club where he's appearing. Go see his act and send a message backstage that you're a comedy writer and would like to talk briefly. Always have material with you, and say so. Sometimes they may not want to see you but might want to read over your stuff.

At the same time, don't be frightened away by the celebrities. The bigger the comic, the more material he needs and the better it has to be. It follows that it's the hardest to get.

Celebrities guard their privacy. It's sometimes hard to reach them, but with persistence and some ingenuity, it's possible. It's probably better to reach these people when they're on the road rather than find their agent's number or their home address. At home, they're bombarded with mail and it sort of overwhelms them. When they have a tantalizing collection to choose from, they naturally concentrate on the most important. A fledgling comedy writer, no matter how good, might not be in that category. But should you find out where they're appearing and send a letter to that club or hotel, it might be the only piece of mail they get there. It's hard to resist opening it.

The weekly *Variety* is a good way of finding out who's appearing where. *Variety* has an extensive listing of nightclub engagements, along with reviews of most of the acts.

I've used this listing to call clubs across the nation. I didn't always reach the celebrity, but I could explain to someone that I had material that I wanted so-and-so to see and was given an address to send it to.

It's possible, too, to talk with people when they come to your hometown. As a beginning writer in Philadelphia, I had pleasant visits with many comics. A few of them even bought some material.

I discovered that most celebrities stayed at one of two or three favorite hotels. When I found out from the papers that they were in town, I'd call those hotels and ask for them. If they were there, I might be connected to the room. If they weren't, I'd be so advised. At least I knew where they weren't.

✔ *Round Table asked Jay Leno for advice for beginning writers.*

My big suggestion to writers is to physically get your material to the person you want to see it.

Also, don't send REAMS of stuff. People will say, "Here're 500 jokes I wrote." Maybe twenty of them are okay, but nobody really wants to read through 500.

Go through it yourself. Take ten of what you think are your best jokes— maybe twenty. Send that as a sample of your work.

Don't send completed scripts. Send something that someone can look at in a minute or two. We get hundreds of submissions and no one will take the time to read a huge, long thing.

Politeness Above All

Don't become a comedy-writing paparazzi who follows celebrities around harassing them by waving pages of typed one-liners in their faces. You'll do yourself only harm by becoming an annoyance.

> ✔ Joan Rivers had this to say about submitting your funniest material:
>
> Boy, when it's funny, it stands out on the page.

I once got a writer a tryout with a well-known comic. This gentleman wrote for the comedian for a while and had many jokes used by the comic …and paid for. However, the writer pushed so hard for acceptance that he became a nuisance and was eventually dropped from the writing team.

In your letters, phone calls, or whatever, be polite, be considerate, and aboveboard. Tell the comics that you have material you'd like them to see and ask if that would be convenient. They can always refuse, but if you're polite and tactful, they can't be offended by the request.

Approaching a Producer

Submitting material for television shows is fairly simple because you just mail it in care of the network to the producers who are credited either at the beginning or the end of the show.

Some producers require a release form with any unsolicited material. Some don't. Again, it's trial and error to find out who will and who won't accept such material. I feel that in this case a letter of inquiry might be self-defeating. It's true that all producers need product, but it's also true that we're basically parochial and a bit lazy. We subconsciously feel that the only really good writers are in New York or Hollywood. We also want to find talent without having to read too much. Consequently, a query letter might be greeted with a polite reply that says "Thanks, but no thanks."

It might be advisable to send your script in and take your chances. If the producers read it, fine. If they return it unopened, you can follow with a letter requesting the proper release forms.

Television, as we discussed earlier, is a difficult medium to begin your career with. You should establish some sort of reputation in other areas of comedy writing before tackling it. However, I include these recommendations because there's no set pattern to attacking your career. You might be ingenious enough to impress a producer with your script. This story might encourage you:

A writer friend of mine began his career by sending a spec script to a producer. The producer read through it and was kind enough to send several pages of criticism. He didn't care for the script and said as much in the letter. The writer, using those notes, immediately began a new script and sent it off to the same producer. The producer read the second script and had his agents sign this writer immediately. They worked together as coproducers of a new sitcom. The producer never realized until much later, that both scripts were from the same person.

One nice thing about being a writer is that your material sells itself. When you go out on a job interview, you have to dress and behave properly. You could well be turned down because of something that has nothing to do with your qualifications. I've always felt sorry for actors who come in for auditions. They put themselves on the line, and when you reject them for a part, you're rejecting a person. But a writer can audition without ever being present. The printed page is his representative.

However, that page is important. It is representing *you*. A strange thing happens when a writer turns in a sketch to a head writer. The head writer will begin to read the script—and automatically reach for a pencil with his free hand. Subconsciously he's saying, "I know something is going to be wrong with this."

Editors are the same with newcomers even though they may be reluctant to admit it. They're looking for a quick reason to turn the manuscript down and not have to read it through. You job is to slam the door on that avenue of escape. The best way is to avoid obvious errors.

The most obvious one is the form your document takes. Any manuscript that is printed out improperly screams "amateur" and is generally quickly abandoned. You must pay attention to format no matter what you write.

Magazines

There has been plenty of material printed on submitting to magazines, and most magazines will send a freelancer a copy of their guidelines on request. The only thing I might add is what will apply for all submissions—they should be neat, typewritten, double spaced, with plenty of margin space allowed.

In sending filler material for magazines, I recommend sending each gag on a separate sheet of paper, preferably a three- by five-inch card. This makes the editor's job easier. If there are one or two worthwhile bits among your submissions and she can separate them from the others quickly and easily, your chances for a sale are increased. Suppose there's a choice between yours and someone else's. The editor, being human, will select the one that makes her job easier—the one that's already separated from the others.

Include your name and address on each card, too. (Your name and return address should be on everything you submit.)

Television Scripts

Scripts are generally in two basic forms—tape and film. I don't know why there's a difference, but there is. Dialogue in tape scripts is double-spaced; in film scripts it's single-spaced. I've included a few pages of a movie script at the back of this book to show you the form. For the tape script, refer to the sketches included in Chapter 16.

Your Writing Is Not All You're Selling

An important part of marketing your comedy material is marketing yourself. You have to let people know you're in the comedy-writing business. Word of mouth can be a surprisingly effective promotion. Tell people you know that you're writing and for whom you'd like to work. It's astounding how quickly a network can form that can lead you to interesting people and assignments.

Alert local newspapers to your success. There aren't a lot of humorists around and you might make good copy. Good copy can get noticed and lead to additional interesting assignments.

Document some of your experiences and sell them to magazines. It's great prestige to have your byline on a magazine article about comedy writing. Some of the things you learn along the way may be of interest to other people making the same journey. You might also have some information that could be useful to writers' magazines.

Believe in Yourself

One facet of marketing that should never be overlooked is your own confidence. You must believe that you can do it.

Now, understand that *believing* you can do it doesn't mean you can do it. (What'd he say?) I said, "*Believing* you can do it doesn't mean you can do it." Remember when you first learned to drive a car? You couldn't drive, but you had no doubt that you could learn, pass your test, and drive as well as anyone on the road. That's the kind of confidence you need to market your writing.

Right now maybe you can't do it yet, but belief in yourself will get you working hard enough to improve. You'll learn how to do it, the same way you learned how to drive.

Then you'll know you're good. When you know you're good, the marketing will happen. Use some of the hints in this book to find some avenues of your own. As you become a better and better writer, people will discover you.

There's an exciting adventure ahead of you. You're about to cut your own distinctive path to writing success. It won't be similar to anyone else's—no two have been the same yet. It is my hope that this book has been some help, but you know the ultimate responsibility is yours. You have to set your own goals. You have to define the disciplines. Above all, you have to write and write and improve and improve. You'll enjoy the rewards.

Comedy is an entertaining profession all along the way. I just hope you'll become successful enough to offer me a job soon.

Good luck—and have fun.

- 23 -

The Answer to the Question Everyone Wants to Ask

In this book, I've tried to explain what comedy writing is, what it entails, how to go about writing humor, and some of the pros and cons of building a career as a comedy writer. My theories are a practical and realistic approach to your career. (We'll talk more about realism as we go on.) As I've said earlier in the text, my approach is not the *only* avenue to a writing career. It may not even be the *best* one. But it is *one way* of building a career. It has worked for more than a few people, and if you honestly evaluate it and experiment with the suggestions, it might work for you.

I hope the previous chapters have answered many of your questions about our profession. However, I know there is one overriding question that everyone who begins to study comedy writing has—"If I want to write comedy and I continue to write, study, practice, and improve, when can I expect success to happen?"

My answer to that is very simple—success happens **RIGHT NOW**. You make yourself a success immediately, right here in this room as you're reading this book. How do you do that? You simply make an announcement to yourself that you are a successful comedy writer.

The chain of events that will lead to your becoming a professional comedy writer begins when you believe in your mind that you have what it takes to become a professional comedy writer.

I said this at a writers' seminar one time and another panelist berated me. "Success," he suggested, "begins when you believe it in your heart." I disagreed then and I disagree now.

Remember, I said that my theories are based in reality. There is a major difference between *wanting* something and *having* something. When you *believe* something, you have it. When you *want* something, no matter how ferociously, you don't have it. By definition you don't have it. If you had it, you wouldn't *want* it.

So the first step to a successful career in comedy is to believe right now that you have a successful career in comedy. The question then is, "Does what you think affect what will happen?" If it doesn't, why bother? And if it does, how does it?

Many learned people say that your thoughts affect your actions and your fate. James Allen wrote a book called *As You Think*. The unfinished part of the title is "So you are." As you think, so you are. Norman Vincent Peale taught and wrote about "The Power of Positive Thinking." It's not a new thought, either. Somewhere around 500 B.C. Buddha taught that "all that we are is the result of what we have thought."

So a lot of people are convinced that what we think affects destiny. But I promised a reality-based program and some might argue that this is self-help gibberish. It has a metaphysical tone to it. Yes, it does, and for all we know, that stuff may work. However, it also has a pragmatic effect. That's what we want to discuss. That's the nuts and bolts "how" of my theory. If this thinking does affect your fate, how does it do that? What's the reality of it?

If you believe you are a successful comedy writer right now, you will begin to act like a comedy writer; you'll think like a comedy writer; and you'll do what a comedy writer would do. That has to produce positive results.

Our tendency is to want to think, act, and perform like a comedy writer when we become a comedy writer. "When they start paying me to write jokes, I'll write jokes." But we may never get that chance if we don't start being a comedy writer now.

Earlier I mentioned Tiger Woods' phenomenal success as a pro golfer. Tiger Woods shot a 49 for nine holes when he was three years old. He has been practicing and playing golf since then. Today he makes a fortune. Why? Because he has been preparing for this career all his life.

How much do you think he'd be making if he said to himself, "I won't pick up and swing a golf club until someone pays me a million dollars to pick up and swing a golf club"?

Tiger was a successful golfer when he was a toddler. That's why he's a phenomenally successful golf pro today.

You have to be what you want to be in your own mind *today*, and then let the rest of the world catch up with your conviction.

That's the other part of the "how" of this belief. When you see yourself as a successful comedy writer, because you think, act, and perform like one, other people will begin to see you in that light also. These are the people who can hire you and help provide the breaks you'll need.

Let me give a practical example of that. When I worked in electrical drafting and engineering, many people from my apprentice class wanted to move up to supervisory positions. Only so many opportunities would open up each year. Naturally, all of us thought we were qualified. Some of us, though, went a step further. We began to be supervisors, in our own minds. We cared about the jobs as a supervisor would, we acted like supervisors, we dressed like supervisors. Others of us said, "No way. I'll work and dress like a supervisor when the company starts paying me supervisor's wages."

Now when a position opened up, whom do you guess was considered for the job? Of course, the ones who looked like they could walk right into the position and perform.

Did that thinking affect their career? Absolutely it did. It earned many of them a raise in status and salary.

So your success should begin right now, in this room, in your own mind. Right now you are a successful, professional comedy writer.

But you may object. "How can I lie to myself like that? I haven't sold a single joke yet" or "I haven't sold many jokes yet." "How can I call myself a successful, professional comedy writer?"

Let me answer this way. Suppose a man is a plumber—a pretty good plumber. He works for a large plumbing organization. They downsize and he's laid off. He now has no income. He's looking for another job. Nevertheless, at no time during that period does he say to himself, "I'm not a plumber." No. He's an out-of-work plumber, but he's still a plumber.

That's what you are—a successful comedy writer who may happen to be between gigs. But being between gigs, even if it's your first real gig you're waiting for, does not mean that you are not a comedy writer.

The first time I met Phyllis Diller was when she was appearing at the Latin Casino. At the time, it was probably the largest nightclub in the country. It held over two thousand people, and they were turning people away. I met her backstage and said, "Phyllis, did you ever imagine success like this?" She said, "Oh, I've known it for a long time. I'm just surprised it took the rest of the world this long to discover it."

You should declare yourself a successful comedy writer immediately. Say it to yourself now and believe it. That'll give the world, and circumstances, a little bit of time to catch up.

Let me play devil's advocate and present another objection to this concept that some may present—"If I declare myself a successful comedy writer right now, doesn't that take away any incentive I might have to study, learn, and improve my writing?" No. In fact, just the opposite is true.

When I worked on *The Carol Burnett Show*, I had lunch with one of the musicians in the orchestra. This gentleman was a successful studio musician and considered one of the finest guitarists in the country. He made a nice living as a studio musician and also had several good-selling records on the market. He had to leave lunch early. I said, "Where are you rushing off to?" He said, "I have to go for my music lesson." Because he was so successful, he felt an obligation to his craft.

We've used Tiger Woods as an example several times in this book. That's because he is one of the most dominant figures in the sports world. He is absolutely the best at what he does. Yet, he probably practices as much or more than the other professionals. Why? How good does he want to be? He is a professional who competes against other professionals. He wants to stay the best. So he practices.

I'm a terrible golfer, but I don't practice or improve that much. Why? Because golf is a pastime with me. It's a diversion. Whether I play well or badly doesn't impact my life that greatly. Therefore, I have no real motivation to work on my swing.

But in a sense, that proves my theory. If I were to suddenly decide on a golfing career and follow my own advice, I'd be declaring right here and right now that I am a successful golfer. What's the first thing I would have to do after making that declaration? I'd have to get my scores down from around 100 to somewhere near par. That's a pretty doggone compelling reason to take some lessons and to spend some time on the practice range.

Being a success in your own mind prompts you to do the things you must do to make that success a probability, or at least, a possibility.

As I said earlier, my approach to building a career is based on reality…and I promised more on reality later. Well, here it is. Being cold-bloodedly realistic is like the cliché joke form—there's good news and there's bad news. Let's deal with the bad news first (although, later we'll see that the bad news is really good news).

The bad news is that no one can do it for you. I can't get into your head and make you a "success" right now. It's your head; it's your belief. I can't make you study to become a better comedy writer. I can't make you set a writing quota. Even if I did, I couldn't make you abide by it. I can't force you to write and write and write so that you'll get better and better and better. I can't make you try out for an assignment when you might fail, but when you also might get the job. Only you can do all that. Only you can force yourself to have what it takes—to do whatever it takes.

I once took a course in music theory and I apologized to my teacher because I didn't complete my homework. He said, "I don't care if you did your homework or not." I was surprised. I was used to teachers berating us for not finishing our assignments. He said, "I give you the knowledge and tell you what you have to do to make that knowledge part of you. If you do it, you'll learn; if you don't do it, you won't learn. Whether you learn music or not doesn't affect me in the least."

That's being cold-blooded. It's also being realistic. If I want to learn music, I have to do whatever it takes to learn music. If I don't, I won't. It's that simple.

However, we have a tendency to dismiss that truth and instead believe any one or several of the myths that swirl up around pursuing a career.

- "It's not what you know; it's who you know."
- "No big-name comedian will ever read my stuff."
- "You can't get into television unless you have connections."
- "If I only had an agent, all my problems would be solved."

And others like those. If you take just a brief minute to honestly reflect, you might find that you have some of those myths in the back of your own head.

The problem with these is that they're easy to accept because they're partly true. Sure, knowing someone may help you land a job. Maybe you don't have the credentials yet to impress a big-name comic. A solid connection might help you get into TV. Certainly, having an agent is a benefit in the writing profession. But they, and other myths like them, are all a result of what you do for yourself. Sell some jokes and you'll get to know influential people, name comedians will be more inclined to read and buy your stuff. Show some promise and TV execs will get to know your work—so will professional agents. So these myths have some validity, but only if you do what it takes to make them apply.

As you progress along your career, you'll surely get help from other people. It's almost a necessity. However, that help will only come, or it will only be beneficial, after you've proven you deserve it.

That's the part that's up to you.

Now what's the good news? The good news is that no one can stop you from doing it. You can sit at a keyboard or pick up a pen and paper and write jokes any time you feel like it. You can watch television and learn how the best shows are written. You can listen to comics and hear brilliant material. You can write and compare your gags to the professionals…and you can keep on writing until you're certain that you're on a par with the best in the business. No one can prevent you from doing any of that. That's the truth.

Again, though, we tend to believe the myths rather than the facts.

- "Agents won't look at new talent."
- "Writers in television keep newcomers out of the profession."
- "Comedians don't want to buy my material; they just want to steal it."

And other similar ones. Again, if you honestly search your mind, you may find some prejudice hidden in there.

These myths are insidious again because they're partly valid. There are agents who won't handle new writers. There are writers who would love to maintain the status quo and not allow new talent into the business. There may be some comics who would read your material, assimilate it, and not pay you for it. However, they can't keep you from reaching your goal. Why? Because there are other agents who will handle new talent. There are writers and producers who not only welcome new writers but go in search of them. There are comics who gladly pay for good material wherever they can find it. Finding those people and impressing them is up to you.

Notice we're right back to you again. This is where we deliver on our promise that the "bad" news we spoke about earlier is really "good" news. The fact that your career is in your own hands is really a blessing, not a curse. No one, not even a person who is sincerely interested in your career, can bring as much dedication and devotion to your work as you can. No one cares about it as much as you do. No one will work as hard at it as you will. An agent won't. A manager won't. A writing mentor won't. It will always mean more to you than it means to anyone else. So it's a good thing—a very good thing—that your career is in your own hands.

There are other facets of a writing career that we could discuss forever—writing techniques, writing exercises, career moves, and the like. However, if you believe:

1. that you are a successful writer right now and that you have the talent, or the potential talent, and the dedication that is required,

2. that you accept the responsibility for your own talent development and career progression,

3. that you refuse to allow anyone, no matter how influential or powerful, to prevent you from pursuing your career,

then all the rest will fall into place. You'll find a way to do whatever you have to do to live up to your belief that you are a successful comedy writer. If you want to be a comedy writer and you keep on writing and improving, you will be a comedy writer.

Sample Movie Script

FADE IN:

EXT. CITY STREETS—MONTAGE—CREDIT SEQUENCE

The OPENING CREDITS ROLL OVER a MONTAGE of scenes showing FATHER BOB walking along the city streets of his parish.

We ESTABLISH that this is a Puerto Rican ghetto area. We can SEE from the storefronts and graffiti and the boarded-up houses that this is a poverty area also.

We ESTABLISH that Father Bob is conversant with most of the people and as much as possible, that he is popular and respected by these people.

We END THE CREDITS, then FOLLOW Father Bob up the steps and into Our Lady of Guadalupe Rectory. He goes inside, and we STAY on the bronze plaque that identifies the building. Then we…

CUT TO:

INT. RECTORY FOYER—DAY

Father Bob goes to a table in the foyer and picks up a stack of mail. He goes through these and selects those that are for him, takes them with him and goes into the kitchen.

INT. RECTORY KITCHEN—DAY

Father Bob enters the kitchen where the housekeeper, JOSEPHINE PINTAVALE, is busy preparing the evening meal.

Father Bob takes out a jar of peanut butter and takes a knife from the drawer.

> JOSEPHINE
> Father, don't eat anything now. I'm preparing a nice meal. Linguini, with meatball sauce...some nice bracciola ...

> BOB
> I'm gonna skip dinner tonight, Josephine. I just want to get a little snack and get a little rest.

He opens a cupboard door and searches for something. He doesn't find it, so he takes down a box of saltines.

As he spreads peanut butter on them and puts them on a plate:

> BOB
> (continuing)
> Josephine, I wish you would buy those little round crackers...you know, the Ritz...instead of these. I keep asking you, but you never buy them.

> JOSEPHINE
> Yes, Father.

Bob cleans out the peanut butter jar and goes over to throw it away. By the trash container he notices a large rock on the counter near the door to the schoolyard.

> BOB
> Josephine, what is this rock for?

261

JOSEPHINE

Father, there's a big dog that comes around here and always goes through our trash. He makes a mess. I'm gonna hit him with this rock.

BOB

Josephine, you can't hit a dog with a rock like that. You could do some serious harm. That poor dog is hungry and it's looking for food.

Bob pours himself a glass of milk.

JOSEPHINE

Why does he have to look for food in our trash?

BOB

Because you make the best food in the whole city. Now, get rid of the rock, please.

JOSEPHINE

Yes, Father.

Bob takes his milk, his letters, and his plate of peanut butter crackers and starts out.

BOB

I'm going to rest awhile, Josephine, but if anyone comes to see me, it's all right to disturb me, all right?

JOSEPHINE

Yes, Father.

Bob exits.

INT. BOB'S APARTMENT—DAY

We SEE Father Bob, in his shorts, asleep on the couch. He is awakened by SHOUTS from outside his room.

> JOSEPHINE (O.S.)
> You can't go up there. Father
> Cosgrove is resting.

> HECTOR (O.S.)
> Father Bob will see me.

> JOSEPHINE (O.S.)
> You go up there, I'll call the police.

> HECTOR (O.S.)
> Let go of me, you old bat.

Father Bob wakes up fully and goes and opens the door.

INT. RECTORY STAIRWAY—DAY

Father Bob comes to the head of the stairs, still in his shorts, while HECTOR and Josephine are fighting partway up the stairs. From Hector's appearance and manner, we see that he is not quite all there.

> JOSEPHINE
> I don't want you disturbing the Father.

> HECTOR
> Father Bob told me to come and see
> him, you stupid macaroni maker.

> BOB
> Josephine...

They both stop fighting and turn to look up. When Josephine sees it is a priest in his shorts, she is horrified.

Index

About the Author

Gene **Perret** began his TV writing career on the staff of *The Jim Nabors Hour*. He has served on the writing staffs of *Laugh-In, The Carol Burnett Show,* and *Mama's Family,* among others. He was head writer and producer for *Welcome Back, Kotter,* and *The Tim Conway Show.*

Perret also wrote for Bob Hope special appearances and television specials from 1969 until Hope's retirement from show business. He traveled with all of the Hope USO shows since 1983 and served as Bob Hope's head comedy writer for the last 12 years of the comedian's career.

Round Table is a newsletter that Gene Perret founded for people who are interested in comedy writing and performing. It's a place where comedy professionals—at all levels—can gather to share ideas, know-how, and laughs.

You can be a part of the Round Table. To get more information go to www.writingcomedy.com or contact Round Table at

Round Table
PO Box 786
Agoura Hills, CA 91376
(818) 865-7833

Gene also teaches e-mail courses on comedy writing and writing humorous articles for magazines. These are limited classes, with Gene providing personal feedback. For a class schedule or for more information contact us through the Web site at www.writingcomedy.com

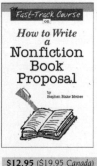